THE **Gardener's**
Problem Solver

THE **Gardener's** Problem Solver

MIRANDA SMITH

COLLINS & BROWN

To Marty, Simone, and Tagore –
the lights in my life

First published in Great Britain in 2004 by
Collins & Brown Ltd
The Chrysalis Building
Bramley Road
London W10 6SP

An imprint of **Chrysalis** Books Group plc

Project Manager: Nicola Hodgson
Editor: Lydia Darbyshire
Designer: Liz Brown
Illustrator: Ian Sidaway

10 9 8 7 6 5 4 3 2 1

British Library Cataloguing-in-Publication
Data:
A catalogue record for this title is available
from the British Library.

ISBN 1–84340–013–8

Printed by Times Printing Group, Malaysia
Reproduced by Classicscan Pte Ltd,
Singapore

Contents

Introduction	7
CHAPTER 1 DESIGN DILEMMAS	**8**
The garden is too small	10
The garden is too large	16
The yard has been neglected	22
The garden design doesn't suit the house	28
An eyesore is prominent	30
The garden is dull in the off-season	34
The strip beside the house is bare	38
The garden backs into a wall	40
The garden is visible from all sides	42
CHAPTER 2 SITE PROBLEMS	**44**
The garden is shady	46
The garden is sunny	50
The garden is damp	52
The garden is dry	54
The garden is windy	58
The garden is cold	60
The garden is by the sea	62
The garden is steeply sloping	64
The garden is in an urban area	66
The garden is rocky	68
The garden is under the eaves	70
CHAPTER 3 SOIL PROBLEMS	**72**
Acid soil	74
Alkaline soil	78
Compacted soil	82
Clay soil	86
Sandy soil	88
Poorly drained soil	90
Boggy soil	92
Low-fertility soil	94
High soluble salt content in soil	98

CHAPTER 4 LAWN PROBLEMS 100

Maintenance is too time-consuming 102
The lawn goes brown 106
Thatch has built up 110
A path has been worn in the lawn 112
The lawn is unattractive 114
Grass won't grow under the trees 116
Insects are eating the grass 118
The lawn has a disease 121
Moles are digging up the lawn 125

CHAPTER 5 PLANT PERFORMANCE 126

The mail-order plants arrived too early 128
The plants won't bloom 130
The plants are slow to bloom 134
The plants have stopped blooming 136
The plants won't bear fruit 138
Plants have difficulty getting established
   in the soil 140
The seeds germinate poorly 142
The container plants look ragged
   by midseason 148
The container plants look nutrient deficient 152

CHAPTER 6 INSECT AND
ANIMAL PESTS 154

Aphids 156
Mexican bean beetles 157
Flea beetles 158
Caterpillars 159
Cutworms 160
Earwigs 161
Nematodes 161
Cucumber beetles 162
Japanese beetles 162
Leafhoppers 163
Mealybugs and scale insects 164
Slugs and snails 165
Spider mites 166
Tarnished plant bugs 167
Thrips 167
Birds 168
Rodents 169
Deer 170

CHAPTER 7 WEEDS AND DISEASES 172

Annual and biennial weeds carpet the
   vegetable garden 174
Perennial weeds sneak into the flower beds 177
Basal rot in bulbs 178
Aster yellows 179
Bacterial wilt 179
Botrytis blight, gray mold 180
Crown gall 181
Damping-off and root rot 181
Rust 182
Scab 182
Downy mildew 183
Fusarium wilt 183
Leaf spot 184
Mosaic diseases 185

Glossary 186
Index 186
Acknowledgements 192

INTRODUCTION

Gardening is almost always challenging. Whether you are trying to outwit an animal pest or create a cohesive design for an entire garden, you're sure to run into some unexpected and puzzling problems. For most of us finding just the right solution to a difficulty is sometimes more fun than implementing it and can even rival enjoying the results.

But no one can imagine every potential solution to every possible problem. Sometimes you get stumped. When this happens, it can be helpful to see how other people have approached a similar situation. Their solutions may inspire you to think about the problem in a new way or could be so relevant to your particular situation that you try to copy them exactly. Don't fear – this isn't cheating. Even if you tried to duplicate a design solution down to the last plant, your garden, climate and growing conditions would make the outcome unique. And in the case of working with hard landscaping elements – laying patio stones or installing a pond liner, for example – you're better off following directions that show how to do these things well.

Garden problems usually have more than one solution. When faced with a consist-ently shady area, for example, your choices can include such things as planting a garden of shade-lovers, climbing-up nearby trees or installing a paved patio. It's worthwhile considering as many of them as possible before you act.

That's where this book comes in. It includes many of the most common garden problems – from difficult sites to harsh climates to tough pests – along with a diverse group of practical solutions to each. In some cases, using one of the solutions prevents you from using any more, but in other cases you can try several approaches simultaneously. You can also begin with the least expensive, easiest or most temporary approach; if that doesn't work, you can always try some of the other remedies. Only you know, of course, what the best option is for you, because only you understand your whole garden and what you want from it.

We've designed this book as a brain-storming tool. So look at the various options you'll find here. Maybe you'll find just the right approach to problems in your garden or be inspired by these ideas to come up with your own solution.

USING THIS BOOK

Beneath each solution you will find icons allowing you to see at a glance whether that particular solution is suitable for your situation, whether in terms of cost, time or energy commitment.

 Suitable for organic growers
Ψ Easy
Ѱ Challenging
 Inexpensive
 Moderately expensive
 Expensive

▯ Low energy commitment
▮ Moderate energy commitment
▮ High energy commitment
🕐 Low time commitment
🕐 Moderate time commitment
🕐 High time commitment

chapter one

DESIGN DILEMMAS

Great gardens are distinguished by two important characteristics: the plants are thriving and healthy, and the design of the garden not only suits the environment but also complements it. Yet even the best gardeners sometimes face design dilemmas. Such problems often occur when a gardener with a lovely and established garden moves into a new home and has to adjust to different and, possibly, less than ideal conditions. The new garden may be too small or too large; it may have been neglected or designed with no thought to its wider environment or the home; or it may have particularly challenging areas, such as a bare, shady spot along one side of the house. No matter what the problem, however, there are many easy and affordable ways to overcome the difficulties.

In the following pages, you will find practical solutions to deal with each of the problems mentioned above and also ways to tackle other commonly encountered dilemmas. There are also lists of plants that will thrive in the particular conditions discussed – sunny, shady, moist or dry – because for the best results you should always choose the plants that will do well in the environmental conditions that you find in your garden.

The garden is too small

Small gardens have many advantages, but if you are frustrated by what appears to be a lack of space, their benefits might escape you.

Details are all important in a small area. Weedy patches might go unnoticed in a large garden, but they will stand out in a small one and be almost impossible to ignore. You are, therefore, more likely to weed a small garden, so it will nearly always look its best.

Small gardens can take little time to maintain if you plan them well. If you prefer to spend your leisure time with family and friends instead of pulling weeds or pruning shrubs, a small garden is almost essential, but whether your garden is small by chance or by choice, it's easy to make the best of it.

solution 1 Extend the house

A garden can appear larger than it is if it seems like an extension of the house. If possible, organize the space so that you can walk directly from a room into the garden or onto a garden deck or patio. Tie the areas together by using the same colours and materials in each. For example, if red cushions are a highlight of the indoor room, carry the theme forward by setting up red garden candles and growing a succession of plants with red blooms close to the doorway or path. Alternatively, paint the deck railing with the same shade of high-gloss paint that was used on the moldings in the room, or paint the flooring of the deck the same colour as the carpet or floor in the room. This will help create the impression that they are the same space.

Carefully selected decorative elements will add to this impression. White wicker in the room might tie into white false wicker outside. Use your imagination to come up with ways to make the transition from the house to the garden as seamless as possible.

solution 2 Use colour for illusion

Hot colours – reds, oranges and yellows – jump out at you. They often look closer than they really are and can also make something look bigger than it is. In contrast, cool colours – blue, green, and gray—tend to recede from the eye and make objects look smaller and farther away.

To make a small garden look larger, use cool colours towards the rear and centre of it. Save the hot colours for the area closest to you. Experiment with colours by setting pots of vividly coloured annuals where you are planning to grow perennials in the same hot colours so that you can judge the success of the arrangement for a few days. A solid border of a bright orange-red may set off the design, or that the area looks better when the bright colour is used to punctuate the planting.

The hot colours in this summer border make it look closer.

See also: **'The garden is in an urban area', page 66; 'Low-fertility soil', page 94; 'Plants won't bloom', page 130**

olution 3 Use balance and scale

'he scale of the plants you choose can make your garden eem larger or smaller. For example, if you create a jungle tmosphere with huge plants that tower over the entrance nd crowd at all the edges, the space will feel small. In ontrast, an open vista with smaller plants and areas evoted to quiet foliage or a patch of lawn can make the rea seem larger.

Whenever you are selecting plants, bear this in mind. Lather than growing a 6-m (20-foot) rambling rose against wall, for example, choose a group of miniature climbing oses, which will grow 1-1.5 m (3-5 feet) high, or a delite plant such as a morning glory climber (*Ipomoea* spp.). imilarly, even though a dwarf fruit tree will not give

the same yields as a standard does, it will look more appropriate because it will not dominate the yard.

Leaf size is as important in creating an illusion as over-all plant size. Large leaves will dwarf a garden, while small ones will help to make it look larger. Look at cultivars and even species and choose those with smaller leaves. Creeping thyme is probably a better ground cover for a small garden than variegated pachysandra, for example, and full-grown azaleas will look better than mature rhododendrons.

Small-leaved plants give a light, airy feeling. Use them wherever you want to add a feeling of space.

solution 4 Layer the plants

Layered gardens are like skyscrapers in that they allow you to make the most of the available real estate. However, you must design such a garden carefully so that each plant receives enough light to allow it to thrive.

Use a trellis to train your top-story plants or grow plants such as sunflowers or bamboo that hold themselves upright. Grow slightly shorter plants that prefer filtered light to fit into the middle layer. (See page 117 for some plants that prefer filtered light.) Shade lovers will grow on the bottom layer. Below is a list of low-growing shade-loving plants suitable for the bottom story in a layered planting.

BOTTOM-STORY PLANTS

Adiantum pedatum (maidenhair fern)

Aegopodium podagraria 'Variegatum' (variegated; ground elder)

Ajuga spp. (bugle)

Anemone hupehensis; A. hybrida (Japanese anemone)

Arisaema triphyllum (Jack-in-the-pulpit)

Asplenium scolopendrium

(Hart's tongue fern)

Astilbe arendsii (false goat's beard)

Athyrium filix-femina (lady fern)

Bergenia spp. (elephant's ear)

Convallaria majalis (lily of the valley)

Hedera helix (English ivy)

Helleborus orientalis (Lenten rose)

Hosta undulata var. *albomarginata;*

H. undulata var. *undulata*

Hyacinthoides hispanica (Spanish bluebell)

Juniperus horizontalis Glauca group (creeping juniper)

Pachysandra procumbens; P. terminalis (mountain spurge)

Primula spp. (primrose)

Vinca minor (lesser periwinkle)

Bergenia (elephant's ear)

Convallaria majalis (lily of the valley)

Ajuga spp. (bugle)

solution 5 Build tiered beds

Tiered beds allow you to increase your growing area and make the garden look larger because of the visual variety they add. You are probably familiar with the three-tiered, circular forms traditionally used for strawberries. However, there is no rule about the number of tiers to use or what to plant in them. Tiered forms make a wonderful home for a collection of herbs, for example, and you might use them for a display of rock garden plants, daylily cultivars, or groups of ornamental grasses. A planting usually grown in a mixed perennial border is also a good choice for tiers.

If you buy a mould, you will probably find a galvanized tin version. Although this material is inexpensive, practical, and weather-resistant, it is not attractive. Make it less obtrusive by painting it with a matte-finish brown that will blend with the colour of the soil or, if you are confident that it will work, turn it into a decorative feature by painting it a high-gloss colour that will complement other elements in your garden.

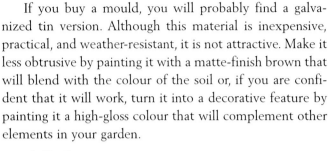

1 Set a large circular metal mould on the lawn or in the garden. These moulds are generally 60 cm (2 feet) tall. Stabilize the mould by pounding short wooden stakes into the soil near its inside perimeter.

2 Fill the mould with soil. Although it is sitting on the ground, this mould is essentially a container. Use a soil mix containing compost for nutrients and additives such as vermiculite and sand for drainage.

3 Set a smaller circular mould on top of the first and fill it with soil. Bury its edges about 8 cm (3 inches) deep and again stabilize it with stakes pounded into the soil. Hide the stakes on the inside edges.

4 Transplant into the mould, starting with the top circle. If you need to step on the soil, stand on a piece of plywood at least 60 cm (2 feet) long and 30 cm (1 foot) wide to spread your weight. Give plants adequate room to grow.

solution 6 Find new spaces

If you are having trouble finding space for all the vegetables that you want to grow in your small garden, use a little ingenuity. You probably already grow as many vegetables as you can on trellises or poles, but you can also grow smaller, low-growing vegetables above the ground. Attach wide plastic or galvanized roof gutters to a fence, at convenient heights, and grow lettuces, herbs, and baby greens in them. Remember to drill drainage holes in the bottom of the gutters before you attach them to the fence so that excess water can drain away.

A few grow-bags or half-baskets hung from a fence or the side of the house can also give you extra space for herbs and salad greens.

Fertilize plants in gutters and space widely enough so that roots can gather adequate water.

solution 7 Get more for your space

In a small garden, every plant counts and, in general, those that bloom the longest count the most. If you truly love a short-flowering perennial, such as a delphinium, by all means plant it, but also include some of the long-flowering perennials listed at right for colour and interest through the season. Look for suggestions for long-blooming annuals on pages 130–133.

⚘ 🐷 ◔ 🥛

Lobelia cardinalis (cardinal flower)

LONG-BLOOMING PERENNIALS

Achillea spp. (yarrow)
Aconitum napellus (monkshood)
Anchusa azurea cvs. (bugloss)
Armeria pseudarmeria (thrift)
Asclepias tuberosa 'Silky Gold',
  'Silky Red' (butterfly weed)
Campanula carpatica (bellflower)
Ceratostigma plumbaginoides (blue
  plumbago, leadwort)
Chelone lyonii (turtlehead)
Dianthus spp. (pinks)
Dicentra spp (bleeding heart;
  Dutchman's breeches)
Echinacea purpurea (purple coneflower)
Echinops ritro (globe thistle)
Eryngium cvs. (sea holly)
Gaillardia grandiflora (blanket flower)
Geum spp. (avens)
Hemerocallis cvs. (daylily)
Heuchera spp. *and* cvs. (alum root)

Hibiscus moscheutos (rose mallow)
Iberis sempervirens (candytuft)
Lathyrus latifolius (sweet pea)
Liatris spp. (gayfeather)
Limonium latifolium (sea lavender)
Liriope muscari (lilyturf)
Lobelia cardinalis (cardinal flower);
  L. siphilitica (blue cardinal flower)
Paeonia spp. *and* cvs. (peony)
Phlox spp.
Physostegia virginiana (obediant plant)
Polygonatum spp. (Solomon's seal)
Potentilla spp. (cinquefoil)
Rudbeckia hirta (black-eyed Susan)
Santolina chamaecyparissus
  (lavender cotton)
Scabiosa caucasica (scabious)
Sedum aizoon; *S. kamtschaticum*;
  S. spectabile 'Autumn Joy' (stonecrop)
Stokesia laevis (Stokes' aster)

solution 8 Change the levels

Introducing variations in level is an excellent way to make a garden look larger than it is, as long as there are not too many levels and they are not built from different materials, which makes them look chaotic. In a small garden, two levels are usually sufficient to be effective, although you can sometimes get away with three if the same materials are used throughout. For example, you can create terraces that are faced with logs or stones or install a two-tier water feature and edge the pond with the same type of stone.

⚘ 🐷 ◑ 🥛

Fill an old compost barrel with soil and plant on several layers to get some extra space in a small garden.

Solution 9 Build terraces

If your garden is small, terracing may be the only way you can transform the area into something you can garden satisfactorily. Terraces offer the same advantages as tiered gardens but are more flexible in terms of design and materials. In most gardens, you can terrace an area yourself. However, if the land is steeply sloped or extremely rocky, you may want to hire a landscaper to do the job. The initial cost will be higher, but the work is likely to hold up longer. Give yourself peace of mind about the project by writing the contract to specify that the landscaper is liable for repairs if a terrace starts to slip.

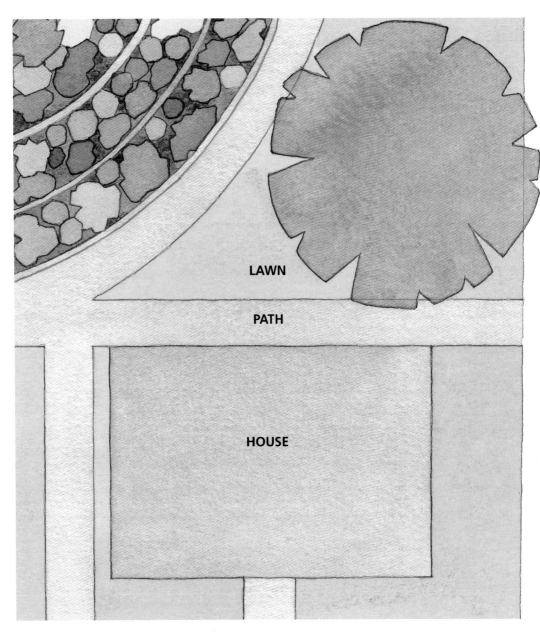

LAWN

PATH

HOUSE

Terraces allow you to plant more closely than you can on the flat, but remember to add stepping stones placed so that you can reach every plant.

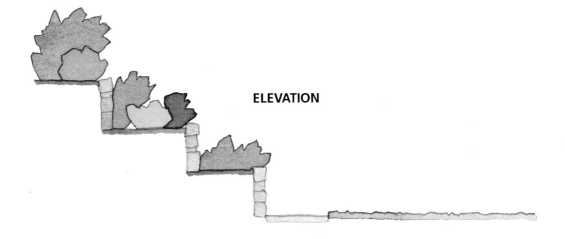

ELEVATION

problem
The garden is too large

Large gardens are a joy for people who never tire of planting, weeding, pruning, and all the other work that a garden entails. You get the space you need to put in orchard crops, a vegetable garden, and any kind of ornamental plantings your heart desires. If you have always wanted a water garden, you can easily fit it into a large garden. But not everyone has the time or inclination to care for a large property. If this is true of you, consider some of the strategies described below to decrease the maintenance time your garden requires.

Even though they enjoy gardening, some people dislike the feeling of a large, open space. They prefer cozier, more intimate areas. It is easy to create an intimate feeling, using hard landscaping or landscaping, in any garden.

solution 1 Use colour for illusion

Just as you can use colour to make a small garden look larger (see page 10), you can also use it to make an area seem smaller. Try planting a border composed of hot pink, red or orange daylilies across a lawn that feels too wide, or carpet the area under trees with impatiens in complementary, hot-coloured shades. If the end of the garden seems too far away, place bright red or orange garden furniture in the spot and grow plants such as trumpet vine (*Campsis grandiflora*) on a trellis or poles that surround the area. Save the blue delphiniums, bachelor's buttons (*Centaurea cyanus*) and balloon flowers (*Platycodon grandiflorus*) for beds around the patio or along the front porch.

Keep hot gardens from being overpowering by adding green or grey foliage and use warm pastels to enliven cool ones.

See also: **'Maintenance is too time-consuming', page 102**

solution 2 Create garden rooms

Large, formal gardens traditionally had at least one 'garden room' formed by a boundary of close-growing hedging plants. Some garden rooms had low walls, enclosed with a boxwood hedge, while others had tall walls composed of plants such as border privet (*Ligustrum obtusifolium*). But no matter what the hedging plants, these rooms not only broke up an expansive area but also provided sitting areas that seemed secluded and offered a measure of privacy.

There is no reason not to copy this style today, as long as you select a hedging plant that requires pruning only once a year and also use some of the labour-saving tricks presented in this book. See pages 20 to 21 and 33 for ideas about using hedges, mulches (including landscape cloth), and easy-care plants, respectively.

Fill a white garden with easy-to-care-for perennials, keep it well-mulched, and add a sitting area so that you can relax and enjoy its peacefulness.

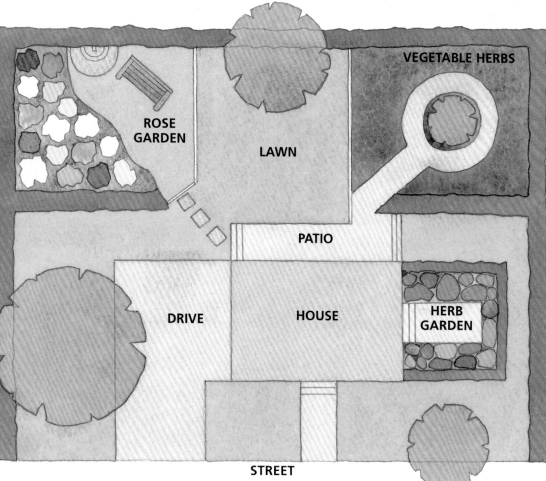

Gardens with lots of different uses sometimes feel chaotic, but you can avoid this by installing hedging to make areas or 'rooms'.

ROSE GARDEN

LAWN

VEGETABLE HERBS

PATIO

DRIVE

HOUSE

HERB GARDEN

STREET

solution 3 Use plants for illusion

Large gardens need large plants, ideally with huge leaves and dramatic blooms. Plants on this scale make a large area feel more lived in. Small plants with tiny leaves are almost unnoticeable in these situations, but if you do see them they make the garden look even bigger than it is. Whenever you are selecting plants for a particular area in a big garden, choose the largest possible specimens. Don't restrict yourself to plants in the list on the opposite page, but do consider growing at least some of them.

The tall, swordlike leaves in this garden are planted to balance each other and also make the space feel intimate.

solution 4 Add paving

Paving can transform a nightmare into a dream. Not only does it look good all year round, but you'll also never have to mow it, fertilize it, or cut it back. You will have to sweep it clear of fallen leaves if you place it under deciduous trees, but there's a trick to avoid that job, too. Spread sheets under the tree and you can bundle up the leaves as they fall.

1 Build a wooden frame for the pavers. Use a T-square and level to square the frame, add stakes to hold it, and add a level layer of crushed stone covered by sand.

2 Set the first stone just beyond the measuring string. Always start in a corner to maintain alignment and press down while you wiggle the stone into place.

3 Check that the paver is level in every direction and also square to the corner of the frame. Set a wooden block under a hammer if you need to correct the level.

4 After checking for square and level, fill the spaces between the stones with mortar. Level the mortar with a flat-edged tool and wash off any spills before they dry.

solution 5 Install crazy paving

1 Excavate the area where the paving is to go to a depth of 10 cm (4 inches). Use strips of thin plywood or Masonite along the edges of the excavated area to make a mould.

2 Lay down a grid of rebar and pour concrete to fill in the area. When the concrete is dry, remove the edging and lay down the stones over the area.

3 Cut the stones so that they fit together. Wear protective goggles and a dust mask and use a circular saw with a diamond-tipped blade for this.

4 Lift each stone and place a bed of mortar under it with a cement trowel. Press the stone into the mortar, making certain that it is firmly seated.

5 Check that the stones are level in all directions. If you find a stone that is raised, use a rubber mallet to pound it down. Continue checking in all directions.

6 Create a clean edge by stretching a string along all the straight edges or a hose along curved ones. Use a pencil to clearly mark this line on the stones.

7 Using the circular saw with the diamond-tipped blade, cut along the pencil line. You want to make the cut smooth so that the edge is not a danger to anyone.

8 Make mortar with 1 part cement and 3 parts sand and push it into the cracks between the stones. Wash off any excess with a wet sponge and water.

olution 6 Add a ground cover

A lawn can be the most time-consuming element in your landscape. Not only do you have to fertilize it, aerate it and dethatch it regularly, but you also have to mow it every seven to ten days when it is growing rapidly. Some people pay someone else to do these chores, but that can get expensive, especially if you have a large lawn. A better alternative is to plant a ground cover.

In a large area, you may be tempted to plant a number of different ground covers. While this can certainly be effective if the plants are well chosen and well positioned, it can also create a messy, patchwork look. It's far safer to begin by planting large patches of one or, at the most, two species. If you do use two, make certain that their colours, forms and flowering seasons coordinate rather than clash.

Choose ground-cover plants according to their appearance. You will be looking at them throughout the season, so it's important that they please you. It's also important to choose them according to the conditions in which they will grow. Some thrive in partial shade, but others need full sun. Some tolerate boggy conditions, although many like well-drained soil. Check the boxes on pages 21, 39, 65, 103 and 116 for appropriate plants.

Use *Anemone nemorosa* (wood anemones) and *Meconopsis cambrica* (Welsh poppies) under trees.

PLANTS FOR ILLUSION

Annuals

Bassia scoparia (summer cypress)

Brugsmansia spp. (angel's trumpet)

Cleome hassleriana (spider flower)

Helianthus annuus (sunflower)

Ricinus communis (castor oil plant)

Tithonia rotundifolia (Mexican sunflower)

Perennials

Aconitum spp. (monkshood)

Aruncus sylvester (goatsbeard)

Baptisia australis (false indigo)

Campanula persicifolia (willow, bellflower, peach bells)

Delphinium elatum

Echinacea purpurea (purple coneflower)

Gaillardia x *grandiflora* (blanket flower)

Helenium autumnale (sneezeweed)

Hemerocallis cvs. (daylily)

Hibiscus cvs.

Hosta spp. *and* cvs.

Liatris scariosa (tall gayfeather)

Lilium spp. (Asiatic and Oriental lilies)

Lobelia cardinalis (cardinal flower)

Monarda didyma (beebalm, bergamot)

Phlox paniculata (garden phlox)

Rudbeckia hirta (black-eyed Susan); *R. lacineata* (golden glow)

Verbascum bombyciferum (felty mullein)

Yucca filamentosa (Adam's needle)

Shrubs

Calycanthus spp. (allspice bush)

Cotinus coggygria (smokebush)

Diervilla lonicera (dwarf honeysuckle)

Euonymus obovatus; E. radicans

Hibiscus syriacus (rose mallow)

Hydrangea spp.

Kolkwitzia amabilis (beauty bush)

Lonicera tatarica (honeysuckle)

Philadelphus spp. (mock orange)

Rhododendron spp.

Salix caprea (goat willow)

Tamarix spp. (tamarisk)

Viburnum opulus (guelder rose)

Wisteria spp.

Vines

Akebia quinata (five-leaf aralia)

Aristolochia macrophylla (Dutchman's pipe vine)

Cobaea scandens (cup-and-saucer vine, monastry bells)

Lablab purpureus (hyacinth bean)

Ipomoea alba (white morning glory)

Lagenaria siceraria (bottle gourd)

solution 7 Decrease maintenance chores

No matter how much you like to garden, you will enjoy your large garden more if you develop some strategies to decrease the amount of time and energy it takes to maintain it. Some, such as using ground cover plants in place of lawn grasses or mulching bare soil between plants, decrease the amount of time you will have to spend on the garden. Others, such as installing paving or tree islands, decrease the size of the area that needs to be maintained.

solution 8 Create a tree island

Trees growing in a large lawn can make its scale less imposing and create a cozier feeling. However, few trees grow well in a lawn and even fewer grasses grow well under trees. In addition, mowing around trunks generally takes more time than it is worth.

A tree island solves all the problems of growing trees in the lawn. Decide where you want to position a grouping of trees and prepare the area by removing the earth. Allow enough space in the island so that each tree will have adequate room when it is mature. If possible, the island should extend far enough out from the eventual drip line of the trees to make it feel like a spacious, parklike spot. Plant the trees as you normally would, but instead of mulching them only to the drip line, cover the entire island with the mulch. For easy maintenance, use fabric covered with a bark or cocoa shell mulch. Edge the island with a mowing strip to make caring for it easier. (See page 104 for installation instructions.)

If the island looks bare because it dwarfs the young trees, position benches, birdbaths, and other garden furniture in it and add some of the easy-care plants listed, at right, to take up space while the trees grow.

Even a single tree can break up a large garden.

Solution 9 Add mulch

Mulches are one of the best ways to decrease the time you spend on weeding, but they also have the benefit of adding a great deal to your garden's appearance. The right mulch can make an ordinary planting look dramatic and will almost always make beds and borders look tidy and well cared for.

In beds and borders, mulches are almost mandatory unless, of course, you can hire an army of gardeners to pluck every weed that takes root. You can choose from a wide range of mulches, from oatstraw for berry bushes to smooth, blue pea stone for a formal entryway. The trick is to match the mulch to the application and lay it down so that it stays in place and doesn't require more topping off than is absolutely necessary.

Straw mulches look good only in hardworking vegetable, herb, small fruit, or cutting gardens. They are not appropriate in ornamental borders and beds, unless you're dressing the plants for winter, when straw makes an ideal mulch for plants such as roses because it insulates while still allowing air movement around the plant's crown, low-

ering the chances of crown rot and other fungal infections.

Bark chips, cedar mulch or cocoa shells, on the other hand, can look good almost anywhere, so use them between enclosed raised beds in a vegetable garden, in a perennial border or around trees and shrubs. To get the most from a loose mulch like chips or shells, enclose it with an edging strip that extends a couple of centimeters (inches) above the mulch. Use brick on end for a handsome look, but if this is impractical simply install the plastic edging strips you can find in any hardware store.

Whenever you are mulching long-lived perennial plants, use a layer of fabric under the mulch. If possible, lay this down before you plant. Cut Xs into it to dig your planting holes, transplant, and cover the cloth with another mulching material. If you are mulching established plants, piece the landscape cloth around each plant and add the second mulch as usual. See page 54 for a list of common mulch materials.

EASY-CARE PLANTS

If you have got a large yard to maintain, the last thing you need is a collection of picky, difficult plants that require a great deal of care. Instead, grow plants that don't ask as much from you. Remember that all plants, even those we call low maintenance, require a little care. Ask neighbours and nursery people for recommendations of plants that thrive with little care in your area and use the list below to get some ideas.

Annuals

Calendula officinalis (pot marigold)
Centaurea cyanus (bachelor's buttons)
Cleome hassleriana (spider flower)
Cosmos bipinnatus
Coreopsis basalis (tickseed)
Eschscholzia californica (California poppy)
Gaillardia pulchella (blanket flower)
Impatiens spp. (busy Lizzie)
Lobularia maritima (sweet alyssum)
Nigella damascena (love-in-a-mist)
Petunia hybrida
Phlox drummondii (annual phlox)

Portulaca grandiflora (rose moss)
Scabiosa atropurpurea (pincushion flower)
Tagetes cvs. (marigold)
Tropaeolium majus (nasturtium)
Viola x *wittrockiana* (pansy)

Ground covers

Ajuga reptans (bugle, carpet bugle)
Convallaria majalis (lily of the valley)
Geranium spp. (cranesbill)
Lysimachia nummularia (creeping Jenny)
Pachysandra procumbens; P. terminalis
Thymus serpyllum (creeping thyme)
Vinca minor (lesser periwinkle)

Perennials

Achillea spp. (yarrow)
Armeria spp. (thrift)
Centaurea macrocephala (knapweed)
Centranthus ruber (red valerian)
Coreopsis verticillata
Dicentra spectabilis (bleeding heart)
Echinacea purpurea (purple coneflower)

Gaillardia grandiflora (blanket flower)
Gaura lindheimeri (white gaura)
Hemerocallis cvs. (daylily)
Perovskia atriplicifolia (Russian sage)
Phlox subulata (moss phlox, moss pink)
Physostegia virginiana (false dragonhead)
Primula spp. (primrose)
Rudbeckia hirta (black-eyed Susan);
  R. laciniata 'Golden Glow'
Salvia farinacea (mealy sage)
Scabiosa caucasica (pincushion flower)
Sedum spp. (stonecrop)
Tanacetum coccineum

Shrubs

Cornus alba (red-barked dogwood)
Forsythia spp.
Fothergilla gardenii (dwarf fothergilla)
Ilex glabra 'Nordic' (inkberry)
Itea virginica (Virginia sweetspire)
Mahonia aquifolium 'Compactum'
  (Oregon grape)
Philadelphus spp. (mock orange)

problem

The garden has been neglected

Neglected gardens are the price many of us pay for a bargain property. Many times, the former owners may have been too old or too busy to keep up with such jobs as pruning deadwood or diseased branches out of trees, over-wintering frost-sensitive plants, or even keeping all the perennial beds weeded.

But don't despair if you have acquired such a property. The fact that you do have to restore it before you can really enjoy it gives you an opportunity to make it into an area suited to your needs and tastes. The task can be daunting, and unless you have a great deal of time and money, it may take a few years to complete. But if you develop a step-by-step restoration plan and keep the goals for each year of your project realistic, you will be able to enjoy the garden while you are transforming it from someone else's problem into your own pride and joy.

solution 1 Develop a long-term plan

Just as it's easier to tackle a huge project at work in small, well-planned steps, it's easier to tackle renovating a garden with a phased plan. It's best to begin at the end: think about what you want the garden to look like when you finish. Once you have that ideal firmly in mind, begin to plan. For example, if you want to create a small pond at one end of the garden, write down each step of building and stocking that pond. If you go through each area of the garden this way, you will soon have a list of jobs that you can use to develop a phased plan. The topics below will help you create a plan that makes sense for your circumstances.

solution 2 Make the design fit your needs

Not everyone wants a backyard barbecue, nor does everyone think a formal herb garden is essential. But you might. No matter what you want, it's essential to begin the revitalization project by making a list of all the ways you want to use the garden. Depending on the amount of space you have, you may need to cut down on your wish list or work out ways to make some areas do double-duty. But even this is a good exercise. You will know what to expect before you get it and won't be disappointed.

Once you have decided what you want, create a list of jobs associated with each area. For example, if a permanent cooking/dining area is important to you but there is no hard surface in the garden, you will have to think about building a paved patio or sturdy deck area before installing a permanent barbecue grill. Write down all the jobs associated with this task. Now do the same for the rest of the garden. When you're finished, map the garden.

solution 3 Map the garden

Site maps are invaluable. They can help you make the best possible use of your space and also allow you to foresee and avoid potential difficulties before they arise.

With a friend, take measurements of all the largest dimensions – house, width and depth of the property, side-path, foundation beds, and so on. You also want to locate fixed elements – trees, for example – that you are going to keep. To locate something like a tree, take measurements from at least two fixed points, say the corner of the house and the shed, to the tree. On the graph paper map, measure the same distance from each point, according to the scale you are using, and draw an arc there. The arcs will intersect where the tree is located.

Once you have your map, you can choose to make multiple photocopies of it or buy a roll of tracing paper to tape over it as you go through the planning process.

On a photocopy or a piece of tracing paper, draw the changes that you want to make. Put a pond where you want it, add a dining area, or sketch in a sandbox for the kids. Draw likely paths, too; you will want to avoid putting a flower bed over a shortcut from one area to another.

When that map is finished, draw the next one. This map will include only the elements that you plan to install in the coming year. Be realistic as you add them; people have only so much time, money, and energy in any one growing season. Go on through the maps this way, adding and subtracting elements as you add photocopies or tracing paper for each year until you have recreated a semblance of the first map you drew. You have now set your goals for each phase of the project, and if you have planned well you won't have any nasty surprises about what the garden will look like at any one time.

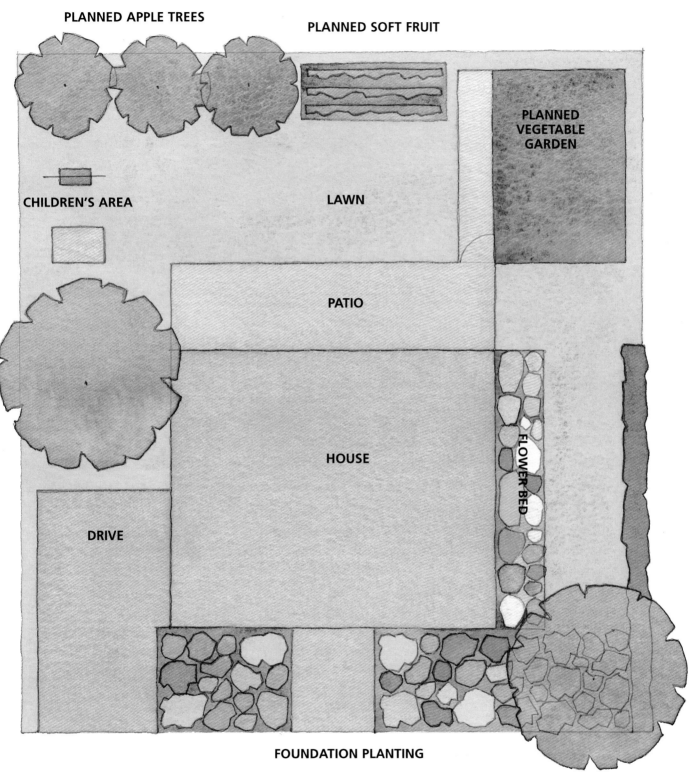

PLANNED APPLE TREES

PLANNED SOFT FRUIT

**PLANNED
VEGETABLE
GARDEN**

CHILDREN'S AREA

LAWN

PATIO

FLOWER BED

HOUSE

DRIVE

FOUNDATION PLANTING

A simple site map like this allows
you to visualize moving between
spaces as well as viewing the garden
from different vantage points.

solution 4 Make cosmetic changes first

No matter what your long-term plans, short-term pleasure is important. A good goal for the first season is making the garden immediately useful and pleasant. After that, you can take on the big jobs. The following small steps make a huge difference.

• Take care of the lawn. It sets the tone for the whole property, and if you have kids they'll need a nice place to play while you're busy renovating both inside and out. Mow the grass and reseed it if necessary. (See Chapter 4 for information about specific lawn problems.)

• Remove weeds in the beds, even those you will eventually pave over. Weed-free areas will do wonders for your state of mind.

• Cut back overgrown plants. Depending on the season, prune woody perennials. (See page 139 to learn when to prune various shrubs and vines.)

• Divide or remove overgrown perennials, as shown in solution 6.

• Paint or spruce up structures and walls. Even if you don't plan to keep a structure, make it look decent in the interim.

• Plant brightly colored annuals. Whether it's just adding some containers at the front door or putting in a small bed in the front garden, add some colour to make the garden look loved.

Even if your garden isn't this grand, you can strive for a lawn that looks smooth and perfect.

Solution 5 Assess existing plants

Even if the garden you're moving into is a total wreck, there are probably some plants worth keeping, so think carefully before making any decisions. Unfortunately, no matter how painful it is, there are times when you have to remove a mature tree. Make the decision easier by applying these guidelines:

• If the tree casts so much shade that you cannot grow anything else in a large portion of the yard, prune it. (See page 48.) If pruning doesn't do the trick and you really can't get anything else to grow, remove the tree (as long as it doesn't have a preservation order on it).

• If the tree is badly infested with a pest or disease, try to control the problem. (See pages 154–187.) If the problem persists after a year of effort, take out the tree.

• If the tree is a nuisance, take it out. Trees that qualify include those that drop small, messy fruit onto patios or parked cars or those that encourage wasps. If the tree is a fruit tree of a kind that you want to grow you may find a more pest- and/or disease-free cultivar to replace it with.

Look at perennials in much the same way. If you dislike a plant or if it is diseased, you can remove it. But if a plant is healthy, fibrous rooted and you like everything but its location, try to move it. Follow the instructions below.

1 In early spring, use a sharp spade to cut through the soil in a circle around the plant. Make deep cuts far enough away from the trunk to keep many of the plant's feeder roots.

2 Recut the circle again in midsummer, going even deeper and beginning to cut the bottom of what will become the root ball. Repeat this again in the fall, before mulching the plant for winter.

3 The following spring, cut again. But this time, use the spade to move the root ball onto a board covered with a large sacking sheet. Once the plant is on the board, wrap it with the sacking.

4 Lower the plant into its new hole and pull the sacking out from under it. Backfill the hole as usual, adding water when it's half-way filled to force out air pockets.

solution 6 Renovate old flower beds

Most flower beds need renovation from time to time, but if you have kept up with winter care, cutting back, adding compost and other additives, weeding, mulching and dividing as plants needed it, you probably won't have to think about this for years after first planting. However, if you have ignored the work or acquired a neglected garden, you will have to renovate.

Begin by digging out all the plants, dividing them into a pile to keep and a pile of those to give or throw away. The only plants you don't want to dig are peonies, because they do not transplant well, and plants that are just too large to move without taking heroic measures. (See page 134 for these.) You will have to work around these as you renovate.

It's best to renovate early in the spring, just after you can see new growth and the ground has thawed enough to dig easily. Wrap the root ball of each plant you want to keep in wet newspaper and place it in a consistently shady spot. Keep the newspaper and root balls wet during the week or two it will take you to renovate.

Test the soil for pH, even if the plants look healthy. If you discover that the pH deviates much from 6.5, apply the recommended amount of either ground limestone or flowers of sulfur to bring it to 6.5, till or spade it into the top few centimetres (inches), and then water. A few days later, add at least 2.5 cm (1 inch) of fully finished compost to the bed, and if you suspect that phosphorus, calcium, potassium or trace elements are low, apply about 2.25 kg (5 pounds) each of rock phosphate and greensand for every 9.3 sq m (100 square feet) of bed area. Again, till or spade this material into the top few inches (centimetres) of the soil and then water.

You can now put the plants back into the ground. Remember to divide any that are too large and plant each one with adequate space to grow for a few years without needing division. If you are worried that the bed will look bare, put in annuals to take up the space. This is also the time to add plants that you have been meaning to grow. Mulch to keep weeds down and walk away knowing that aside from regular maintenance, you won't have to worry about that bed for a good five years or so.

1 Dig the crowded daylily clump when the weather is relatively cool and you expect good rainfall. Place the roots on a scrap of plywood or piece of cardboard.

2 Insert two spading forks, back to back, into the centre of the root ball. Force the spading forks apart – the roots and bulbs will separate without much damage.

olution 7 Make new garden beds

's more than likely that you will want to make a few new
arden beds. If you are transforming a lawn area into a gar-
en, you can remove the grass before you begin or put
heet mulch on top of it. Your choice should depend on the
ypes of weeds and grasses you will be replacing. If there
are a lot of plants that spread by runners or rhizomes, it's
best to remove them. But if most of them are fibrous-root-
ed species that spread by seeds, sheet composting will
work. This is illustrated below.

1 Cover the area where you want to make a
new bed with cardboard, overlapping the edges.

2 Shovel compost or a mix of topsoil and compost over the cardboard plus any additives.

3 Smooth the area and add a deep layer of
mulch. You can plant in it the following spring.

Once established, flower beds are
easy to maintain and care for.

problem
The garden design doesn't suit the house

Few people try to plan a garden to suit the architectural style and feeling of the house it complements. It's common to see overgrown cottage-style gardens in front of formal brick buildings, for example, or asymmetrical flower beds on only one side of a central path leading to such a home. Less common are formal gardens in the front of cottages, but it could happen. While it's certainly possible to design a garden in opposition to the style of a building, it's difficult to make it look appropriate. Your garden will look much better if it conforms to the feeling of your house, so it's worth taking the time to design it that way.

solution 1 Make a planting formal

Formal gardens are characterized by symmetry and balance and are usually geometric in outline. Many people recoil from this design style because they think it has to be cold, rigid and unimaginative. Nothing could be farther from the truth, however. Once you have satisfied the needs for balance, symmetry and a well-defined outline, you can have as much latitude as you want with the other elements of the design.

A simple way to begin experimenting with this style is to plan gardens to flank the front path and entrance. By giving the gardens straight edges and corners with right angles, making them identical on both sides, and planning so that mature plants will be in scale with the size of the house, you have satisfied the requirements of a formal design. If you want to include vividly colored annuals and perennials with lavish leaves, feel free to do so. Formal gardens don't have to be confined to plants with blue, white and soft mauve flowers.

Only a formal garden would complement this house. But formal gardens also suit smaller homes with symmetrical lines.

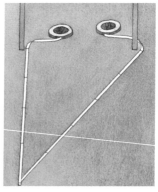

Make a right angle with the 3, 4, 5 rule: measure 1m (3 feet) on one side of a stake, 1.25m (4 feet) to the other side. The distance between these points will be 1.5m (5 feet) if the angle is square.

solution 2 Match the colours

If your house is painted in neutral colours, you can plant whatever your heart desires in the front garden. However, if the walls, shutters, roof or door are a noticeable colour, pay attention to the other colours you introduce. Without advance planning, you might find out how easy it is to create a horror show of clashing hues. A combination of reds and pinks will probably fight with brick-coloured roof tiles, for example, but oranges and yellows can supply the same warm feeling and also fit into the colour scheme of the home.

Colour matching is especially important when it comes to window boxes and foundation plantings. Even if you decide to get a little experimental out at the front, try to make the colours in the areas close to your home similar to or compatible with the major colours of the house.

Solution 3 Make a planting informal

Informal gardens can range from tightly packed cottage gardens, where plants sprawl over each other and volunteer seedlings are welcome, to well-planned beds filled with any number of plants. The only requirement of an informal planting is that it is not designed along formal lines.

These gardens suit most modern homes, particularly those with asymmetrical design elements. They are also appropriate on plots where curves—from the street or a drive, for example—are prominent. But don't assume that you can just plant a hotchpotch collection of plants in any configuration and succeed in making a beautiful garden. Instead, try to echo the lines of the house, drive, or street in its outline. By working within these confines, you can make your informal garden complement rather than detract from your home.

A second misconception about informal gardens is that they are easier to care for because they can be chaotic in design. While it's true that they can be more forgiving about when you weed them, maintaining them can be more time-consuming because they are more complicated. Make your informal garden practical by planting through fabric and mulching. (See page 21.)

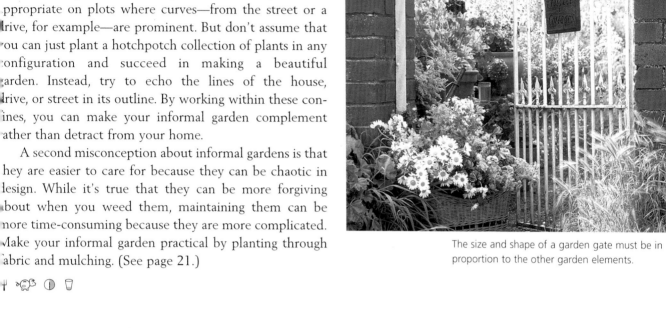

The size and shape of a garden gate must be in proportion to the other garden elements.

Solution 4 Match the scale

Scale is always important when it comes to garden design. A big house needs big plants and large gardens, while a small one looks far better with daintier plantings. If you are moving into a large new house, one without any plantings at all, you might wonder how to create a big look in a hurry. After all, it takes trees years and years to mature to the point where they look in scale with a large house.

One of the best tricks is creating a large garden of hot-coloured plants in a prominent location. For example, if you have a long drive leading to this big house, you can plant a collection of warm-coloured daylilies along its length. Make the planting at least 1.2 – 1.5 m (4 or 5 feet) deep to give it the presence you want.

A tree island (see page 20) is another way to create an instant garden in scale with the house. Even though the trees will take some time to grow to any size, the mulched area is large enough to count for a lot of visual weight. Patios, gazebos, arbours, garden furniture, and water features can all fill out the garden and make the house seem a part of a landscape rather than the dominant feature of it.

The opposite problem, working with a small house, calls for a different approach. Simplicity is your best ally. For example, rather than planting a border of daylilies of various hot colours, put in a long monochromatic planting. It could be daylilies, certainly, but it would be more successful if it was a narrow border of a lemon-coloured cultivar. See pages 10 to 11 for design tricks for small gardens.

Cottage gardens can take more work than formal ones. Use mulches and choose easy-care plants to decrease labour time.

problem
An eyesore is prominent

More often than not, the view from a garden is less than ideal. Given people's proximity to each other, you might be ab
to see the neighbours' rubbish bins or the back of their garage. Fortunately, the best solutions to this problem all mak
your own garden more beautiful. And depending on your choice of plant, they can also give you delicious fruit.

Your choice of solution will depend on the size of the area to be camouflaged. If it's extensive, you might as well plar
a thick, tall hedge. But if it's simply a utility area, a 2-m (6-foot) fence will hide it, as will a plant-covered trellis. You ca
also use trellises and screens to conceal your own utility areas, turning them into assets rather than liabilities.

solution 1 Build a wooden trellis

Wooden trellises have the virtue of being extremely flexible. You can build them as long and as high as the situation demands. Just by varying the footing of the supporting posts they hang from, you can also make them a temporary or a permanent feature of the garden. And best of all, no matter where you put your up trellis – in full light or filtered shade – there's sure to be a climbing plant that will thrive on it.

Try to decide what plant you are going to grow before you put up your trellis. Climbers have different ways of attaching themselves to their supports; the plant you want may not be able to climb your trellis unless you plan ahead. See 'Climbing styles', opposite, for information to help you match the climber to its support.

Size and sturdiness are also considerations. If you are putting in a trellis for a wisteria plant, set 2 x 2 m (6 x 6 foot) posts in concrete; these plants need the strongest possible trellis. Small perennial plants, such as kiwi, don't require such a strong trellis, but they do need one that will last for years. It doesn't hurt to set the supporting posts in concrete, as shown on page 30. Trellises for small annual plants don't need to be as large or long

lasting. The illustrations opposite show how to install trellis for a light annual plant such as a morning glory o sweet pea.

A wooden trellis can be so striking, even without climbing plants, that it effectively stops the eye from travelling beyond it.

Solution 2   Build a screen

A screen is simply a trellis that is more tightly woven and thus less see-through than a trellis. It might be just the right way to disguise whatever you are trying to hide because you really can't see through it, even in winter when the leaves are off the plants. However, it's wise to think about what kind of plant to grow on it

Plants that climb with 'holdfasts' or aerial rootlets can generally climb a screen, particularly if it has a little texture for them to cling to. However, before you decide to plant something like this, think about humidity levels and weight.

If you live in a humid climate, you may be asking for trouble by growing a plant right against a screen. This will not be a problem if the screen allows air to move through it, but, if it doesn't, humidity levels around the plant could be high enough to cause diseases.

Many plants are heavier than they appear. English ivy, for example, is a weighty plant because, as it ages, its stems become woody. If your screen is heavy and you have installed it with posts set in concrete, this shouldn't be a problem.

If you have any doubt about either humidity or strength, save yourself future grief by setting up a trellis just beyond the screen. Plants can grow on this structure, and the screen will still be there to provide a pleasant view all through the year.

1 Protect your trellis by installing a nylon screen about 30 cm (1 foot) in front of it for vines to climb. The space allows air circulation.

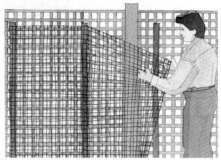

2 Attach the nylon net trellis to the stakes with staples or tie them in place, at close intervals, with strong wire.

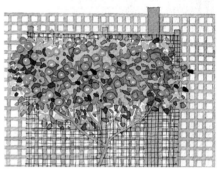

3 Plant a perennial or annual climbing vine 15–30 cm (0.5–1 foot) in front of the nylon trellis and tie it in place.

Vining styles

Aerial rootlets – *Hedera helix* (English ivy)
Aerial rootlets grow from the stem of the plant and attach themselves to crevices in their support. In the wild, they can climb trees, but they are equally at home on brick and rough wood walls.

Twining stems – *Wisteria*
Plants with twining stems curl around any support they can find while they are growing. Most require thin supports that are easy to encircle, but large, heavy plants, such as wisteria, require stout ones.

Tendrils – *Lathyrus odoratus* (sweet peas)
Many of the plants that hold onto their supports with tendrils have stems that also twine around whatever they can. The small tendrils need slender supports, such as nylon netting or small wood trellises.

Holdfasts – *Parthenocissus quinquefolia* (Virginia creeper) or *P. tricuspidata* (Boston ivy)
The holdfasts on most vines are shaped like small suction cups. They adhere to the surfaces by secreting an adhesive substance. This makes them able to climb smooth walls.

Scandent – climbing rose
Some of the plants we call climbing actually lean against their supports rather than climb them. Climbing roses are an excellent example. You will have to tie them to their supports to keep them in place.

solution 3 Build a wooden fence

Fences are sometimes the best way to obscure an unsightly view. If your yard looks over an abandoned lot, chances are that you don't want to have to look at it every day. A fence, with boards placed tight against each other, will hide it. This kind of fence can also keep some, but not all, of the problems that grow on the lot from blowing onto your property. Low-flying weed seeds, disease spores, and pest insects will tend to get trapped on that side of the fence, minimizing the troubles your garden could acquire.

While you can grow many plants right up against a fence, it's not a good idea. Plants give off moisture, which can damage the fence after a few years, and, mor important, the moisture they release can create the kind o environment that makes them susceptible to funga diseases. Good air circulation is the best preventativ measure against these problems. If you want to grow plant against the fence, use 20–30cm (8–12 inches eyescrews to attach a wooden or plastic trellis, nylo netting, or even strings for twining plants to climb. Th distance guarantees that some air can move behind th climbing plants.

1 Dig a straight-sided hole by hand or use a post-hole digger. Make the hole about 20cm (8 inches) wider than the post and 20cm (8 inches) deeper than you will set it.

2 Use a level to check that the pole is standing straight. Add about 10cm (4 inches) of soil and tamp it down to hold the post in position while you mix the concrete.

3 Check level again, pour concrete to fill the hole half-way, check level again, add water to help the concrete set quickly, and finish filling with concrete.

4 Wait at least a day for th concrete to finish setting. Once it dry, screw fencing panels betwee the posts. Again, use a level t make true lines.

solution 4 Plant a distraction

Plants alone, without any hardscaping, can serve as a distraction. A group of bamboo, for example, can add a graceful note to any yard. If you plant ornamental grasses or other lovely foliage plants in front of them, they will act as a living wall behind those plants, and observers will rarely look beyond them.

Other tall, bushy plants can also distract the eye. Mexican sunflower (*Tithonia rotundifolia*), with its velvety, dark green, heart-shaped leaves and brilliant orange-red blooms, is such a vivid plant that no one looks beyond it. Again, if you need to create a distraction at its feet, use a spreading foliage plant, such as a hosta, or grow impatiens in a color that doesn't fight with the brillian flowers above.

Shrubs can also serve this purpose. Some, such as wil roses (*Rosa rugosa*), can serve double duty in thes locations. Not only will they shield the viewer from th sights beyond, but their thorny stems will also preven small animals from crossing the boundary. Just use you imagination to come up with a planting that will suit th environment while also acting as a visual distraction.

...lution 5 Plant a hedge

...dges can offer several benefits to the garden. First of all, ...y can form a screen that totally obscures the view ...yond them. In addition, they can create a gentle ...dbreak that moderates wind enough so that some ten-... plants are helped to withstand winter weather. Hedges ...ir the street can absorb a great deal of noise and also ...p some of the pollution from traffic out of your garden. ...d from a purely decorative point of view, a hedge can ...vide a dark green living 'wall' that sets off the ...uty of the plants in front of it.

You can choose either a deciduous or an evergreen ...nt for your hedge. You can make it dense by planting a ...uble staggered row, or keep it simpler by planting only a single row. Depending on your taste and the design needs of the garden, you can make it formal by pruning it to a rigid shape, or informal by pruning only to make it bushier and keep it in bounds. If you wish, you can choose a hedge that will feed the birds with berries in the autumn and winter or one that will be so prickly that it discourages visits from wandering animals.

No matter what sort of hedge you decide on, plan ahead. Learn how tall and wide the hedge will eventually become so that you can avoid problems with the neighbours. If it might grow onto their property, assume the worst. Plant it far enough away from the property line so that trespass never becomes an issue. It's also wise to collect other sorts of information. What exposure will the plant stand? What soil conditions does it prefer? How much moisture does it need? Is it resistant to pests and diseases or will it draw them like a magnet? How frequently and severely do you have to prune it? Is it poisonous? Does it drop fruits that can become a nuisance? Use the chart below as you begin to research possible plants for your hedge.

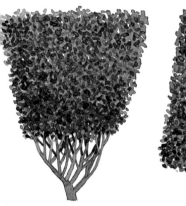

...you prune so that the top is ...vider than the bottom, the ...ottom leaves will fall off.

Pruning so the top is narrower than the bottom allows light to reach the whole plant and snow can slide off easily in winter.

Pruning so that the whole plant is the same width allows light to reach all parts.

HEDGING PLANTS

Deciduous	Height m (ft)	Rate of growth	Exposure	Pruning time
Berberis spp. (barberry)	1.2–2.2 (4–7)	Moderate	Sun or partial shade	Early spring
Cotoneaster lucidus (hedge cotoneaster)	1.5–4.5 (5–15)	Rapid	Sun or partial shade	Spring or summer
Rosa rugosa (wild rose)	2–2.2 (6–7)	Rapid	Full sun	Early spring
Spiraea spp.	2.6 (9)	Rapid	Sun or partial shade	Early spring
Evergreen				
Buxus spp. (boxwood)	0.9–2.4 (3–8)	Slow	Sun or shade	Early spring
Euonymus japonicus (evergreen euonymus)	2–3 (6–10)	Moderate	Sun or partial shade	Late spring
Ilex spp. (holly)	0.3–6 (1–20)	Moderate	Sun or partial shade	Late spring
Ligustrum spp. (privet)	2–4.5 (6–15)	Rapid	Sun or partial shade	As needed
Annually				
Pseudotsuga menziesii (Douglas fir)	6 (20)	Rapid	Full sun	Early spring
Pyracantha coccinea (scarlet firethorn)	2–4.2 (6–14)	Rapid	Full sun	As needed

problem

The garden is dull in the off-season

The first frost may herald more than a change of season in your garden; it could also mean that it's beauty is finished f
the year. This is often the case in gardens devoted primarily to annuals and herbaceous perennials. Once the blooms a
gone, the garden becomes dull.

Don't let this happen in your garden. Even in the cooler climes, there are too many fine days when a brisk walk ou
side or even a short spell of sitting in the garden is just what you need. It's also a treat to be able to look out the window
at a constantly changing and evolving landscape with good looks no matter what time of year.

You can create such a landscape by paying attention to the basic design, including some woody plants, adding som
garden furniture, and choosing plants that remain lovely through more than one season.

solution 1 Add structural elements

What garden is complete without some furniture? Even
if your garden is primarily practical – a place to grow
vegetables, fruit and cut flowers – it's a pleasure to have a
simple bench or a nook with a table and chair. Birdbaths
add the pleasure of watching birds in all seasons, but many
of the birds they attract do more than look beautiful. They
are some of the best insect pest controls in all of nature. No
matter how small the area, you're sure to be able to fit in
a garden structure or two if you give it some thought. And
not only will you enjoy the structure during the season,
you will also like the dimension it gives to the out-of-
season garden.

LEFT Gazebos add a
romantic touch to any
garden, even the most
practical. Think carefully
about its location before
adding it – put it where
you'll want to sit in all
seasons.

BELOW LEFT Use attractive
trellises in climates where
they'll be bare for part of
the year.

BELOW RIGHT Metal benche
look good in any season.
Use a cushion to enjoy the
bench in winter.

olution 2 Add autumn colour

Autumn gardens can easily be as bright and colourful as any in spring or summer. Many species bloom in autumn and others sport leaves in vivid oranges, yellows and reds. Berries and rose hips shine out from bushes, and trellises and bare branches add an architectural look to any garden.

Plan for autumn when you design your garden. Use the following list as a starting point for choosing plants that come into their own once the days are short and temperatures are falling.

♉ ⋊🐑 ◑ 🥛

PLANTS FOR AUTUMN INTEREST

Perennials

Allium cristophii (ornamental onion)

Cyclamen hederifolium (hardy cyclamen)

Dictamnus albus var. *purpureus* (burning bush, dittany, fraxinella)

Epimedium x *versicolor* 'Sulphureum' (barrenwort, bishop's mitre)

Eryngium bourgatii (sea holly)

Shrubs

Berberis thunbergii 'Rose Glow' (Thunberg's barberry)

Callicarpa bodinieri var. *giraldii* 'Profusion' (beauty berry)

Calluna vulgaris 'Robert Chapman' (heather)

Cornus sanguinea 'Winter Berry' (common dogwood)

Cotoneaster lacteus (evergreen cotoneaster)

Euonymus alatus (winged spindle)

Fothergilla major (mountain witch hazel)

Hydrangea quercifolia (oak-leaved hydrangea)

Viburnum opulus 'Xanthocarpum' (guelder rose)

Climbers

Clematis 'Rosy O'Grady' (downy clematis); C. *tangutica* (lemon peel clematis)

Cotoneaster horizontalis (fishbone cotoneaster)

Parthenocissus henryana (Virginia creeper)

Pyracantha 'Orange Glow' (firethorn)

Complement the bright autumn colours of a maple tree with some equally vivid *Pyracantha* 'Orange Glow' for autumn drama.

solution 3 Add winter interest

Many of the plants that add interest to the autumn garden also look good in winter. Similarly, if a plant looks good in winter, you can be sure it also adds a dimension to the autumn garden. Fortunately, most of these plants are as good in the summer as they are in the autumn and winter.

If you don't know what some of these species look like take a trip to a local nursery with a list in hand. Ask what they have; you may be pleasantly surprised to find some real treasures for your garden.

PLANTS FOR WINTER INTEREST

The curving design of these plants adds to the effect they create on dreary winter days.

Perennials

Bergenia 'Sunningdale' (elephant's ear)
Helleborus foetidus (stinking hellebore)

Shrubs

Cornus mas (Cornelian cherry)
Erica carnea 'Golden Starlet' (winter heath)
Hamamelis x *intermedia* 'Jelena' (witch hazel)
Mahonia japonica

Vines

Hedera helix (English ivy)
Wisteria spp.

solution 4 Install a Zen garden

Zen gardens are becoming more and more popular as increasing numbers of gardeners see them in the media. A broad expanse of sand or pea stone, punctuated by a boulder or two, a simple planting of ornamental grasses or stark bamboo, and a sleek water feature is immensely calming. As ourlives become ever more hurried, our appreciation for this sort of garden grows.

You will enjoy this garden all through the year. During the growing season, it will offer a respite from the bright colours and busyness of the rest of the garden, but you may be surprised to find that you love it best of all in winter. The forms of this garden remain intact even if snow covers the landscape, and the quiet becomes more complete. It can be a place to forget the pressures of everyday life.

To make your Zen garden, pick a flat, out-of-the-way area of the yard. Clear it of sod (see page 64). If you want boulders in the garden, set them in place and bury the bottoms about 15cm (6 inches) deep to keep them in place. It's best to lay fabric over the bare soil you will be covering with sand or pea stone. Not only does it minimize the amount of sand that washes down into the soil when it rains, but it also prevents any grasses that spread by rhizomes from growing through it. Similarly, if you have a water feature, set it down into the soil and surround it with the fabric and sand or pea stone.

Less is always more in a Zen garden. Keep it simple to make it effective.

olution 5 Make spring gardens vibrant

pring makes the blood of every gardener run faster.
he first snowdrops, the crocuses that push through the
nelting slush by the front door, the tiny green shoots that
how where the ground is suddenly bare – it's all
vonderfully exciting. But after the first excitement, some
ardens can be rather an anticlimax. Instead of bursting
vith spring colour and new growth, they look barren and a
•it dingy.

Fortunately, spring gardens can be lovely, thanks
o some tricks to make them so. First of all, use garden
tructures and the forms of woody plants in your garden
or the backbone of a good design. Next, plant some of the
pecies suggested for winter interest (see opposite page).
This will set a good stage for spring flowers.

A few bulbs scattered here and there don't look
inspiring, but masses of them create a real show. Naturalize
as many early-blooming daffodils as you can possibly afford
in a tree island or anywhere else that you can avoid
mowing for a few weeks.

Make your mixed bulb gardens more inviting by
planting in tiers. Take advantage of the fact that you plant
larger bulbs, such as daffodils, as much as 20cm (8 inches)
below the soil surface, but smaller ones, such as grape
hyacinths, only a few inches down. You can plant a layer of
daffodils, cover them with enough soil to place the grape
hyacinths at the correct depth, and then cover the grape
hyacinths. In spring, you will have a pretty mixed planting.

BULB COMPANIONS

Make your bulb plantings more interesting
by planting a companion that will bloom
at the same time or not long after they do.
You can also plant your bulbs in an area
where perennials will soon grow large
enough to hide the yellowing leaves. Good
bulb companions include the following:

Alchemilla mollis (lady's mantle)
Bellis perennis (English daisy)
Helleborus niger (Christmas rose)
Myosotis alpestris (alpine forget-me-not);
 M. sylvatica (forget-me-not)
Oenothera speciosa (evening primrose)

Primula marginata (primrose)
Viola tricolor (pansy, viola)

Don't be afraid to pair forget-me-nots with
tulips – no matter how often you see this
combination, it's always lovely.

problem
The strip beside the house is bare

Many homes are built on relatively narrow plots and are often positioned on the site so that a narrow strip of grass is left on one side of the house. Depending on the house's orientation and the proximity of neighbouring homes, this strip can be extremely shady or sunny for a good part of the day. More often than not, it's a place where nothing but grass grows. You probably don't use the lawn there because the area is too narrow or too exposed, but you do mow it. If you have been wondering what use you could make of this space, use the suggestions below to stimulate your imagination.

solution 1 Create a narrow border

A narrow border running along the side of the house may be just what you want to liven up the property. Because you won't want to mow at all in this spot, begin by installing some sort of permanent pathway. You could use bricks, stones or a thick layer of bark chips, but it should be wide enough so that you can work from it with ease. It should also allow you to reach every plant in the border. It may be a good idea to put the path beside the house and the border against the property boundary so that the plants or moisture from them doesn't interfere with the house's wall.

Your choice of plants depends entirely on the environment in the strip. Chances are that it is sheltered from the wind, but it may be shady or sunny, arid or quite moist. Check the index of this book to find lists of appropriate plants for its conditions.

Large leaves and tall plants add drama.

solution 2 Grow fruits or vegetables

Vegetable and fruit plants are often so lovely that you can use them as part of the landscape. You don't need to have a special garden for them. However, not all of them are pretty, and if you want an appreciable quantity of a particular crop, it would certainly look odd as part of the foundation planting.

Depending on the environment in the strip beside the house, this may be just the place to grow some fruits or vegetables. If sun hits it for at least six hours a day, you can set up a trellis or use the fence to grow raspberries, or lay down fabric and put in a crop of strawberries. As long as the area receives reflected light for a good part of the day or direct light for two hours or so, a little shade needn't discourage you. Plant a group of cool-loving herbs, both medicinal and culinary, as well as lettuce and other greens for salads. The list to the right can get you started.

Space-saving containers can add interest.

Solution 3 Plant a four-season ground cover

Ground cover plants are often the best solution to a landscaping problem. They have the advantage of being extremely low maintenance once they are established, and if you choose wisely they can look good all year.

No matter what ground cover you choose, reduce weeding by laying down fabric and cutting holes in the appropriate spots to plant. If the ground cover will take some time to cover the area completely and you don't like the look of the landscape cloth, put down mulch to hide it. Choose from among the plants listed below.

FOUR-SEASON GROUND PLANTS

Ajuga reptans (bugle, carpet bugle)

Arabis alpina subsp: caucasica (mountain rockcress, wallcress)

Bergenia spp. (elephant's ear)

Erica spp. (heath)

Euonymus fortunei and cvs.

Hedera helix (English ivy)

Juniperus horizontalis (creeping juniper)

Leucothoe spp.

Mahonia aquifolium (Oregon grape)

Microbiota decussata

Pachysandra terminalis cvs.

Taxus baccata 'Repandens' (yew)

Vinca minor and cvs. (lesser periwinkle)

Pachysandra terminalis

HERBS AND VEGETABLES FOR PARTIAL SHADE

Anthriscus cerefolium (chervil)

Galium odoratum (sweet woodruff)

Levisticum officinale (lovage)

Mentha spp. (mint)

Monarda didyma (beebalm, bergamot)

Origanum majorana (sweet marjoram)

Petroselinum crispum (parsley)

Tanacetum vulgare var. *crispum* (tansy)

Thymus spp. (thyme)

Brassica hirta (mustard)

Brassica rapa var. *nipposinica* (Japanese greens, mizuna)

Claytonia perfoliata (miner's lettuce)

Eruca vesicaria var. *sativa* (rocket)

Lactuca sativa (lettuce)

Rumex scutatus (sorrel)

Spinacia oleracea (spinach)

Valerianella locusta (Mache)

problem
The garden backs into a wall

In urban areas, it's inevitable that some gardens will back right into a wall. This has the advantage of increasing the privacy, but it certainly doesn't make an attractive view. If the wall belongs to your neighbour, you will need to get permission before putting some of these solutions in place. However, since none of them will damage the wall, that shouldn't be a tall order.

Before you plant anything, think about painting the wall. If you put up a trellis for screening plants, you won't see much of the wall once the plants are full grown, but that will take a few years, and even then the colour of the wall will peek out between the leaves. So paint the wall a colour you can live with and that won't fight with whatever plants you eventually grow. Pale tan, green, blue and grey are all reasonable choices. White and off-white can also look good in the right circumstances.

solution 1 Attach a trellis to a wall

Walls can give wonderful support to almost any kind of trellis, but to protect both the wall and the plants you will need to attach them so that there is 20 – 30 cm (8 – 12 inches) between the wall and the trellis. This space will allow air to move between the plants and the wall, blowing off and drying the moisture that the leaves give off.

1 To make a long-lasting trellis to cover a brick wall, you'll need to attach it to the masonry. Ask for special masonry screws at the hardware store to attach the lathing strips securely to the bricks.

2 Add a second lathing strip to those you've attached to the wall to add some air circulation behind the trellis. Attach a wooden trellis with galvanized outdoor screws.

3 Remember to use a level at every step to check that lines are true. Even though plants or pots may eventually cover the trellis, a crooked installation will bother the eye.

Solution 2 Grow a border of screening plants

Screening plants can do a great deal to cover a wall. But rather than sticking to just one type of plant, you may want to develop what amounts to a border of tall plants. This solution requires a deep area, because the plants you will be using all require some space.

Depending on your taste, you can plant one species, perhaps a dark-coloured hedging plant such as Canadian hemlock (Tsuga Canadersis), at the rear and then add complementary flowering hedging plants in front of it. Alternatively, after painting the wall a neutral colour that you like, plant a mixed group of tall flowering plants. In addition to the hedging and screening plants listed on page 33, think about using some of the species listed here.

FLOWERING HEDGE PLANTS
Abelia x *grandiflora* (glossy abelia)
Chaenomeles speciosa (flowering quince)
Clethra alnifolia (sweet pepper bush)
Forsythia intermedia
Hibiscus syriacus (rose mallow)
Nerium oleander (oleander)
Weigela florida

Solution 3 Use half-baskets and grow-bags

Some walls are attractive so they don't need hiding, but you can always do something to add to their charm. If you consider the wall you back into an important element in your landscape, you can either leave it as it is or use it to house a collection of ornamental and useful plants.

Two types of containers are ideal for walls like this: half-baskets and grow-bags. Half-baskets are shaped like hanging baskets, but they are a half-circle rather than a full one so you can place the flat side against a wall. Grow-bags are plastic bags with drainage holes and Xs cut into the plastic to show where to transplant your seedlings. They are available from several seed companies and mail-order gardening catalogues.

Plan a collection of plants that harmonize with each other as well as with the wall. Remember, they will need frequent watering because they are in containers. Learn how to apply foliar feeds and fertilize them through the season. (See pages 148 to 149 for information about container growing.)

A group of half-baskets and container plants hides this wall as well as a climber would.

problem
The garden is visible from all sides

Gardens that are visible from all sides are sometimes perplexing to design. Most gardeners are used to working against a boundary of some sort, so they plan gardens with the tallest plants at the rear and progressively shorter ones toward the front. But this plan just doesn't work when there isn't a rear—all sides become equal.

There are several approaches to this problem, depending on what you want to grow. If you have a large garden and plan to include vegetables and fruit as well as ornamentals, plant them as usual, but set this garden off from its surroundings with a mowing strip or a short hedge as a boundary all around it.

solution 1 Hide maintenance paths

Maintenance paths are essential in any garden; you must be able to reach all parts of every plant and the soil below them. In a garden that backs up against a boundary of some sort, paths are easy to hide. Plants in front of them will obscure them and no one need ever be the wiser that they are there. However, in a garden that you view from all sides, you will have to show a little more ingenuity with their placement. If you set them up in straight lines – from the perimeter to the centre of the bed, for example – they'll look awkward in irregularly shaped gardens and like a pie chart in a circular one. Instead, make them zigzag a bit. Set a large stone where you can step on it easily from the perimeter of the garden and then set others in the garden, at convenient distances from each other, but in a seemingly random pattern.

solution 2 Design in a circle

A circular garden can be lovely, particularly when it is used as an island planting in a large garden. The trick to making it a garden you love is placing plants well. Because there is no 'rear' of the garden, you must develop a new way of thinking about border designs. Imagine that you can pick up a border that you admire and curl it into a circle. The plants that were at the rear are now in the centre. Cascading away from them in all directions are the shorter plants. Just as with a traditional border, you must be careful to keep the garden from looking too regimented. Put the tallest plants in the middle, but on the second and third tiers make sure that there is a plant slightly out of place every so often. This design makes the bed look less manicured and adds to its charm.

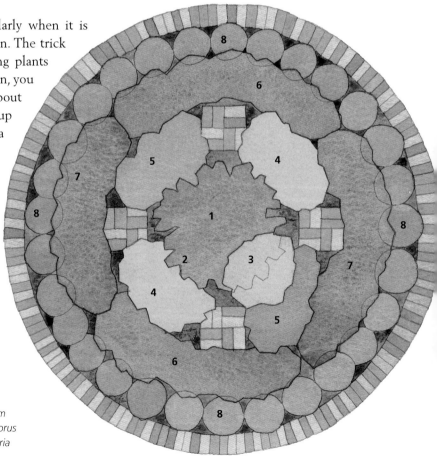

KEY TO PLANTS

1. *Buddleja davidii*
2. Spring bulbs
3. *Clematis maxim*
4. *C. maximowicziana*
5. *Artemisia absinthium*
6. *Platycodon grandiflorus*
7. *Armeria pseudarmeria*
8. *Lavandula* spp.

Circular beds add interest to large gardens. If they are large, their size compensates for the time it takes to mow around them.

chapter two

SITE PROBLEMS

A garden site can present problems that are a challenge to overcome. As every gardener knows, it's impossible to grow some plants in shade and equally impossible to grow others in sun. Consistently damp soil demands special treatment and special plants, just as extremely rocky soil does. Urban environments can be difficult, particularly if there are high levels of pollution in the area; the soil and air in seaside gardens are often too salty for many plants; and only selected species grow well in windy spots.

No matter what the problem with the site, nature has provided a number of plants that prefer those particular conditions, and gardeners can also use a number of techniques and tricks to mitigate the conditions prevailing in their own yards. Between the solutions presented below and the lists of suggested plants, you should be able to find a solution to whatever site problems your garden gives you.

problem
The garden is shady

Plants that require full sun simply won't grow in shady sites. If you yearn for a garden of California poppies (*Eschscholt* *californica*) and portulaca (*Portulaca* spp.), lavender (*Lavandula* spp.) and rosemary (*Rosmarinus officinalis*), you'll need find another spot to plant them. But shade needn't stop you from creating a truly beautiful garden full of other floweri plants. A huge variety of plants grow beautifully in shaded conditions. All it takes for success is understanding the type shade your site experiences, modifying it if necessary, and choosing plants that will thrive in it.

solution 1 Suit plants to shade type

Not all shade is equal. Shade from buildings and walls is deep. However, the orientation of the wall makes all the difference. Plants growing along an east–west wall, for example, receive some light every day. If a plant thrives in partial shade, it is likely to grow well in this location. Plants growing to the north of a wall receive almost no light in winter. However, since they get indirect light in summer, perennials that die back in winter and shade-loving summer annuals can do well in these spots.

Shade under trees varies according to the density of the leaf canopy. Trees such as Norway maples and hemlocks cast such a deep shade that almost no plant will grow under them. But paper birches and mountain ashes cast a dappled shade welcomed by many plants.

Campanulas are pretty flowers that add a splash of color to stark areas. While the taller varieties flower best in full sun, *C. glomerata*, shown here, will do well in dappled shade.

TREE	TIMING OF LEAVES	SHADE QUALITY
Acer griseum (paper bark maple)	Late	Light
Acer platanoides (Norway maple)	Early	Dense
Betula pendula (silver birch)	Early	Light
Fagus sylvatica (beech)	Early	Dense
Malus spp. (flowering crab)	Early	Dense

solution 2 Create reflective surfaces

If a wall is responsible for the shade your plants are experiencing, you can turn this to their advantage by painting the wall bright white. The white will reflect any light that strikes it, providing the plants with good illumination even if they don't have direct sunlight. This trick will be particularly effective with a north-facing wall.

If it's not possible for you to paint the wall, you could get round the problem by securing a light-coloured screen between the wall and the plants. Screens with a smoot surface are more effective than those with texture, but a light-colored backgrounds will reflect some light.

Once the background is reflective, remember tha plants must be able to 'see' the light it reflects. Don plant tall plants and expect small plants in front of ther to prosper.

See also: **'Cultivating compacted soil', page 82; 'Planting bulbs', page 47; 'Plant performance', pages 126–153**

Solution 3 Grow flowering plants

If your shade is dappled from shadows cast by deciduous trees, you can plant a colorful spring garden of sun-loving plants. The earliest bulbs, such as snowdrops, crocus, early daffodils and bluebells, all grow well under almost any deciduous tree. Bulbs that bloom in mid-spring, such as many daffodils, corydalis, and windflowers (*Anemone blanda*), grow best under trees that come into leaf late. Early-blooming perennials, such as astilbe (*Astilbe* x *arendsii*), American columbine (*Aquilegia canadensis*),

Virginia bluebells (*Mertensia virginica*) and primroses (*Primula* spp.), will also thrive under trees that come into leaf late in the spring. Many of these spring-flowering plants become lovely focal points later in the season thanks to their foliage.

You will find that spring flowers, such as bluebells, daffodils and crocus, grow well under the cover of almost any deciduous tree.

solution 4 Prune nearby trees

If low-hanging tree branches are casting shade on your garden, the answer is to carry out some careful pruning.

In late winter or very early spring, remove the bottom branches from the offending trees. If you cut just beyond the collar it ensures that the wound will heal quickly. Remove only a few branches from each tree, taking care that the growth is balanced around the trunk and that y• leave enough branches to keep it healthy.

You may want to hire a professional for this job wi greater expertise and the tools required.

1 Remove any small and spindly branches growing from the main trunk, using a sharp pair of pruning shears. Take care not to damage the bark on the tree trunk.

2 Remove the bulk of any large branches using a bow saw. Cut the branch from underneath, 8–15cm (3–6) inches from the point where it joins the tree trunk.

3 Next, saw from above, 8cm (3 inches) fart from the trunk. As you saw, the branch will s to the first cut without tearing the uncut bran

solution 5 Brighten dark areas with whites and pastels

Dark corners can seem to disappear, making the garden seem smaller than it is. If you want to brighten them up and make them a part of the visual landscape, you'll have to create some illusions with colourful plants.

White and pastel flowers, as well as plants with grey leaves, can make these areas more prominent. Choose a tall background plant, such as foxglove (*Digitalis grandiflora*) or kirengeshoma (*Kirengeshoma palmata*) for a site with damp soil and fairy lanterns (*Disporum flavum*) for a dry one. Using the Shade-Loving Plants lists, opposite, as well as other resources, fill in the area with a selection of white and pale-blooming plants that will brighten it up.

White and creamy yellow flowers and foliage brighten dark corners that may be overshadowed by trees.

olution 6 Grow shade-loving plants

Choosing appropriate plants for your site is your best guarantee of success. In addition to knowing if a plant grows well in shaded conditions, you must also know whether it grows well in damp or dry conditions. The following plants are divided into these categories to help you plan. These lists are not inclusive; try growing other shade-loving plants too.

PLANTS FOR DAMP SHADE

Annuals and biennials

Begonia semperflorens-cultorum hybrids (wax begonias)
Coleus x *hybridus*
Digitalis purpurea (foxglove)
Hesperis matronalis (dame's violet, sweet rocket)
Impatiens balsamina (balsam); *I. wallerana* (busy Lizzie)
Torenia fournieri (wishbone flower)

Bulbs

Anemone blanda (windflower)
Begonia x *tuberhybrida* (tuberous begonia)
Caladium x *hortulanum*
Chionodoxa spp. (glory of the snow)
Crocus

Eranthis hyemalis (winter aconite)
Galanthus nivalis (snowdrop)
Puschkinia scilloides (striped squill)

Ground cover plants

Hedera spp. (ivy)
Liriope muscari (lilyturf)
Pachysandra procumbens (Allegheny spurge); *P. terminalis* (mountain spurge)

Perennials

Alchemilla mollis (lady's mantle)
Aquilegia spp. (columbine)
Arisaema triphyllum (Jack-in-the-pulpit)
Brunnera macrophylla (bugloss)
Convallaria majalis (lily of the valley)
Dicentra spp. (bleeding heart)

Ferns, all
Geranium spp.
Hosta spp.
Hyacinthoides non-scripta (bluebell)
Kirengeshoma palmata
Polygonatum spp. (Solomon's seal)
Primula spp. (primrose)

Shrubs

Camellia japonica (camellia)
Fatsia japonica (fatsia)
Rhododendron spp. (rhododendron)
Taxus baccata (yew)
Viburnum davidii (viburnum) Wishbone Flower (Torenia fournieri)

PLANTS FOR DRY SHADE

Annuals and biennials

Dianthus spp. (pinks)
Lunaria annua (honesty)

Ground cover plants

Aegopodium podagraria 'Variegatum' (variegated ground elder)
Hedera spp. (ivy)
Lamium maculatum (dead nettle)
Liriope platyphylla; L. spicata (creeping lilyturf)
Vinca major; V. minor (periwinkle)

Perennials

Acanthus mollis, A. spinosus, A. spinosissimus (bear's breeches)
Alchemilla mollis (lady's mantle)
Disporum flavum (fairy bells)
Helleborus spp. (hellebore)
Iris foetidissima (stinking iris)

Shrubs

Aegopodium podagraria 'Variegatum' (Goutweed)
Cotoneaster 'Cornubia'
Euonymus spp.
Lamium maculatum (dead nettle)
Liriope platyphylla; L. spicata
Mahonia aquifolium (Oregon grape)
Symphoricarpus spp. (snowberry)

ABOVE *Digitalis* spp. (foxgloves)

LEFT *Galanthus nivalis* (snowdrops)

problem
The garden is sunny

Few gardens are too sunny for many ornamentals and most fruits and vegetables, but this certainly isn't true for peopl
Although most of us enjoy some time in the sun, we all need a certain amount of shade to enjoy fully the garden whe
we are using it to relax or entertain.

If you are enterprising, you can create shade with garden structures. A pergola or gazebo with a roof will shade yo
through the hottest part of the day, while a well-placed trellis or hedge can cast shade when the sun is at a particular heigh
and angle. And once you have created this shade, you can go ahead and plant some of the species that, like you, prefer
little shade.

solution 1 Create shade with plants

You may discover that you cannot grow good lettuce during the middle of the summer in the vegetable garden because it is just too hot and sunny. Many other crops will also react poorly to constant sunlight. Astilbes, black cohosh (*Cimicifuga racemosa*), balloon flowers (*Platycodon grandiflora*), and pansies (*Viola* x *wittrockiana*) are some of the perennials that don't fare well without some shade.

In the vegetable garden, you can use shade cloth, of course, but the expense is unwarranted unless you are a commercial grower. It is more economical (and attractive)

to use plants to create your shade. This solution is close t invisible, and it will take a sharp observer to notice that a the midsummer lettuce is growing in the shade of the pol beans and that a bed of partial shade loving perennials just to the northeast of the trellised trumpet vines. B simply planning ahead and leaving room where tall plant will cast their shade, you can grow almost any plant yo wish, even those that like a bit of shade.

Shade brings out the best in these plants and also allows you to enjoy being in the garden when the sun is high and hot.

See also: **'Good urban plants that are tolerant of dry heat, dry soil', page 66**

olution 2 Create shade with structures

We usually think of a trellis as a structure meant to provide support for a climbing plant. This is true, certainly, but the same trellis can do double duty by creating a partially shaded environment for plants. Other structures can be used in the same way. If you have the space, you can put up a gazebo, for example, and grow plants to the north and east of it. This placement ensures that they get good morning light but that afternoon light is blocked.

In the vegetable garden, you can use compost bins and a storage shed the same way. Place them where the shade that they cast is thrown on a spot where you can grow some midsummer vegetables.

PLANTS FOR SUNNY SPOTS

When choosing a plant for a sunny spot, take soil moisture levels into account. Many plants that like dry, sunny spots would die in moist, sunny areas. This list is divided into those categories.

DRY SOIL
Perennials
Acanthus mollis (bear's breeches)
Achillea filipendulina (yarrow)
Allium spp. (ornamental onion)
Anthemis tinctoria (chamomile, ox eye)
Artemisia absinthium (wormwood)
Asclepias tuberosa (butterfly weed)
Centranthus ruber (red valerian)
Echinops ritro (globe thistle)
Eryngium bourgatii (sea holly)
Iris cvs. (bearded iris)
Lavandula angustifolia (lavender)
Penstemon hirsutus

Perovskia atriplicifolia (Russian sage)
Scabiosa caucasica (pincushion flower)

Shrubs
Aesculus parviflora (bottlebrush-buckeye)
Cercis canadensis (redbud)
Cornus mas (Cornelian cherry)
Kerria japonica (Japanese kerria)
Viburnum spp.
Vitex agnus-castus (Abraham's balm, chaste tree)

MOIST SOIL
Perennials
Anemone spp.
Astrantia major; A. maxima
Baptisia australis (false indigo)
Coreopsis verticillata (tickseed)
Digitalis grandiflora (yellow foxglove)

Echinacea purpurea (purple coneflower)
Filipendula palmata (meadowsweet)
Hemerocallis cvs. (daylily)
Heuchera americana (albumroot, rock geranium, satinroot)
Phlomis russeliana (Jerusalem sage)
Phlox paniculata
Platycodon grandiflorus (balloon flower)
Trollius x *cultorum* (globeflower)

Shrubs
Abelia x *grandiflora* (glossy abelia)
Caryopteris x *clandonensis* (blue mist spiraea)
Chionanthus retusus (Chinese fringe tree)
Cotinus coggygria (smokebush)
Kolkwitzia amabilis (beauty bush)
Pieris japonica (lily-of-the-valley bush)

ABOVE *Cornus mas* (Cornelian cherry)
RIGHT *Digitalis grandiflora* (yellow foxglove)
FAR RIGHT *Kolkwitzia amabilis* (beauty bush)

problem
The garden is damp

Damp gardens can be difficult to manage. It's wonderful to have a damp spot where you can put in bog plants and othe[r] moisture lovers, but it's another thing entirely when the whole garden is damp. A great many diseases, most of them fungal, prefer high levels of humidity around plant leaves. Similarly, constantly wet soil can lead to root rots and other diseases.

It's certainly possible to have a lovely garden growing nothing but plants that prefer damp soil. However, it's also possible, and well worth the effort, to create some areas without these conditions.

solution 1 Build raised beds

Raised beds can go a long way toward solving the problem of constantly damp soil. By raising the soil up and away from the groundwater and the surrounding ground soil, you are increasing its ability to drain well. If you build a raised bed that isn't enclosed with boards or logs, wind hitting the sides will also tend to dry it.

In vegetable gardens, unenclosed raised beds are ideal. However, they can look quite sloppy by the end of the season, so you may want to enclose them in the ornamental garden.

Raised beds are ideal in a herb garden, particularly for species that hail from dry, well-drained soils.

1 Measure the area where you want the bed, aligning it with the house or other elements in view. Set wooden or composite boards on top of each other, staggering the corners as shown.

2 Pound wooden stakes on the inside of each 'wall' near the corner and at intervals along the sides to stabilize the boards and prevent the soil you'll add from pushing them out of place.

3 Use nails or screws to attach the stakes to the walls of the bed. Make certain to attach them to both boards. To prevent the stakes from rotting over time, cover them with clear latex paint.

4 Fill the bed with a rich soil mix that contains compost for nutrients and beneficial micro-organisms, a drainage material such as sand, perlite or vermiculite, and native top soil.

solution 2 Choose appropriate plants

Some plants thrive in damp conditions. Rather than contracting diseases and weakening to the point where they attract insect pests, they grow without difficulty. Fortunately, you will be able to find any type of plant your design calls for – shrubs, perennials or annuals. Appropriate plants are listed on pages 14, 19 and 21.

Solution 3 Use prevailing winds

Winds are the gardener's best ally when it comes to blowing moisture away from plant leaves. In most areas, it tends to come from one direction unless there is a storm. Pay attention to the wind patterns in your yard. Go outside at different times of day and just stand there. You will feel where the wind is coming from. Once you have a good idea of the prevailing wind patterns, you can make use of them. Design your gardens so that wind blows through the plants. If you have rows of something like raspberries, set the trellis to follow the line of wind rather than crossing it. Follow this same idea in perennial borders and other dense plantings. This simple planting pattern can make a big difference to the health of the garden.

Solution 4 Give your plants space

Good spacing also helps to minimize the chances that plants will contract fungal diseases. When air can circulate freely around the leaves, it dries them. If you have a damp garden and have had troubles with fungal diseases, one of the best remedies possible is to take out some of the plants and move them to a spot with more space.

Judicious pruning can also give your plants some breathing room. If leaves or branches threaten to touch those of neighboring plants, head them back at the appropriate time – early spring if the plant blooms on new wood or after it blooms if it blooms on old wood.

Good spacing prevents this garden from feeling overgrown and crowded and also helps to keep plants healthy because it allows good air circulation.

problem
The garden is dry

Dry soils usually require a great deal of attention, particularly when it comes to watering. The best way around the problem is to grow plants that thrive in low-moisture conditions. Some of these plants, particularly all the grey-leaved Mediterranean species, are so lovely that some people without dry soils work to create conditions where they will grow.

Once you broaden your gardening horizons to include plants that aren't suited to your dry soils, you will have to plan ahead to keep them moist enough. Some of the solutions below can help you make good conditions for them without giving yourself excessive work.

solution 1   Make use of mulches

Mulches are a gardener's best friend, in any climate and on any soil type, but this is particularly so when it comes to dry soils. Not only do mulches keep weeds down, reducing maintenance time, but they also hold moisture in the soil. Added to that is the improvement that they can make to the soil itself. If you use an organic mulch, it will increase the water-holding capacity of the soil once it decomposes and turns into humus.

The only times you should not mulch plants is during wet periods and close to tree trunks in winter. When it's wet, slugs live in the mulch so they can hide close to your plants. Plants are also more susceptible to fungal diseases when it is wet, and this is particularly so if a mulch is holding moisture over their crowns. In winter, mice often use mulches as cover while they eat tree bark.

Mulches not only improve the appearance of a garden, they also hold in moisture.

COMMON MULCH MATERIALS		
Material	**Characteristics**	**Best uses**
Bark & cedar chips	Attractive	Paths, ornamental borders
Buckwheat hulls	Attractive	Everywhere but the vegetable garden
Cardboard	Unattractive	Paths, new ground
Cedar	Attractive	Paths, borders
Cocoa bean hulls	Attractive	Everywhere but the vegetable garden
Compost	Can be attractive	Only where nutrients are needed
Felt	Unattractive	Paths, under another mulch
Hay, spoiled	Attractive	With annuals because it can bring in weed seeds
Landscape fabric	Unattractive: cover with other mulch	Under perennials
Leaf mould	Attractive	Where humus and water retention are needed
Leaves, shredded	Can be attractive	Robs soil of nitrogen
Newspaper	Unattractive	Paths and new ground
Pine needles	Attractive	Use with acid lovers and other perennials
Plastic film, black	Unattractive	Prevents weed growth
Sawdust	Attractive	Paths; robs soil of nitrogen
Seaweed, washed	Unattractive	Adds trace elements N and K
Stone, pea	Attractive	Use with perennial trees and shrubs
Straw	Attractive	Use in annual and vegetable gardens
Wood chips	Attractive	Use in areas with adequate nutrients
Wood shavings	Attractive	Robs soil of nitrogen

Solution 2 Build a water feature

A water feature won't help your soil become more moist or keep your plants any wetter, but it will certainly add interest to your yard. You can choose between installing a preformed plastic liner for the pond or a thick, flexible liner. Consult with water garden experts in your area as well as other homeowners before making a choice. Both types of liners will give you years of service without any trouble if you install them correctly and maintain them well. Also think about adding a small fountain if you live in a dry climate. The water you lose to evaporation will be more than made up for by the pleasure of listening to the water splashing.

1 Dig a hole for your preformed plastic pond liner. As always, make certain that the hole is aligned with other garden features.

2 Remove rocks or sharp objects from the hole and set the form in place. Check in numerous spots to make sure it's level.

3 As you fill the pond, fill the space between the liner and surrounding area with sand or top soil. Choose sand if the soil is likely to bring in lots of weed seeds.

4 For good drainage, add a layer of sand about 25cm (10 in) beyond the edge of the liner. Build up the sand layer close to the pond, making it slightly angle away from the water.

5 Set flat paving stones over the sand. Leave 5–8cm) (2–3 inches) between the stones and let them overhang the pond by at least 8cm (3 inches). Make their slope uniform.

6 Sift compost or a very rich potting soil in the spaces between the stones. Nutrients are more important than drainage in this spot. Mist it with a fine nozzle to moisten.

7 Transplant small, creeping plants that are easy to control into the prepared areas. Creeping thyme is always a good choice because it withstands foot traffic well.

8 If you've filled the pond with city water, wait a week to 10 days to place potted plants or fish in it. This wait gives chlorinating agents time to evaporate.

Solution 3 Install drip irrigation for garden areas

Drip irrigation is almost essential for gardeners with dry soils, particularly in hot, arid climates. When you use a sprinkler, a great deal of the water evaporates before it penetrates the soil, but when you use a drip system, even one that sits on the soil surface rather than being buried, the droplets sink into the soil. The convenience of having a drip system can't be overemphasized. If you set it up on an automatic timer, you can be sure that the garden will be watered when it needs it, even if you aren't home.

Look at companies and suppliers before you buy a system. Several companies offer free consulting to help you design a suitable system and offer you phone assistance if you need it while you are installing the system, and if you have any trouble with it after it's in operation. These services are invaluable, particularly if this is your first experience with a drip system.

solution 4 Shade the vegetable garden

Many vegetables will grow well with six hours a day of direct sunlight rather than the 10 to 12 that some gardens provide at midsummer. If your soil is dry, extra hours of direct light will make it even drier. Creating shade is the answer to this problem. Some plants, such as lettuce and other cool-lovers, will thrive under a tunnel made of commercially available shade fabric or simple dressmaker's canvas. Not only will the soil stay moister, but the reduced light levels will keep the plants cooler.

Plants that grow well with high light, such as cucumbers, melons and tomatoes, can also benefit from some midsummer shade. But rather than covering them with shading, it's best to set up a screen that shades them from the sun in the middle of the afternoon. A row plants, such as pole beans on a trellis, can provide th shade, but you may find it more convenient to set u temporary screens covered with an opaque material. Plac them where they will block afternoon light and stak them securely.

Take advantage of a well-positioned fence to provide afternoon shade for cool-loving vegetables and herbs.

solution 5 Conserve water with rocks

Rocks or pea stones make an excellent mulch because they are attractive, keep down weeds, and also conserve water. To use them for weed control, layer them several centimeters (inches) deep. Because some weed seeds may blow in from surrounding areas and sift down to the soil beneath the stones, remember to patrol for weeds every few weeks and pull them as you spot them.

The rocks act to conserve water when you use them around a tree trunk or the stems of a shrub. Form a small bowl or depression in the soil around the trunk and place the stones so that any water that hits them will naturally roll down the slight slope to the tree trunk. The stones will help to direct rainwater to the plant and will also collect dew during the night.

Rocks used in this way will keep water for longer around a plant.

PLANTS FOR DRY SOILS

In addition to the plants listed on page 51, the following species are good choices.

Perennials

Armeria spp. (thrift)
Arum italicum 'Pictum' (lords and ladies)
Aubrieta deltoidea
Aurinia saxatilis (golddust, madwort)
Bergenia cordifolia (elephant's ear)
Campanula carpatica (Carpathian bellflower)
Crocus speciosus (autumn crocus)
Erysimum cheiri (wallflower)

Eschscholzia californica (California poppy)
Euphorbia myrsinites (spurge)
Geranium cvs. (cranesbill, hardy geranium)
Helleborus spp.
Iberis sempervirens (candytuft)
Linum narbonense (flax)
Sedum spp. (stonecrop)
Stachys byzantina (lamb's ears)

Shrubs

Berberis thunbergii (Thungberg's barberry)
Euphorbia characias subsp. *wulfenii* (spurge)

Helianthemum nummularium (rock rose)
Jasminum nudiflorum (winter jasmine)
Mahonia aquifolium (Oregon grape);
  M. japonica
Poncirus trifoliata (Japanese bitter orange)
Potentilla fruticosa
Santolina chamaecyparissus (lavender cotton)
Skimmia japonica
Viburnum spp.
Vitex agnus-castus (chaste tree, Abraham's balm)

---

solution 6 Install drip irrigation for containers

Containerized plants must be watered at least once a day in most climates, and sometimes more frequently in dry areas. Consequently, some people decide not to have containers because they don't want to be tied to a watering schedule. However, a drip system can make all the difference. When you install a drip system in the garden, ask the supplier about systems for containers. You may be pleasantly surprised to discover that a small header pipe, a timer, and a bunch of spaghetti tubes and emitters are all you need to keep a group of container plants watered without your daily attention. You have two options to make this system truly foolproof. You can use containers of roughly the same size that contain plants with similar moisture requirements. This plan lets you be certain that each plant is receiving just what it needs. However, you can have a more varied planting without worrying. Simply add one or two more spaghetti tubes to each container holding moisture-loving plants.

problem
The garden is windy

Wind can be one of the most difficult factors in a garden. While breezes are invaluable for minimizing fungal diseases and also helping to pollinate some plants, wind can be destructive. If it is too strong, it will interfere with pollinating insects: they aren't able to fight it to get to the flowers, they will go elsewhere.

Wind also increases plants' water needs by blowing off the water they release from their leaves. The plant compensates by pulling more water from the roots. If it can't pull adequate water quickly enough, the leaf dries. This particularly common when the ground is frozen. What we call winterkill is actually a form of drought. Plants can't take u water from frozen soil, so on sunny days when they release some water from their leaves a high wind can damage them It's relatively easy to solve these problems, however, so you need not despair if you are on a windy site.

solution 1   Plant windbreaks

A band of trees and shrubs, growing at different heights will moderate all but the strongest winds. Air currents los velocity as they hit the leaves, spending a great deal of thei power before they emerge on the other side. Engineer have measured the effect of hedgerows and report tha there is a 75 percent reduction in windspeed at a distanc of twice the height of the hedgerow. That is, if the talles plants in the hedgerow measure 4.5m (15ft) high, 32kph (20mph) wind will turn into a 8kph (5mph) win 9m (30ft) away from the hedgerow. At five times th distance from the hedgerow, there is a 66 percen reduction, and at ten times, a 50 percent reduction. A these figures show, a hedgerow is well worth a fair bit o time, trouble and expense.

In gardens, it's best to plant the smallest possibl shrubs that will do the trick. Consider evergreen specie such as yew (*Taxus baccata*) or a holly (*Ilex* spp.) an fill in the spaces between the plants with smaller shrubs Don't forget that these plants will be subjected to wind too, and may need protection when they are small Use screens, as described opposite, until they ar well established.

A decorative trellis adds so much beauty that you'll soon forget you installed it to be a very practical windbreak.

Solution 2 Create windscreens

Windscreens also protect plants from harsh winds and have the added advantage of being extremely versatile. You can set up a small windscreen around an exposed planting on a hill while it is getting established, or use one as a permanent part of the yard. Remember that wind will go around barriers as well as to the top of them, so make the windscreen wider than the area you are trying to protect.

As illustrated below, the best windscreens allow air to pass through them rather than travel above and to their sides. Use tightly woven panels from a home improvement store or set up something as simple as a canvas screen. If the area is quite windy, it's important to stake the windscreen well. Sink the posts into concrete if the screen is to be permanent. If it's only temporary, sink the posts to a depth of at least 30cm (1ft) and also stake the screen.

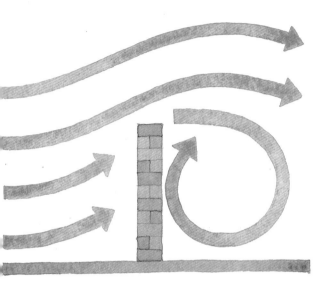

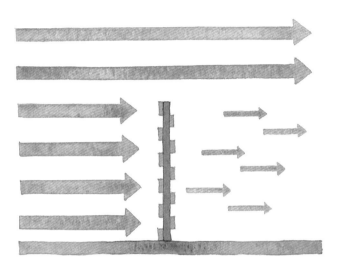

Solid walls do not make good windbreaks. As shown above, wind traveling toward a wall is forced over and above it. Wind that drops to the ground creates an area of turbulence that can be stronger than the initial wind.

Walls with spaces that allow air to move through them don't create turbulence because most of the wind passes through the spaces. As it does so, wind speed is decreased enough so that plants don't suffer from it.

WIND-TOLERANT PLANTS

As a rule, some characteristics predispose plants to surviving well in windy conditions. Choose those with narrow leaves and a base wider than the top growth, preferably from a low-humidity environment. As a start, select from the following species.

Perennials

Achillea filipendulina (yarrow)
Anemone hupehensis; A. x hybrida (Japanese anemone)
Coreopsis verticillata (tickseed)
Ornamental grasses (various species)
Penstemon spp.
Phlox subulata (moss phlox, moss pink, mountain phlox)
Veronica spicata (spiked speedwell)

Shrubs

Bamboo (various species)
Calluna vulgaris (heather)
Chamaecyparis obtusa 'Nana' (dwarf Hinoki cypress)
Erica carnea (winter or spring heath)
Ilex aquifolium and other spp. (holly)
Juniperus chinensis 'Echiniformis' (hedgehog juniper)
Ligustrum ovalifolium (privet)
Potentilla fruticosa
Rhododendron impeditum (Yunan rhododendron)
Sambucus nigra (elderberry)
Spartium junceum (Spanish broom)

Trees

Crataegus monogyna (hawthorn)
Fagus sylvatica (beech)
Pinus mugo (mountain pine)
Sorbus aucuparia (mountain ash)

problem
The garden is cold

Cold is a fact of life in most of the north, but northern gardeners soon adjust to their environment and learn that they ca
have gardens just as beautiful and productive as those of their southern neighbours.

If you are new to these conditions, it is worth knowing the following. Frost is more likely when the air is dry, becau.
moisture in the air keeps heat close to the ground from escaping. Bare soil freezes more quickly than soil where plants
mulch cover the surface, and dry soil freezes more quickly than moist soil. When frost does strike, you may be able to sa
your plants if you sprinkle them with water as the sun is coming up and during the time it first strikes them. The wat
droplets slow down the rate at which they'll thaw and keeps cells from bursting.

solution 1 Configure the soil for warming

South-facing slopes are known for their early warming in
the spring. They tend to be terrible places to grow fruits
because their orientation stimulates early blooming, which
is vulnerable to late frosts, but they are excellent places to
grow cold-hardy annuals.

If you don't have such a spot on your property, you can
still benefit from a south-facing slope. When you put the
annual garden to bed in the autumn, till it or spade it into
ridges or wide beds that slope to the south. Then plant a
crop of oats to cover the soil during the winter. The oats
will die from the cold, but their roots will remain in place,
keeping the slopes intact. In spring, after the snow has
melted, pull back the dead oat straw on the southernmost
sides of your beds to let the sun heat the soil. Plant your
first crops into these areas as soon as the soil is warm.

1 Heap up the soil where you plan
to grow warm-loving annuals, such
as courgettes, the following year.
Slope it so that rain won't break
it down.

2 Plant an annual cover crop lor
enough before a frost so it ca
grow a root system extensi
enough to hold the soil in plac
over the winter.

solution 2 Avoid frost pockets

Frost pockets are areas where frost collects. On a marginally
frosty night, only the plants sitting in a frost pocket may
freeze. So it pays to learn where these sites are in your garden.

As the illustration at right shows, cold air moves down
a hill. Whenever it hits an obstruction, such as a fence or
hedge, a great deal of it gets trapped. But if there are no
obstructions, it just keeps going.

If at all possible, don't plant at the bottom of a hill.
Instead, place plants midway down the slope. But if you
have no choice and your entire property sits in a frost
pocket, use some of the tricks on the opposite page to keep
your plants from freezing for as long as possible.

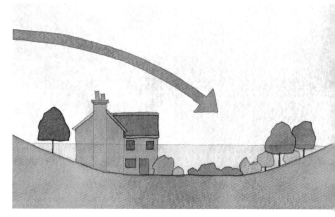

If your house sits in a frost pocket, plant warm-loving crops
on the top of the slope and cold-hardy ones at the bottom.

Solution 3 Use walls, fences and hedges to advantage

Walls, fences and hedges can all help to protect plants from frost. Choose the most appropriate structure for your situation and place it where it can trap the frosty air as it moves down the hill. Do this only if the plants you want to protect are at the lowest point in the area. Otherwise, it's better to let the frost roll on through.

A hedge or woven fence is as effective as a solid wall. If you have no other use for this structure you may want to make it solid.

♉ ⚘ 🕐 🥛

Solution 4 Use row covers and plastic

Extension devices – fleece, plastic tunnels and cloches – are commonly used in the vegetable garden to protect plants against the first or last frosts of the season. Gardeners rarely use them in ornamental plantings, probably because they are not attractive. However, if you do cover a bed when you expect a frost and uncover it again the next morning, you could be gaining a couple more weeks of beauty from the garden.

The most appropriate covers for ornamental beds are plastic sheeting and fleece material. The two materials are different. Plastic traps moisture along with air, so it's important to pull it off before the sun gets high or plants may contract fungal diseases. Fleece lets moisture escape, so you can leave it in place if you are expecting another frost the following evening. However, a single layer only gives 1–2 degrees Celsius (3–5 degrees Fahrenheit) of protection, so it's best to use at least two, and sometimes three, layers over the bed.

♉ ⚘ 🕐 🥛

COLD-HARDY PLANTS

Wise plant choice is the best possible defence against the cold enough to cope with some degree of frost.

Perennials

Achillea millefolium (yarrow)
Allium spp. (ornamental onion)
Asclepias tuberosa (butterfly weed)
Aster Michaelmas daisy x frikartii;
  A. novae-angliae; A. novi-belgii
Baptisia australis (false indigo)
Boltonia asteroides (false aster)
Campanula spp. (bellflower)
Coreopsis verticillata (tickseed)
Delphinium elatum
Eryngium amethystinum; E. planum
  (sea holly)
Liatris scariosa (tall gayfeather)
Myosotis scorpioides (water forget-
  me-not)
Phlox paniculata (garden phlox)
Primula elatior (primrose); P. veris;
  P. vulgaris

Rudbeckia hirta (black-eyed Susan,
  coneflower)
Trollius europaeus (globeflower)

Shrubs

Arctostaphylos uva-ursi (mountain box,
  red bearberry)
Clethra alnifolia (sweet pepper bush)

Euonymus alatus (winged spindle)
Kerria japonica (Japanese kerria)
Spiraea thunbergii (bridal wreath)

Allium spp. (ornamental onion)

Campanula persifolia (bellflower)

problem
The garden is by the sea

Seaside gardens pose two major problems: wind and salt. Both can be a problem, but when you put them together, th[ey] become even more drying than each would be alone. The wind draws moisture from the leaves (see page 53), and s[alt] always draws water out of the materials it touches.

The soil in these areas can't help but contain the salt that years and years of prevailing wind and spray ha[ve] deposited. Increasingly, breeders are working to develop vegetable cultivars that tolerate higher than normal salt leve[ls.] Seaside gardeners can check with nurseries in their areas to learn if any of these plants or seeds are available. The solutio[ns] suggested here will go some way towards alleviating the negative effects of the wind and salt on your garden.

solution 1 Plant a barrier

Nowhere is a screening hedge more valuable than at the edge of the ocean. The right plants will not only screen the rest of the garden from salt and wind but will also help to create a calm, sheltered place for you to sit. Follow the directions for planting a hedge (see page 33), but select plants that are suited to the environment. Choose plants from the list opposite, but also check with local nurseries and garden associations to learn which plants do especially well in your area.

Just as you must protect plants in a windbreak for the first few years after planting, you will have to protect your barrier plants. Put up a screen as discussed, opposite, to shield them from the wind until they are well established.

This lovely stone wall not only defines the end of a seaside property, it also reduces the amount of sea-spray garden plants receive.

See also: **'Build raised beds', page 52; 'Plant a windbreak', page 58; 'Build a wooden fence', page 32**

olution 2 Install screens or walls

creens are as useful as barrier plants when it comes to rotecting your plants from salty breezes. Set them up as ou do other trellises, but make them sturdy. If you plan to eep them in place for a long time, it is worth setting their osts in concrete (see page 31). Otherwise, bury their posts eeply and use guy wires to support them further.

If you decide to build a wall rather than a screen, member that air will try to move around and above it. uild it sufficiently high and wide so that it really does rotect your plants.

Screens, on the other hand, must allow air to move through them or they will never stand up to strong wind. Take some care with the selection of your screening material. Woven plastic sheeting is comparatively unobtrusive but not attractive. If you can't find this, fit canvas or bamboo shades to the framework of the screen. You may have to replace this material each year, but its good looks will be an asset to the garden.

SEASIDE PLANTS

The best way to find out if a plant will grow in your seaside garden, particularly if you have put up some kind of protection from the sea spray, is to try it out, and this you can do with annuals and bedding plants. Save yourself potential grief and unnecessary expense when it comes to selecting shrubs and perennials, however. Check with local nurseries and gardening societies for suggestions, and use some of the plants from the following list, which will all thrive in seaside conditions.

Perennials

Armeria pseudarmeria (thrift)
Bupleurum fruticosum (shrubby hare's ear)
Centranthus ruber 'Albus' (white valerian)
Chasmanthium latifolium (northern sea oats)
Crambe maritima (sea kale)
Elymus arenarius (lyme grass)
Festuca glauca 'Elijah Blue' (blue fescue)
Kniphofia cvs. (red-hot poker)
Opuntia compressa (prickly pear cactus)
Pennisetum alopecuroides (fountain grass)

Phragmites australis 'Variegatus'
Solidago sempervirens (seaside goldenrod)

Shrubs

Baccharis halimifolia (bush groundsel)
Calluna vulgaris (heather)
Ceanothus spp. (California lilac)
Chamaecyparis spp. (cypress)
Euphorbia characias (spurge)
Hippophae rhamnoides (sea buckthorn)
Hydrangea macrophylla 'Compacta'
Ligustrum ovalifolium (privet)
Myrica pensylvanica (bayberry, candleberry)
Prunus maritima (beach plum)
Pyracantha spp. (firethorn)
Rosmarinus spp. (rosemary)
Santolina chamaecyparissus 'Small Ness'
Tamarix spp. (tamarisk)
Viburnum trilobum (highbush cranberry)

ABOVE *Elymus arenarius* (lyme grass)

LEFT *Chamaecyparis* spp. (cypress)

RIGHT *Opuntia compressa* (prickly pear cactus)

problem
The garden is steeply sloping

Steep slopes can create a great many garden problems. The soil on slopes erodes easily if there isn't a good network of roots to hold it in place. Nutrients travel with the soil, so slopes are often nutrient-deficient. Water can run right down the slope, too, so, unless you live in a wet area or your slope is well covered with vegetation, expect the soil to be dry.

If you are growing lawn on a slope, mowing can be a nightmare. Some people gamely tie ropes to the handle of the lawnmower so they can let it travel down the hill and then pull it back up without going down the hill themselves. Unfortunately, this is not a solution; it's a different kind of problem.

solution 1   Grow ground cover plants

Ground cover plants are the best way to tackle a steep slope. Once you plant them, you need to do little to maintain them. You don't need to mow them or deadhead them, and if you plant a species that is hardy to your climate they won't need special winter care. You may need to do a little judicious pruning of ground-cover shrubs once a year, but you certainly won't have to do more than that. Meanwhile, your easy-care planting will be protecting the soil from erosion, creating a haven for wildlife, and creating a lovely view for you and your visitors.

Take some care in choosing ground-cover plants for a steep slope. To protect yourself against future disaster, choose cultivars that are hardy to an area colder than the one in which they will grow. Insulating snow cover is steady enough in most years to offer protection. However, if some unexpected January thaw brings a total melt, throw some evergreen boughs or straw over the planting if you are concerned about its survival.

Plants that tolerate drought are also wise choices simply because any kind of rain but a gentle 'soaker' tends to run off a slope, especially if the soil is already dry. The plants listed on the opposite page as good plants for slopes are all suited to dry conditions.

solution 2   Mulch to clear sod

Tilling a slope to clear it of grasses and weeds can be extremely difficult. If you are using a large tilling machine, it can also be dangerous because you might not be able to control the machine on the steepest areas. Instead, take a year to mulch out the problem. Lay several layers of newspaper over the area and water. Cover the newspaper with overlapping sheets of cardboard and water again. If you need to hold the cardboard in place, use ground staples because rocks will only slip down the slope. If your local garden supplier doesn't have ground staples, make them by bending 43cm- (17inch-) long pieces of 9- or 10-gauge wire into U- shapes. Push the staple through the cardboard and into the soil wherever it threatens to drift. Cover the cardboard with a layer of straw or woodchips. If you think these materials will migrate, stretch a piece of plastic net trellis, as illustrated, right, over the mulch and use ground staples to secure it. After a year, the underlying vegetation will die. Cut holes in what remains of the cardboard and plant your ground cover through the netting and mulch.

1 'Spot-mulching' is also effective. Cover the area that will be under your plant's drip line with land-scape fabric.

2 Dig out the grass where you plant. Transplant as usual, and then cover the whole area with bark mulch.

See also: **'Build terraces', page 15; 'Build raised beds', page 52**

Solution 3 Plant through plastic netting

One of the easiest ways to plant a ground cover is through nylon plastic netting. This solution not only helps you space plants correctly but also helps to stabilize the soil. If you have filled a slope rather than mulched it, the soil may tend to drift down to the bottom of the hill. Covering it with a plastic trellis will minimize this to some extent. If you are concerned about the appearance of the net before plants cover it, use a nylon netting and dye it in a strong solution of coffee before using it.

1 Use plastic or nylon trellis netting to secure the soil on a steep slope or anywhere you are putting in a group of the same plants that demand precision planting.

2 Use the holes in the netting to plant in a staggered pattern. The netting forces you to space uniformly and also holds the soil while slow-growing plants cover it.

GOOD PLANTS FOR SLOPES

Ground covers
Ajuga reptans (bugle)
Armeria plumbaginaceae (thrift)
Epimedium alpinum (alpine barrenwort)
Euonymus fortunei
Festuca spp. (fescue)
Hemerocallis cvs. (daylily)
Hypericum calycinum (creeping
   St John's wort)

Liriope muscari (lilyturf)
Oenothera speciosa 'Rosea'
   (evening primrose)
Thymus serpyllum (creeping thyme)
Vinca minor (lesser periwinkle)

Shrubs
Arctostaphylos uva-ursi (mountain box,
   red bearberry)

Artemisia stellariana (beach wormwood,
   dusty miller)
Cotoneaster salicifolia (willowleaf
   cotoneaster)
Juniperus horizontalis 'Wiltonii'
   (creeping juniper)
Lavandula spp. (lavender)
Potentilla tabernaemontani
   (spring cinquefoil)

Cotoneaster salicifolia (willowleaf cotoneaster)

Ajuga reptans (bugle)

Lavandula spp. (lavender)

problem
The garden is in an urban area

Living in an urban area can be exciting and stimulating, and contrary to what many people think, it doesn't mean that yo can't have a garden. But you do have to plan it carefully.

Urban air quality is often poor, especially in gardens close to busy streets. It's important to limit yourself to fruiting cro such as tomatoes or corn if you want to grow edibles, because leafy crops and roots pick up more pollutants from the and soil than fruit crops do.

Heat is usually more extreme in the city, too. During the daytime, light-coloured surfaces reflect light all around the increasing surrounding temperatures. At night, the concrete and masonry release the heat they absorbed earli moderating the night-time lows. But this increased heat can be too much for some plants, particularly those that pref cooler temperatures, and it can drastically increase water needs.

solution 1 Choose plants tolerant of poor air quality

Three types of air pollution commonly affect plants: high ozone levels, peroxyacetyl nitrate (PAN) and high levels of sulfur dioxide.

Most people discover plants that are resistant and tolerant to poor air quality by trial and error. If there is no other cause for cells to collapse and die in plant leaves, for example, it's possible that ozone damage is to blame. PAN causes silvering or a tan glazing on the lower leaf surfaces, and sulfur dioxide damage shows as ivory to brown areas between the veins on plant leaves and at the margins.

If you suspect that your plants are suffering fro: pollutants, grow some of the species listed opposite.

GOOD URBAN PLANTS THAT ARE TOLERANT OF HIGH HEAT AND DRY SOIL

Annuals and tender perennials

Antirrhinum majus (snapdragon)

Arctotis acaulis (African daisy)

Bracteantha bracteata (everlasting strawflower)

Brugmansia spp. (angel's trumpet)

Portulaca grandiflora (purslane, rose moss)

Xeranthemum bracteatum (strawflower)

Ground covers

Pachysandra procumbens; P. terminalis (mountain spurge)

Perennials

Alstroemeria aurea (Peruvian lily)

Baptisia australis (false indigo)

Calamintha grandiflora; C. nepeta (calamint)

Catananche caerulea (cupid's dart)

Coreopsis spp. (tickseed)

Crambe cordifolia (seakale)

Crepis incana (hawk's-beard)

Dictamnus albus; D. albus var. *purpureus* (dittany, gas plant)

Digitalis grandiflora (yellow foxglove)

Gaura spp.

Gypsophila paniculata (baby's breath)

Hesperis matronalis (sweet rocket)

Limonium spp. (statice, sea lavender)

Lupinus spp. (lupin)

Lychnis coronaria (dusty miller, rose campion)

Phlox subulata (moss phlox, moss pink)

Shrubs

Amorpha spp. (lead plant)

Buddleja davidii (butterfly bush)

Caragana arborescens (Siberian pea shrub)

Kolkwitzia amabilis (beautybush)

Lantana camera (shrub verbena)

Poncirus trifoliata (Japanese bitter orange)

See also: 'An eyesore is prominent', page 30; 'Install drip irrigation for garden areas', page 55; 'Install drip irrigation for containers', page 57; 'Mulches', page 54; 'Make use of mulches', page 54; 'Common mulch materials', page 54; 'Plants for sunny spots', page 54; 'Plants for dry soils', page 57

Solution 2 Choose plants tolerant of hot, dry conditions

Plants growing near pavements are likely to be exposed to heat and high light reflected from the surrounding light coloured concrete surfaces. This kind of environment dries soil quickly, too, so plants will require a great deal of water. Install drip irrigation if you possibly can (see page 55). With a good system, you can grow any plant that normally grows in your zone. However, if you don't have a drip system, make your soil as moisture-retentive as possible by adding copious amounts of compost before you plant. Mulch with a material that retains moisture and remember to water in the morning, before the sun is high. But the most effective measure you can take is choosing plants that can tolerate this environment. In addition to the species listed in 'Plants for sunny spots, dry soil' (page 51) and 'Plants for dry soil' (page 57), choose from the plants in the list on the opposite page.

Solution 3 Design for privacy

City gardens can be true refuges from the world outside their boundaries. But you must plan for privacy. If you don't have walls around the garden, you may want to build them, put up trellises, or plant a hedge. Each of these structures has pros and cons. Depending on how tall it is, a wall can give you a great deal of privacy. It blocks wind but can create turbulence (see page 59). It can give the kind of warm shelter that would allow you to grow a plant that is only marginally hardy in your climate. But it does create shade.

A hedge can provide almost as much privacy as a wall does. It also gives protection against wind without creating a turbulent spot and creates a sheltered environment. But in an urban setting, its most important attribute is as a noise buffer. So much sound gets trapped in the many air spaces between the small leaves of a hedge that you can almost forget the city street beyond it.

A screen of plants growing on a trellis is well-suited for giving you a certain amount of visual privacy. Depending on the plants—evergreen or deciduous, lush or sparse—you can feel quite apart from your surroundings. Even though it won't work to buffer noise and it can't provide a great deal of shelter, it can create the feeling of being alone in your garden.

A paved courtyard makes an urban garden feel luxurious.

PLANTS TOLERANT OF AIR POLLUTANTS

In the following table, plants marked O_3 are tolerant of ozone; those marked SO_2 are tolerant of sulfur dioxide; those marked PAN are tolerant of peroxyacetyl nitrate; and those marked ALL are generally tolerant or resistant to damage from air pollutants.

Herbaceous plants	Chemicals tolerated
Aquilegia spp. (columbine)	O_3 and PAN
Begonia spp.	PAN
Calendula officinalis (pot marigold)	PAN
Callistephus chinensis (china aster)	O_3
Chrysanthemum and *Dendranthema* spp.	O_3 and PAN
Dianthus spp. (pinks)	SO_2
Eschscholzia californica (California poppy)	O_3 and PAN
Gaillardia x *grandiflora* (blanket flower)	PAN
Geranium spp. (cranesbill)	O_3
Heuchera spp. and cvs. (alum root, coralbells)	O_3 and PAN
Hibiscus spp.	SO_2
Impatiens spp. (busy Lizzie)	SO_2
Lilium spp. (lily)	O_3 and PAN
Lobelia spp.	O_3
Narcissus spp. (daffodil)	O_3 and PAN
Solenostemon spp.	PAN
Tropaeolum majus (nasturtium)	SO_2
Viola x *wittrockiana* (pansy)	PAN
Zinnia spp.	SO_2

Trees	
Abies balsamea (fir, balsam)	All
Betula pendula (European white birch, silver birch)	All
Cornus florida (common white dogwood)	All
Gingko biloba	All
Ilex spp. (holly)	All

problem
The garden is rocky

Rocky soil can try the patience of a gardening saint. Depending on how rocky it is, digging can be close to impossible ar it can be frustrating to use even a small hand tool. Tines of garden forks break off, blades need sharpening every time yc use them, and you're likely to put more than one big dent in shovels and spades.

Rocky soils also drain quickly. Not only does this make it more difficult to keep soils moist enough, but it al: increases the rate at which soluble nutrients leach away. Your gardening jobs will be a great deal easier if you dig as litt as possible and add nutrient-holding materials wherever you can.

solution 1 Water-in fertilizers

Rocky soils usually demand fertilizing during the season because nutrients leach so easily from them. Don't apply a one-rate-suits-all fertilizer spray to every plant in the garden, however. Remember that plants such as those listed opposite in 'Rock garden plants' grow well in low-fertility areas. Instead, save the fertilizer for plants that show symptoms such as slow growth, leaves that turn yellow, and stems and leaves that become purple or bronze.

Choose from a number of liquid fertilizers made up of liquid seaweed and fish emulsion, or mix the ingredients yourself according to the ratios listed on their containers.

Applying the liquid can pose some challenges. If you are fertilizing only a few plants, simply mix up the solution in a 2-litre (5-gallon) bucket and use some kind of container to scoop out two cups for plants with high nutrient demands and one cup for plants with moderate needs. Pour the nutrient around the base of the stem.

You can also buy an attachment for the hose that mixes the nutrient to the correct proportion. Look for a small plastic jar with a dial on the lid or a tube with what loo' like an irrigation nozzle at one end. Each of these devic will allow you to apply the correct dilution of nutrients your plants.

Fertilizers can easily be watered into your garden plants.

solution 2 Pick rocks seasonally

Rock picking is a time-honoured job everywhere that rocks abound. But it's best to pick rocks when the soil is not so wet that you will be compacting it by walking on it or by hauling a heavy load of rocks over it. In most areas, this means that springtime is no time to pick rocks, no matter how much the sight of them annoys you. If you can avoid stepping on growing areas while you pick, you can ignore this advice, of course, but otherwise take the caution seriously. Instead, pick rocks when all good farmers do – in late summer and autumn.

Late summer, when you are removing the debris fror annual crops from the garden, is an ideal time because th soil is usually not wet. Continue picking up however man you can manage until the fall rains begin to get serious an the soil gets saturated again. Because rocks will continue t move up through the soil each time the ground freezes an thaws during the winter, expect to repeat this proces annually.

See also: 'Grow ground covers', page 64; 'Make compost', page 95; 'Low-fertility soil', page 94; 'Test soil pH', page 74

Solution 3 Adjust pH

Increasing soil acidity can also be a problem in rocky soils. As base nutrients such as calcium, magnesium and potassium drain away, the soil will become progressively more acidic unless you add lime to it. Test the soil frequently so that you can adjust it before the problem becomes severe.

Because digging lime into the soil can be difficult in rocky areas, let the fast drainage that caused the problem help to solve it. Sprinkle the recommended amount of limestone on the soil surface and use the hose or a sprinkler to water it in. It will drain down to the root zone right away.

Solution 4 Develop a rock garden

Rock gardens are truly beautiful solutions to the problem of a rocky soil. Choose the site carefully. A slope with a northern or eastern exposure is ideal because it protects plants from some of the temperature extremes that rocky areas on southern or northern slopes experience. Don't despair if you have only flat ground. If your soil is truly rocky and freely draining, the plants should do well.

Do some research to discover the needs of the plants you want to grow. True alpine species, such as edelweiss (*Leontopodium alpinum*) and gentian (*Gentiana* spp.), fare best in moist but well-drained soils with a neutral to slightly alkaline pH, as do the plants in the list below. However, you may wish to grow some plants that are adapted to well-drained soils but require more acid conditions. If you want a mixture of types, segregate them. Amend the soil for each group in a separate section of the plot and put the most versatile plants at the boundary between the two areas. Remember to test the pH once a year so that you can adjust it as needed.

Rock gardens allow tremendous creativity in design and plant choice.

ROCK GARDEN PLANTS

Perennials

Achillea clavennae (yarrow)

Aethionema grandiflorum (Persian stonecress)

Alyssum montanum

Aquilegia canadensis; A. saximontana (columbine)

Arabis spp. (rockcress)

Armeria juniperifolia; A. maritima (thrift)

Leontopodium alpinum (edelweiss)

Minuartia verna (spring sandwort)

Sedum spp. (stonecrop)

Teucrium chamaedrys (germander)

Veronica prostrata; V. spicata (speedwell)

Shrubs

Calluna vulgaris (heather)

Chamaecyparis obtusa (Hinoki cypress)

Erica carnea (heath)

Juniperus chinensis 'Echiniformis' (hedgehog juniper)

Rhododendron impeditum

Erica carnea (heath)

problem
The garden is under the eaves

Foundation plantings placed under deep eaves often suffer from drought. This can be true even in rainy climates because the eaves can prevent rainwater from reaching the soil under the overhang.

Foundation plants tend to be tough. Few people give them much care aside from an annual pruning and some mulch and fertilizer once a year. Given how busy most people are, this level of care seems appropriate as long as the plants don't suffer. But if you have deep eaves that keep water from falling on them, you may have to do some extra work to keep them healthy. The suggestions below are designed to make their care as convenient as possible.

solution 1 Mulch deeply and often

Mulch can be your best ally in keeping the soil around foundation plants moist enough to promote good growth. Choose a mulch that is attractive in combination with the materials and colours of your house. If possible, use a layer of fully finished compost under another mulch because it will increase the water-holding capacity of the soil. Do not pile the mulch too thickly. It's better to add to it a couple of times a year than put so much on that it offers a safe haven for rodents.

Cedar mulch can be used for plants growing near the house to increase the amount of water they receive.

solution 2 Install a rain barrel

Rain barrels are wonderful inventions. They fit under a gutter and collect water running off the roof. A tap at the bottom of the barrel allows you to drain the water into a watering can or hose. You can also fit the tap to work with a drip irrigation system that is connected to an automatic timer. This system will allow you to water the foundation plants almost effortlessly during consistently rainy periods.

You can use any extra water for houseplants and areas where you want to spot water rather than use a drip or a hose.

Rain barrels can protect plants from being washed out by heavy rains and also give a ready source of chlorine-free water for delicate seedlings.

See also: 'Install drip irrigation', pages 55–57; 'Plants for dry soils', page 57; 'Mulch', page 54; 'Make use of mulches', page 54; 'Common mulch materials', page 54; 'Plants for dry soils', page 57

Solution 3 Direct the gutter flow

Rain gutters can lead right into the area where foundation plants grow. However, because the flow can be so strong, it can wash out plants or lead to waterlogged soils.

If you live in an area with light rainfall, directing the gutter flow into the foundation garden makes sense. But protect the plants by creating an area of gravel, 8–10cm (3–4 inches) deep, directly in front of the outlet. And keep watch over the area to make certain that the plants aren't suffering in any way. To mask the view of the gutter and outlet, plant bushy species towards the front of the garden.

Ψ 🐢 ◑ 🥛

FOUNDATION PLANTS FOR DRY SOILS

Berberis spp. (barberry)

Cotoneaster spp.

Euonymus fortunei

Ilex verticillata (winterberry)

Juniperus horizontalis (creeping juniper)

Mahonia spp.

Rhododendron spp.

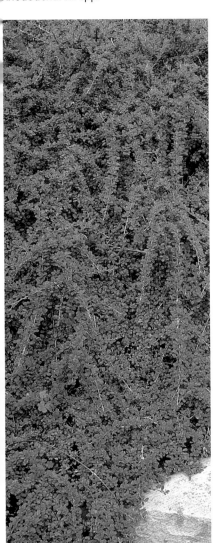

ABOVE *Juniperis horizontalis* (creeping juniper)

LEFT *Cotoneaster horizontalis*

BELOW *Rhododendron* spp.

chapter three

SOIL PROBLEMS

Soil is one of the most important elements of your garden. Without good soil,
you could have a lovely exposure, just enough rainfall, gentle breezes that blow
disease spores into the next state, a totally pest-free environment, and still be
unable to grow a thing. Soil is the plant's source of moisture and nutrients as well
as the closest thing it has to an immune system; it always determines how a plant
will grow.

Ideal soils are rare, and one of the most important tasks of any gardener is
learning about the soil in his or her garden. You will want to know what kind of
texture – sandy, loamy or clayey – it has, whether it has a compacted or friable
structure, what the pH is, whether or not it drains well, if it's rocky, and if it's
fertile or not. Once you know all that, you can set about improving it. The
problems in this section are common, and you are likely to encounter more than
one of them in your gardening life. The solutions are all designed to make your
gardening more successful for years to come.

problem
Acid soil

The pH level of soil – its acidity or alkalinity – affects everything else about that soil, from its microbial population and structure to its drainage and the nutrients that are available. Neutral soil has a pH of 7, but for most garden plants the ideal soil has a pH between 6.8 and 6.5—that is, one that is just slightly acid. Most of the plants you will grow will tolerate soil more acid than this, but when there is a pH below 6.0 you are likely to see a few problems, and if the pH is 5.5 or below you will encounter severe problems.

Acid soils interfere with nutrient absorption by plants partly because they make some of the trace elements excessively available. Manganese, boron and aluminium all fall into this category. In high concentrations, some aluminium compounds are toxic to plants, and plants often take up manganese and boron in preference to some of the other nutrients they need. This results in deficiencies of nutrients such as nitrogen and phosphorus. Soil micro-organisms can also be adversely affected. Without high populations of diverse organisms, organic matter cannot be changed into forms that are available to plants, and the soil's capacity to hold both air and water diminishes. For all these reasons, it's wise to correct pH problems before they become severe.

solution 1   Test pH with a meter or kit

When you send your soil to a lab for a nutrient analysis, you will also receive results of a pH test. They will tell you the pH of the soil and, if it is too acid, how much lime you need to add to it to bring the pH to 6.5. If the condition is not serious, you will be able to adjust the soil in a single season. However, if the pH is 5.5 or lower, it may take a couple of years to bring it up to ideal levels. Continue to test so that you have an idea of the progress you are making. If you don't want to pay an outside lab to test for you through this process, you can do it yourself.

Begin by saving a sample of the soil that you initially sent off to the lab. You will want this to set a benchmark.

Test it with one of the methods shown below so that you can compare your results to the lab results. They may be only slightly different, but they could be as much as half point apart. In the future, when you do a soil test, you can add or subtract the difference between the lab's results and your own to determine what the pH is. While any difference between the results could vary between acidity levels, it won't be so serious that you can't use this technique to adjust any inaccuracies in the home test.

1 Take soil samples from several spots in your yard. Scrape off the top layer of sod and roots and take a 15-cm (6-inch) deep slice with a plastic or stainless-steel trowel.

2 Place the soil in a stainless-steel or plastic bowl and let it dry. Mix and crumble it with your hands, again being certain not to touch it with a tin or aluminium tool.

3 Read the directions that came with your test kit to see how much soil to add to the test vial. Again, if you use a tool, make sure it's plastic or stainless steel.

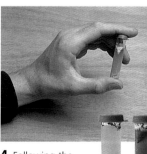

4 Following the kit's directions, add the reagent or tablet and distilled water to the vial and shake it for the suggested time. Results depend on precision. Determine the pH by matching the colour against the kit's chart.

See also: **'Build a raised bed', page 52**

solution 2 Look for indicator plants

Various plants have evolved to live in just about every environment that can be found on the earth's surface. As a consequence, certain plants can indicate what the soil conditions are likely to be in a particular site – wet, dry, acid or alkaline. These plants aren't always present and they won't tell you exactly how acid, wet, dry or alkaline the soil is, but if you do find them they can give you a clue that the condition exists. The plants listed below are all acid indicators. If some of them tend to come into your gardens or lawn as weeds or if they grow in wild places on your land, you would be wise to test the soil's pH (see opposite page).

Azaleas thrive in acid soil.

ACID INDICATOR PLANTS

Grasses

Agrostis spp. (common bentgrass)

Festuca ovina (sheep's fescue)

Shrubs

Crataegus spp. (hawthorn)

Ilex spp. (holly)

Rhododendron spp.

Ribes spp. (brambles)

Sambucus spp. (elderberry)

Vaccinium spp. (blueberry)

Viburnum trilobum (highbush cranberry)

Weeds and wildflowers

Anemone nemorosa (wood anemone)

Angelica archangelica

Campanula rotundifolia (blue bellflower)

Filipendula ulmaria (meadowsweet)

Fragaria vesca (wild strawberry)

Leucanthemum vulgare (ox-eye daisy)

Oxalis spp. (sorrel)

Plantago spp. (plantain)

Ranunculus ficaria (lesser celandine)

Rumex crispus (curly dock)

Silene dioica (red campion)

Stellaria media (chickweed)

Taraxacum officinale (dandelion)

solution 3 Add lime

Ground limestone is generally used to reduce soil acidity. It works because it contains many nutrient elements that carry a positive charge. Soil becomes acid when too many of the negatively charged ions on clay particles and organic matter hold hydrogen rather than one of the other positively charged cations – forms of calcium, potassium, magnesium and some types of nitrogen. Limestone changes this balance because it is full of calcium and, depending on the type, magnesium. Once these elements enter the soil, they displace some of the hydrogen.

Adding lime is not a one-time, fix-all solution. The positively charged elements leach out of soils easily. The more decomposed the organic matter in the soil, the less quickly they leach, but nevertheless, they disappear over a period of time. If you live in an area that receives a lot of rain, it's likely that your soils will try to revert to being too acid for garden plants. Guard against this by testing for pH every other year once levels are 6.5.

Choose the lime you use carefully, too. Look at yo[ur] soil test to determine the levels of magnesium in your so[il]. It's possible to have excessive magnesium and still ha[ve] acid conditions. If the magnesium is high, use calci[tic] limestone. However, if it is low, use dolomitic limesto[ne]. Do not use gypsum to correct soil acidity. It contains a ty[pe] of calcium that does not alter the pH of the soil, so it's use[d] only to correct calcium deficiency in soils with optimu[m] pH levels.

Remember to apply limestone on a calm day. Th[e] particles are so small that they drift easily. Many peop[le] also wait two weeks after liming to apply compost or age[d] manure because lime can cause available nitrogen in the materials to evaporate and blow away.

1 Determine how much lime to add by measuring the garden's size. Calculate by using the table below for soil type and amount for each 9.3 sq m (100 sq ft).

2 Weigh the lime on a scale and sprinkle it over the area. If you are adding more than 2.25kg (5lb), divide both the area and the lime into manageable amounts.

3 Rake the lime into the soil immediately to keep it from blowing away. You can also set a tiller to the shallowest depth and move slowly to incorporate it.

4 Water immediately so it w[ill] begin reacting with the soil a[nd] also to let the calcium leach in[to] the root zone area. Wait about tw[o] weeks before planting.

HOW MUCH LIME?

A soil lab will recommend an appropriate application rate of limestone to correct acidity in your soil. However, if you are working without a lab report, you can use the following chart as a guide. Note that the application rate is dependent on the type of soil you have – a sandy soil with a pH of 5.8 will require less lime than a clay one with the same pH to bring it up to 6.5. The amounts show[n] below are standard to bring up the pH one point – from 5.5 to 6.5, for example. If your soil is more acid that this, it would be better to add the suggested quantity in the early spring and then to add additional limestone in the autumn or the following spring.

Application rates

Type of lime	Soil type	Pounds (per 100 square feet)
Calcitic	Clay soil	9.0
	Loam	6.5
	Sandy soil	2.5
Dolomitic	Clay soil	7.75
	Loam	6.0
	Sandy soil	2.0

Solution 4 Choose plants tolerant of acid conditions

If your soil is very acid, there will be only so much you can do to correct it. The minute you let down your guard or stop spreading lime, it will become acid again. You can fight this battle in the vegetable garden and for a few selected specimen plants, but you might also consider simply growing acid-tolerant plants wherever possible. They will save you a lot of time, trouble and grief. Use the list below to guide you in some lovely choices.

PLANTS FOR ACID SOILS

Annuals and perennials

Ajuga spp. (bugle)

Asclepias tuberosa (butterfly weed)

Chrysanthemum and *Dendranthema* spp.

Convallaria majalis (lily-of-the-valley)

Hemerocallis cvs. (daylily)

Iris spp.

Liatris spp. (gayfeather)

Lilium spp. (lily)

Lobelia cardinalis (cardinal flower)

Lupinus spp. (lupin)

Nicotiana spp. (tobacco plant)

Platycodon grandiflorus (balloon flower)

Primula spp. (primrose)

Rudbeckia hirta (black-eyed Susan)

Sedum spp. (stonecrop)

Tagetes cvs. (marigold)

Tiarella spp. (foamflower)

Viola x *wittrockiana* (pansy)

Shrubs

Amelanchier spp. (snowy mespilus)

Arctostaphylos uva-ursi (mountain box, red bearberry)

Calluna vulgaris cvs. (heather)

Erica spp. (heath)

Euonymus spp.

Gaultheria procumbens (checkerberry, creeping wintergreen)

Kalmia latifolia (calico bush)

Myrica spp. (bayberry, candleberry)

Rhododendron spp. (rhododendrons and azaleas)

Rosa rugosa (Japanese apple rose)

Trees

Abies spp. (fir)

Carya illinoiensis (hickory, pecan)

Cedrus spp. (cedar)

Cornus spp. (dogwood)

Malus spp. (crab apple)

Oxydendrum arboreum (sourwood)

Pinus spp. (pine)

Quercus spp. (oak)

Rhododendron

problem
Alkaline soil

Highly alkaline—or base—soils occur most frequently in dry areas. Additionally, if you are gardening in a spot where lar
concentrations of fertilizers were used, you may have soil that is both alkaline and saline, or salty. This gives you tw
problems to solve, not just one. (See 'High soluble salt content in soil,' page 98, for help with high salts.)

The problems associated with alkaline soils are similar to those encountered with high acid soils: Plants can't pick u
the nutrients they require to grow well and stay healthy. But the elements differ. Alkaline conditions prevent plants fro
acquiring adequate levels of phosphorus and most of the trace elements. Both sodium and selenium can be excessive
available and kill plants at high levels. Most microorganisms require slightly acid soils, so decomposition and nutrient cyclir
processes are disrupted. It's well worth the effort to try to correct the problem.

solution 1 Detect alkaline conditions

Because alkaline soils lead to various nutrient deficiencies, you would be wise to have it tested if a number of plants have yellow discolouration on green leaves – the telltale symptom of iron deficiency. If you think you have really alkaline soil, get the kids to do an experiment for you. Have them mix a tablespoon of soil with a tablespoon of vinegar. If the mixture fizzes, the soil is definitely alkaline. You can test it yourself, but it's wise to begin with a laboratory test.

Follow the directions in 'Test pH with a meter or kit' (se
page 74) for using the lab test as a benchmark when usir
a home pH test.

solution 2 Apply flowers of sulfur

Sulfur helps to lower the pH of alkaline soils, but it must be applied correctly. For every 9.3 sq m (100 sq ft), apply no more than 0.5kg (1 lb) of flowers of sulfur. This amount will lower the pH one unit, say from 8.0 to 7.0 in most soils.

Don't be tempted to add more than this, even if your soil needs to be lowered more than one unit. Larger amounts will disrupt micro-organisms and soil animals, harming your soil more than it helps. Instead, apply additional sulfur the following year.

It's important to water immediately after applying the sulfur. Because it will work better if the soil contains high levels of organic matter, it's wise to apply a layer of compost, about 13mm (½ inch) deep, at the same time as you apply the sulfur.

Cichorium intybus (chicory)

See also: **Test pH with a meter or kit', page 74**

INDICATOR PLANTS FOR ALKALINE SOILS

Some plants that grow well in cooler, wetter areas of the country prefer alkaline conditions, too. The following plants fall into this category. Remember that they can grow well on a range of soils, so don't assume that your soil is alkaline just because it hosts Queen Anne's lace and chickweed. Test to be certain.

Chenopodium bonus-henricus (good King Henry, goosefoot)
Cichorium intybus (chicory)
Cynodon dactylon (Bermuda grass)
Daucus carota (Queen Anne's lace, wild carrot)
Euphorbia maculata (spotted spurge)
Filipendula ulmaria (meadowsweet)
Stellaria media (chickweed)

RIGHT *Chenopodium bonus-henricus* (good King Henry)
BELOW *Filipendula ulmaria* (meadowsweet)

Solution 3 Water for a quick fix

If you have a plant that is suffering from alkaline conditions in mid- to late season, you can give it a quick fix when you water. Simply replace one watering a week with common white vinegar, which contains 5 percent acetic acid. Remember to apply enough to penetrate the soil, down to the area where the roots are actively growing and taking in moisture and nutrients. Monitor the soil with a home test to be sure you aren't making it too acid, and stop when the pH reaches a level between 6.8 and 6.5.

Vinegar is fairly inexpensive when you are making pickles, but if you have more than a plant or two that needs this treatment, it could prove expensive. Check with your local pharmacist and explain what you plan to do. He or she may be able to give you a 10 percent solution at a much lower price. Dilute it by half to make it 5 percent acetic acid; percentages higher than this can injure plant roots and disrupt soil life.

solution 4 Choose acidifying mulches

If your soil is excessively alkaline, you can change it slightly through your choice of organic mulches. Don't expect to change the pH in any significant way with a mulch, but if you have added flowers of sulfur to a garden bed and want to slow down its movement back to an alkaline state, a mulch can help. The list right includes materials that are good for winter cover as well as for annual and perennial beds during the growing season.

ACIDIFYING MULCHES

Mulch	Best uses
Bark, chips	Paths and perennial beds; all seasons
Bark, shredded	Paths and perennial beds; all seasons
Coffee grounds	Small containers; summer
Evergreen boughs	Winter cover for perennials
Leaves, shredded	Winter cover for perennials; annual beds in summer
Pine needles	Paths and perennial beds; all seasons
Sawdust	Annuals and perennials; all seasons
Sugarcane (bagasse)	All areas; all seasons

PLANTS TOLERANT OF ALKALINE CONDITIONS

Annuals and perennials
Alcea rosea (hollyhock)
Alchemilla mollis (lady's mantle)
Aquilegia spp. (columbine)
Bergenia spp. (elephant's ear)
Chrysanthemum and Dendranthema spp.
Cosmos spp.
Geum spp. (avens)
Gypsophila paniculata (baby's breath)
Helianthus spp. and cvs. (sunflower)

Iris spp.
Lathyrus odoratus (sweet pea)
Lobelia spp.
Penstemon spp.
Petunia hybrida
Phlox spp.
Reseda odorata (mignonette)
Salvia spp. (ornamental sage)
Scabiosa spp. (scabious)
Tropaeolum majus (nasturtium)

Trees
Acer negundo (box elder); A. saccharum subsp. nigrum (black maple)
Catalpa spp. (Indian bean)
Fagus sylvatica (beech)
Gleditsia triacanthos (honey locust)
Platanus spp. (sycamore, plane)
Quercus macrocarpa (bur oak)

Shrubs
Berberis thunbergii (Thunberg's barberry)
Buddleja davidii (butterfly bush)
Celtis spp. (hackberry, nettle tree)
Clematis spp.
Crataegus spp. (hawthorn)
Elaeagnus angustifolia (oleaster)
Helianthemum spp. (rock rose)
Lavandula spp. (lavender)
Lonicera spp. (honeysuckle)
Mahonia spp.
Philadelphus spp. (mock orange)
Spiraea prunifolia (bridal wreath)

Buddleja davidii (butterfly bush)

Aquilegia spp. (columbine)

Solution 5 Choose plants tolerant of alkaline conditions

Some soils are unrelentingly alkaline. Even with yearly applications of sulfur, they drift back to an alkaline state by the end of the season. You can continue to fight them by applying treatments twice a year, watering with vinegar, and using acidifying mulches, but it's much easier to plant alkaline-tolerant plants in as many areas of the garden as possible (see opposite page).

Berberis thunbergii (Japanese barberry)

problem
Compacted soil

Compacted soils cause many problems for plants. The lack of air spaces around the roots means a lack of oxygen, witho
which both micro-organisms and plant roots suffer. Nutrient deficiencies are common, and organic matter doesn't bre
down properly. In completely compacted soil, only a few species will grow. But less severe and less obvious compaction al
affects plants adversely. In soils with a fairly loose top layer but a compacted hardpan 15–20cm (6–8 inches) below t
surface, plant roots grow horizontally because they can't penetrate the hardpan layer. With high soil nutrition and adequa
moisture levels, they can continue growing in this fashion all season. But otherwise, they will suffer drought and/
deficiencies as the horizontal layer becomes congested with roots from many plants. Lack of support is the other probler
because when roots grow near the surface of the soil a strong wind can blow them over, tearing them from the soil.

solution 1 Check drainage

If you aren't sure whether your soil is compacted or not, you can do some diagnostic work. One of the best ways to detect slight compaction is to check the drainage. Compacted soils simply cannot drain quickly; they lack the pore spaces for water to filter through.

1 Using a sharp spade, dig a hole at least 30cm (1ft) deep in the area where you want to check drainage. Don't tamp the bottom or sides.

2 Slowly pour water in the hole. Don't ju dump a bucket-full into it – you don't want make the sides of the hole collapse.

3 Let the water drain completely out of the hole. This can happen quickly or slowly, depending on the weather and soil conditions.

4 Immediately fill it again and let it drain. more than 5cm (2 inches) remain after 24 hou you'll know that drainage is poor.

See also: **'Build raised beds', page 52**

Solution 2 Aerate mechanically

If your soil is only moderately compacted, you can solve the problem mechanically by poking holes into the compacted layer of the soil. You will want to use a digging fork or a U-bar as shown. Make deep holes at close intervals. If your compaction problems are severe, you may want to go over the area several times, on consecutive days and/or weeks. Add organic matter (see below) after you have broken through the compacted layers.

Use a digging fork to pierce holes in the soil. Do this on a day when you have a lot of patience – it's best to make the holes at close intervals and to go over the area in several directions.

Solution 3 Add organic matter

Organic matter helps to solve compaction problems by adding micro-organisms to the soil. As microbes break down organic matter, they create soil aggregates – that is, small, jagged lumps of soil particles. Rather than lying flat against each other, these aggregates pile up like bread-crumbs, with spaces for air and water between them.

Organic matter also feeds earthworms, which help to counter soil compaction by tunneling through the soil, leaving long channels for air and moisture to move between the surface and the lower depths.

Apply a layer, 13–25 mm (½–1 inch) deep, of good finished compost to the soil in early spring and work it into the top few centimetres with a digging fork or U-bar. Where appropriate, mulch with an organic material, such as straw or cocoa bean hulls, which also have spaces for a great deal of air, rather than sawdust or autumn leaves, which themselves compact easily.

solution 4 Grow deep-rooted cover crops

Farmers who have a field with compacted soil often take it out of production for up to 18 months. During this time, they grow a tough, deep-rooted cover crop. Their first choice is often alfalfa because it grows roots as deep as 7.5m (25ft) into the soil over an 18-month period and penetrates most compacted soils. It also adds a great deal of nitrogen to the soil while it is breaking up the compaction. Because the roots quest for nutrients deep in the soil, they also recapture potassium as well as various trace elements and bring them up to the root zone of garden crops. Crops with tough roots, such as daikon radish, break through shallow but rigid hardpans. They c[ ] not add any nitrogen, but they do add organic matter.

When you are using a crop to break up so[ ] compaction, it's important to make as dense a planting [ ] possible. Most of these plants do well at densities of 3–5c[ ] (1½–2 inches) between seeds. Plant the seed from spring [ ] late summer, but leave perennials in place for at least [ ] year. If you can let them stay in the ground f[ ] 18 months, you will get even more benefits. Till under [ ] the early spring, taking care to set the tiller at differe[ ] depths if you need to go over the ground more than onc[ ]

**COVER CROPS
FOR COMPACTED SOILS**

Brassica juncea (mustard);
 B. napus (rape)
Coronilla varia (crown vetch)
Lupinus angustifolius (lupin)
Medicago sativa (alfalfa)
Raphanus sativus (daikon
 radish)
Trifolium pratense
 (red clover)

Alfalfa makes a wonderful cover crop as long as your soil has a pH close to neutral. If you want to plant it in an acid area, amend with lime several weeks before seeding.

Solution 5 Double-dig the garden

Double-digging garden beds is the most effective way around the problem of compacted soils. But make no mistake about it, it's hard work. Fortunately, once you have double-dug a bed, you don't have to do it again if you treat it well. Don't till it or break it down in any way, at any time. At the end of the season, simply pull the roots and plant a cover crop or apply a mulch. If you plant a cover crop, use an annual such as oats (*Avena* spp.), which will die during the winter so you don't have to destroy the bed to get rid of it in the spring.

Begin double-digging by digging a 0.34-m (1-ft) wide and deep trench. Reserve the soil from the trench. Use a spading fork to aerate the subsoil at the bottom of the trench. Dig a second trench next to the first and put the soil from this one into the first trench. Aerate the subsoil in the second trench and go on in this fashion, finishing by using the soil from the first trench to fill the last trench after you have aerated its subsoil.

problem
Clay soil

Clay particles are tiny and flat, and if the soil lacks organic matter, these particles are likely to pile up against each othe trapping water and leaving no space for air. The result is a compacted, wet soil.

If you make the mistake of trying to dig in the garden when this soil is wet, it may form clods. When the soil drie these clods will be nearly impossible to break apart. Plant roots certainly can't penetrate them. The surface of a clay s also cracks when it dries, and because clay tends to shed water, it's hard to rehydrate.

The good thing about clay soils is that they hold nutrients well. If you can modify this soil with one of the solutio described below, your plants grow well in it.

solution 1 Add sharp sand

Sharp sand will help to modify a clay soil. But you can't add just a little bit. If you do, the soil will be even harder to work than it was without the sand. To make a significant difference, it takes an addition of 3–5 tonnes of sand for every 93 sq m (1,000 sq ft) of garden area. But sand alone is not as effective as a mixture of sand and organic matter. Apply at least 2.5cm (1 inch) of finished compost to the top of the soil, just after you spread the sand in an even layer, and work both materials into the first few centimetres. Be sure to wait until the clay soil is dry enough to work before starting this procedure.

 Be sure to get washed sand; you don't want to add salt.

solution 2 Try peat moss

Large quantities of peat moss worked into the top layers of the soil also help to improve its texture. Most peat moss is acid, however, so this solution is useful only in an alkaline soil.

Test your soil before adding the peat moss. You should feel secure about adding peat moss if the pH tests well above 7. If it does not come above 7, use sharp sand.

The layer of peat moss should be at least 15cr (6 inches) thick. Sprinkle it only enough to keep it fror flying as you incorporate it into the soil. Work it into th top 20–30cm (8–12 inches) of soil with a spading fork. the soil's dry, add water to make the soil and pe mixture damp.

Let the soil sit for a week and then test again. Th second test will give you a good idea of the way the pe moss has affected the pH.

Peat moss can clump, but you can avoid this by crumbling it with your fingers as you add it.

See also: **'Check drainage', page 82; 'Build a raised bed', page 52; 'Add organic matter', page 83; 'Double-dig the garden', page 85; 'Mulch', pages 54 and 21**

Solution 3 Use gypsum

Gypsum affects clay in the same way that decomposed organic matter does. It draws particles together into aggregates. Because the aggregates are unevenly shaped, they create some pore spaces in the soil.

Although gypsum contains high levels of calcium, it does not affect pH. You can add it if the soil is deficient in calcium. It's also useful if your soil is high in magnesium, which is a common problem in clay soils. By adding more calcium, you can balance these nutrients.

Other mineral sources, such as greensand or azomite, help to modify the soil structure indirectly. Their balanced trace elements stimulate microbial activity, and this, in turn, leads to an increase in decomposition of organic matter. The more organic matter there is in your soil, the better the aggregate structure and drainage.

Solution 4 Choose plants tolerant of heavy soils

Even if you add huge quantities of sharp sand, peat moss, and/or gypsum, your soil is likely to remain heavy. As always, your plants will be healthier if they are adapted to clay soils. The selection below is not inclusive, but it will give you a good starting point because all of the species listed tolerate soils with high clay content.

PLANTS TOLERANT OF CLAY SOILS

Perennials

Alchemilla mollis (lady's mantle)
Baptisia australis (false indigo)
Bergenia spp. (elephant's ear)
Epimedium spp. (barrenwort)
Geranium spp. (cranesbill)
Helleborus spp. (hellebore)
Hemerocallis cvs. (daylily)
Liatris pycnostachya (Kansas gayfeather)
Monarda fistulosa (beebalm, bergamot)
Rudbeckia hirta (black-eyed Susan)
Solidago spp. (goldenrod)

Trees and shrubs

Amelanchier spp. (serviceberry)
Berberis spp. (barberry)
Cornus spp. (dogwood)
Elaeagnus angustifolia (oleaster)
Euonymus europaeus (European
  spindle tree)
Potentilla fruticosa
Spiraea spp.
Syringa spp (lilac)
Viburnum spp.

Potentilla fruticosa (potentilla)

Syringa spp. (lilac)

Alchemilla mollis (lady's mantle)

problem
Sandy soil

Sandy soils are difficult to work with because they simply don't hold water or nutrients. Organic matter that you add breaks down right away and nutrients in the soil solution drain off because there is so little humus in the soil to hold them in place.

These soils also get quite hot under the sun but cool off at night because, as they don't hold moisture, they don't buffer temperatures. Roots are exposed to more extremes in a sandy soil than they are in a clay one.

Even with these problems, sandy soils are easier to handle than clay ones. If you add lots of compost and keep the soil mulched with organic materials all through the year, you can increase the water- and nutrient-holding capacity of these soils enough so you can appreciate their benefits. They warm and dry quickly in the spring, they don't form clods if you happen to work them when they're a bit wet, they drain quickly, and it's easy to change the pH.

solution 1 Fertilize frequently

Sandy soils don't hold nutrients well, so you must fertilize them differently than you do a clay or even a loam soil. Begin the year by adding a layer of compost over the entire soil surface. On sandy soil a layer 5cm (2 inches) deep is more appropriate than the 2.5-cm (1-inch) layer gardeners add to loam soils. Once plants are growing well, mulch with as thick a layer as practical of an organic material that breaks down fairly rapidly. Use straw in vegetable and herb gardens and, if possible, grass clippings in the flower gardens. If clippings aren't available, try compost or fully finished leaf mold, both of which add water- and nutrient-holding humus to the soil.

By midseason, some plants may need a nutritional boost. You can sidedress with more compost, putting a 2.5–5cm (1–2 inches) thick layer around plants after you pull back the mulch. You can also give them a liquid boost by watering in a solution of liquid seaweed and fish emulsion, mixed as directed on their bottles.

If you live in an area with cold winters, remember not to fertilize perennials in late summer. Extra nutrition at that time might stimulate late growth, which will not have time to harden before winter.

Apply compost to a sandy soil every spring as well as at intervals during the growing season

solution 2 Modify your irrigation system

Sandy soil drains quickly and water coming into it it tends to move almost straight down through the soil. In contrast, when water enters a soil with more organic matter, silt and clay particles, it moves in a more horizontal fashion before it penetrates to lower depths.

Most drip irrigation systems have emitters spaced for an average – that is, loamy – soil. You cannot change the placement of holes in a drip line, but you can modify the way you use it. For example, if the company recommends placing two drip lines on a 1.25-m (4-ft wide) bed, consider using at least three, possibly four, lines. You will need to place a line by every row of plants.

If you are using a system that depends on adding spaghetti hoses and small emitters to a header line, simply add extras. Place three emitters by each large plant instead of the recommended two, for example.

Watering times will also change. You can water for less time in a sandy soil than in a loamy one. If you are using automatic controls, begin by seeing how long it takes water to penetrate 15–20cm (6–8 inches) below the surface. Don't water beyond this time, because the plants won't use it and you will just be giving yourself a higher water bill.

olution 3 Choose plants tolerant of sandy conditions

Many plants thrive in sandy soils. Because these soils tend to be dry, you can be sure that any desert-type plants will do well in your garden. If you want to include plants outside this category, look at the plant's root system. In general, plants with a deep taproot survive droughts and dry soils better than those with a fibrous root system, because a deep root can grow down into the soil where water supplies are likely to be more plentiful. The list below contains species that do well in sandy, but not desert-like, soils.

⚓ 🐛 ① 🥛

PLANTS FOR SANDY SOILS

Annuals and perennials

Achillea spp. (yarrow)

Artemisia spp. (wormwood)

Asclepias tuberosa (butterfly weed)

Aster spp.

Celosia spp.

Centaurea cyanus (bachelor's buttons)

Coreopsis spp. (tickseed); *C. basalis*

Hibiscus syriacus (rose of Sharon)

Kniphofia uvaria (red-hot poker, torch lily)

Lavatera spp. (tree mallow)

Limonium latifolium (sea lavender)

Perovskia atriplicifolia (Russian sage)

Portulaca grandiflora (rose moss, sun plant)

Santolina spp. (lavender cotton)

Sedum spp. (stonecrop)

Tropaeolum spp. (nasturtium)

Verbena spp.

Yucca spp.

Trees and shrubs

Berberis spp. (barberry)

Buddleia davidii (butterfly bush)

Calluna vulgaris cvs. (heather)

Chaenomeles spp. (flowering quince)

Cistus spp. (sun rose)

Cotinus coggygria (smokebush)

Cytisus spp. (broom)

Elaeagnus umbellata (autumn olive)

Gleditsia triacanthos (honey locust)

Hamamelis spp. (witch hazel)

Juniperus spp. (juniper)

Ligustrum spp. (privet)

Myrica pensylvanica (bayberry, candleberry)

Pinus spp. (pine)

Potentilla spp. (cinquefoil)

Rosa rugosa (Japanese apple rose)

Yucca filamentosa (Adam's needle)

Cytisus spp. (Scotch broom)

Yucca filamentosa (Adam's needle)

problem
Poorly drained soil

Poorly drained soils cause many of the same problems that clay soils do—the soil stays too wet to work in the early spring and you can compact the soil simply by walking on it. But not all poorly drained soils are clay; poor drainage can happen as easily on a sandy soil as it does on a clay one.

Hardpan, whether it is naturally occurring or caused by poor tillage techniques, can lead to poor drainage. Even though water filters down through the top layers of the soil, it stops when it gets to the hardpan. Because it can't go anywhere it collects and then wicks upward. Other causes of poor drainage include high water tables or rock ledges under the soil as well as poor grading. You can't do a thing about a high water table or a rock ledge, but you can certainly modify the grading on your land.

solution 1 Create berms

Berms are simply small hills or humps in the soil, like a small embankment, and they serve two purposes in poorly drained soils: They can form an obstacle to running water or function as quasi-raised beds. If you are building one to direct runoff away from a particular area, begin by watching how the water runs onto the garden. You will want to build your berm so that any water hitting it will be directed to a spot where it can do no harm, such as a storm sewer. But remember that water always seeks the lowest spot, so you must make certain that you are directing it downhill. If the ground is level, dig it out enough to make a trough for the water to flow. It's also important that your berm cannot wash away. Once you have it positioned just where it can do the most good, plant a low ground cover on it to hold the soil in place. Don't use grass; you can't mow it on a berm and its seeds will become a weed problem if the grass isn't mowed.

Berms work like raised beds, too. If you want to grow a hedge along one side of the garden, for example, you can build a berm to plant into. It's best to import good topsoil or a mixture of compost and topsoil for this berm. After you mix the soil for the berm, test it for drainage by filling

4 litres (1 gallon) pot with it and then pouring the same amount of water into it. It should drain quickly. If it does not, add sand to the mixture until it does, and mix the balance of the soil for the berm using the same ratio of sand to soil.

Construct the berm so that it is nearly as wide as the drip line of the mature hedging plants and make it at least 60cm (2ft) high. If you are worried that it will wash away, plant an understory ground cover, such as sweet woodruff, violets or myrtle (*Vinca minor*), to hold it in place.

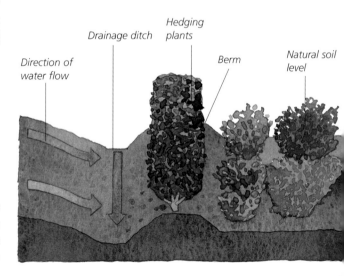

Direction of water flow | Drainage ditch | Hedging plants | Berm | Natural soil level

This berm fulfills the double purpose of directing runoff from rain and melting snow away from the garden while also giving the hedging plants a well-drained spot to grow.

See also: **'Compacted soil', page 82; 'Clay soil', page 86; 'Double-dig your garden', page 85; 'Build raised beds', page 52; 'Check pH', page 74; 'Add organic matter', page 83; 'Good bog plants', page 93**

PLANTS FOR POORLY DRAINED SOILS		
Annuals and perennials	*Iris pseudacorus* (yellow flag)	**Shrubs**
Aconitum spp. (monkshood)	*Lamium* spp. (deadnettle)	*Clethra acuminata* (cinnamon clethra);
Ajuga reptans (bugle)	*Lobelia cardinalis* (cardinal flower)	C. *alnifolia* (sweet pepper bush)
Arisaema spp. (arum);	*Mimulus luteus* (monkey flower);	*Cyrilla racemiflora* (swamp cyrilla)
Astilbe spp. (false goat's beard)	*Onoclea* spp. (sensitive fern)	*Euonymus americana*
Calla palustris (bog arum)	*Osmunda regale* (royal fern)	(American euonymus)
Cardamine spp. (cuckoo flower)	*Polygonatum* spp. (Solomon's seal)	*Fothergilla* spp.
Chelone glabra (turtlehead)	*Salvia uliginosa* (bog sage)	*Hibiscus syriacus* (rose of Sharon)
Crinum pedunculatum	*Schizostylis coccinea* (river lily, kaffir lily)	*Myrica* spp. (bayberry)
Euphorbia spp. (spurge)	*Thelypteris* spp. (marsh fern)	*Rhododendron vaseyi* (azalea);
Filipendula spp. (meadowsweet)	*Trollius* spp. (globeflower)	R. *viscosum* (azalea)
Galanthus spp. (snowdrop)	*Veratrum* spp. (veratrum lily)	*Rosa virginiana* (Virginia rose)

Solution 2 Put in ditches

Ditches can direct runoff water as well as any berm. Your choice between the two depends as much on the look you want to create in the yard as the function that the berm or ditch will play. Ditches tend to look less formal than berms, although you can form them in such a way that they become a focal point of your yard.

If you are fortunate to have a garden on a slope and have plenty of rocks, you can make a ditch that looks more like a streambed than a functional part of the landscape. Dig the ditch where it will catch runoff and then lead it down the hill. It doesn't have to take a straight course. Instead, let it meander as a real streambed does. Place rocks all along the bottom and sides of the ditch. You don't have to make them level. Water flowing down a waterway with some obstacles will create lovely little waterfalls. Plant water-loving plants along the sides of the ditch to complete the picture.

Ditches can look as lovely as streams.

Solution 3 Choose plants tolerant of poorly drained soil

Some plants thrive in wet, poorly drained soils, while others prefer boggy conditions, the difference being that plants in poorly drained soils do not have their roots in wet soil all the time, while bog-garden plants thrive in permamently damp conditions. The plants listed at top will tolerate consistently wet soils. Some of these plants will also tolerate boggy conditions. For plants that grow in bogs, see page 93.

Clethra alnifolia (sweet pepper bush) is suited to poorly drained soils.

problem
Boggy soil

Boggy soil has its advantages, but they don't include such things as vegetable gardens, orchards, strawberries or traditional flower gardens. If you look at the cultural requirements for most plants, you will see that 'well-drained soil' is at the top of the list. If you try to grow these plants in a bog, they will sicken and die.

Boggy areas can be as different as meadows; some are in shade, some in sun. Some form at the headwaters of a creek and some are runoff from a river or lake. The water in most is fairly shallow and somewhat stagnant. True bogs are covered with sphagnum moss and are highly acid. Depending on your climate, a bog is the perfect environment for some of the loveliest plants you can grow. Once you discover what marvels you can grow in a bog garden, you will never again wish it away.

solution 1 Eliminate mosquitoes benignly

Mosquitoes are one of the disadvantages of bogs. Standing water looks like a comfortable nursery to a mother mosquito, so people with bogs often have mosquitoes.

Fortunately, you don't need to get out a poison spray or eat dinner in a haze of citronella smoke to get rid of them. A form of *Bacillus thuringiensis*, or Bt, is as effective as any poison and totally harmless to other organisms in the bog.

Look in a garden centres or in garden catalogues for the Bt. It is usually packaged in what looks like a sawdust doughnut. Follow the instructions on the package to work out how many of these doughnuts to put into your bog and at what intervals to replace them. The disease attacks the larvae and cleans up your problems.

Bats and martins are also good mosquito controls, but of the adults, not the larvae. They don't control a mosquito problem as well as Bt does, but they take care of many adults who fly in looking for a nice place to lay eggs. You have to do some work to attract either bats or martins, both of which need specialized homes. You can buy them ready-made, from garden suppliers.

solution 2 Plant in containers

If you have no well-drained soil and want to grow vegetables or flowers that require it, consider using containers. With a good potting soil and a container of the correct size, you can grow just about anything. If you are growing vegetables in pots, you will need to fertilize regularly, but most herbs and many annual flowers need fertilization only once or twice per season.

Watering is the major chore when you grow in containers, but you can make it easier by grouping the pots close together. Not only does this reduce your walking time, but it also reduces the speed with which they will dry, because, apart from the outermost pots, they act as insulation for each other. See pages 148–151 for solutions to common problems with container growing.

solution 3 Grow carnivorous plants

Carnivorous plants are common in bogs because they prey on insects for their nutrient needs rather than counting on the low-fertility soil. These plants intrigue most people, especially children. The plants lure insects onto their leaves with odours, some of them fetid. Plants such as sundews have sticky tentacles that hold an insect while the rest of the tentacles close over it, and others are shaped so that the insect simply falls into the area where the plant can digest it. They eat slowly, so a small population will not solve insect problems, but they are certainly a conversation starter.

See also: **'Build raised beds', page 52**

olution 4 Plant a bog garden

og gardens can be beautiful as well as an endless source of
iscination. No matter how well planned they are and how
much maintenance work you do to keep them under
ontrol, they are always a little bit wild. For one thing, the
reatures that the garden attracts will vary through the
ear and you won't have too much control over them.
ovely darting dragonflies will become an everyday sight,
nd frogs will serenade you at night. Migrating waterbirds
re likely to stop for a semiannual visit. If you have
hildren, this garden can become a living lab for them.

The plants that live in bogs must be able to survive in
cid, low fertility, and wet spots. Some bog plants have
volved to live with their roots and crowns under water,
vhile others prefer a marginal position, growing in the wet
oil at the edges of the bog. You will want a variety of
lants for this garden. The plants for poorly drained soils
sted on page 91 will thrive at the margins of your bog.
"hose listed below will grow well, even if the water covers
heir crowns, either periodically or on a permanent basis.

Make the best of boggy soil by choosing plants that will thrive there.

GOOD BOG PLANTS

Acorus calamus (Japanese rush, sweet flag)

Alisma plantago-aquatica (water plantain)

Butomus umbellatus (flowering rush)

Calla palustris (water arum)

Calluna vulgaris (heather)

Caltha palustris (marsh marigold)

Carex aquitilis (water sedge); *C. oligosperma* (bog sedge)

Carex grayi (mace sedge)

Chamaedaphne calyculata (leatherleaf)

Chelone glabra (turtlehead)

Dactylorhiza elata (robust marsh orchid)

Drosera spp. (sundew)

Equisetum scirpoides (bushy horsetail)

Erica spp. (heath)

Eriophorum virginicum (tawny cottongrass)

Iris pseudacorus (yellow flag)

J. effusus f. *spiralis* (corkscrew rush)

Ledum groenlandicum (Labrador tea)

Mazus pumilo (purple swamp mazus)

Myosotis scorpiodes (water forget-me-not)

Pontederia cordata (pickerel weed)

Rhododendron viscosum (swamp azalea)

Sagittaria sagittifolia (arrowhead)

Sarracenia purpurea (pitcher plant)

Salix babylonica (weeping willow)

Typha spp. (reedmace)

ABOVE *Iris pseudacorus* (yellow flag).

LEFT *Salix babylonica* (weeping willow).

problem
Low-fertility soil

Low-fertility soils can always be transformed into soils with adequate, if not superb, fertility. This is, however, scar consolation during the years it takes to make this transformation. Without good fertility, plants simply don't grow wel They are smaller than they should be and they sometimes show specific deficiency symptoms, such as yellowing leaves a a consequence of nitrogen deficiency or purplish leaves because phosphorus levels are too low. They are also much mor vulnerable to pests and diseases. Many pest species prey first on weak plants, and some diseases won't attack unless th plant is stressed, either because it is old or because it lacks adequate nutrition.

Diagnosing a fertility problem can be difficult, and this is especially true of gardens that slowly decline. You may notic that plants don't seem as vigorous as they should be and that the incidence of pests and diseases is rising instead of falling Each of these symptoms is a warning sign that the soil might be losing fertility.

solution 1   Test for nutrients

When plants show deficiency symptoms, such as slow and/or stunted growth, yellowing or purpling colouration, or tip burn or die back, you can be pretty sure the soil is suffering from a nutrient deficiency. Instead of diagnosing and treating the problem simply by looking at the plants, however, make use of some technological tools. For one thing, various deficiencies can mask other problems, and an excess of one nutrient can cause others to be deficient. The only way to determine exactly what's going on in the soil is to do a soil test.

You can send a soil sample to a laboratory or buy a home test kit and do it yourself. A professionally done sample will come with recommendations for the types and amounts of fertilizers and amendments to use to adjust the

soil, and you can be pretty sure that the test was we conducted, too. No test is a totally accurate picture of wha nutrients are and are not available to plants because the use a different acid than plants do to extract the nutrient Nonetheless, workers in a laboratory are trained to inter pret the results and give good recommendations.

Home tests can be good if you conduct them well. It a good idea to take a soil sample as shown on page 74 an send half of the sample to a lab and keep the balance t test yourself. Compare the results to learn if your tes results are similar to the lab's.

solution 2   Use bagged additives

The line between additives and fertilizers is vague, but, for the purposes of this discussion, soil additives are materials that stimulate microbial activity, enhance the physical qualities of the soil, and/or contribute nutrients. In most cases, the majority of the nutrients in a soil additives are unavailable – micro-organisms must break them down and transform them before plants can use them. The chart on page 96 lists some common additives along with their average analysis and the amount to apply on soils with adequate, medium, and low levels of the nutrient in question.

If you are uncertain whether to add an additives or fertilizer, base your decision on your soil. If it's full c organic matter, choose a fertilizer. However, if not, add a amendment. Remember that you can use an additives an a fertilizer together.

See also: 'Add organic matter', page 83; 'Mulch', pages 21 and 54; 'Plants for sandy soil', page 88

Solution 3 Apply foliar feed

Plants can take in nutrients through their stomata (epidermal pores) in their leaves as well as through their roots. You can use this characteristic when a plant needs a quick fix. If you suddenly notice that a plant looks nutrient-deficient, you can deal with it immediately.

Liquid seaweed and fish emulsion are both good foliar fertilizers. Mix them at half the rate recommended on the bottle for soil application. Spray early in the morning, before the sun is up. If bright light hits the leaves when the droplets are still wet, the material can burn little spots in the leaves. Don't spray in the evening because the stomata may be closed at that time. You can also use nettle tea and compost tea as foliar feeds.

Solution 4 Make compost

Compost is truly a miracle substance. It increases the water- and nutrient-holding capacity of your soil, it improves soil structure, it adds micro-organisms that prey on pests and diseases as well as make nutrients available to your plants, and it adds nutrients both in available forms and in forms ready for microbes to attack and transform.

The advantages to making your own compost include being able to recycle wastes from the garaden and kitchen as well as being able to do your own quality control. Once you become adept at the process, you can even make specialized composts. If you completely compost a fair amount of hardwood bark, for example, the resulting material will kill many soil-borne damping-off and rotting disease organisms. You can add rock phosphate to increase the phosphorus content in the compost or seaweed to increase the trace element content. But before you get too elaborate, learn to make a good compost.

Decomposing micro-organisms require adequate oxygen, water and food sources. Additionally, they work best when a pile contains more carbon than nitrogen. A pile with about 6 parts of dry material to every 1 part of green material usually gives the right ratio. The materials should be about as damp as a wrung-out kitchen sponge and bulky enough to make plenty of air spaces. The centre of a pile like this will heat up to 70°C (160°F) in a few days. When it begins to cool, turn it inside out to add more air and water it if necessary. Keep doing this until the pile no longer heats after turning.

Layer composting materials into a bin. If possible, stockpile each type – dry and carbonaceous, green and nitrogen-filled, and rich, finished manure – until you can fill the bin.

2 Use approximately 6 parts dry material to 1 part green, covered with 2.5 cm (1 inch) of manure to build the pile in the beginning. Let this mixture 'cook' before mixing the layers.

3 Mix every two weeks or so, moving the pile from one bin to the next or the outside to the inside every time. When the pile stops heating and smells sweet, cover and let cure for a month.

solution 5 Use fertilizers

Fertilizers are necessary in many situations. You might think that a well-composted soil that you continue to build with organic mulches and cover crops can take care of its own nutrient supplies, but this is true only if the soil is already in good nutritional balance. Few soils start out this way; it takes an average of seven to ten years of care to get a soil into balance. In the meantime, fertilizers – used in combination with soil amendments – can help build the soil while also providing the nutrients that plants need.

The selection of fertilizers is amazingly wide, even among those we call 'organic'. Given this, there is no reason to use a synthetic fertilizer. No matter what your soil needs, you can find an organic formulation to supply it.

Organic fertilizers are superior because they add much more than just the nutrients in question. Often, they add needed trace elements, but, more than that, most supply organic matter and the micro-organisms necessary to break it down. The numbers of available nutrients in these blends tend to be lower than those in synthetic fertilizer meaning that they will not burn roots. With the exception of materials that contain large amounts of bat guano, blood meal, feather meal, horn and hoof meal, and leather dust the available nitrogen in an organic product will be 8 percent or less, and the total percentages of available nitrogen, phosphorus, and potassium will be 15 percent or less. Never be tempted to double up on a fertilizer. If you are used to using a 10-10-10 on your garden but buy a 5-5-5, use only the recommended amount. Remember that as the season progresses, microbes will make much more of each nutrient available to your plants.

If you are looking for a fertilizer supplier, it is worth checking the internet for somewhere that is local to you

COMMON FERTILIZERS

The following is a small selection of available fertilizers. Inclusion in this list is not necessarily an endorsement of the product. Apply fertilizers using the rates recommended on the packaging.

Fertilizer Company	Fertilizer Name	Analysis	Notes
J. Arthur Bowers	Growmore	7–7–7	Inorganic multi-purpose fertilizer.
J. Arthur Bowers	Once	14–9–14	Slow-release inorganic fertilizer – once a season.
J. Arthur Bowers	Liquid ericaceous	5–4–7	Fast-acting inorganic fertilizer for ericaceous plants.
Chase Organics	Hoof and horn	13– 0–0	Slow-release inorganic fertilizer – base dressing.
Chase Organics	Lawn fertilizer – spring	9–3–3	Slow release nitrogen-rich organic fertilizer.
Chase Organics	Lawn fertilizer – autumn	4–6–12	Organic fertilizer – guarantees a healthy lawn.
Chase Organics	Organic potash	0–0–20	Organic fertilizer for correcting deficiencies.
Chase Organics	Organic fertilizer	6–5–7	Balanced multi-purpose organic fertilizer.
Chase Organics	Potato fertilizer	6–5–10	Also good for roses and other flowers.
Chase Organics	Rock phosphate	0–27–0	An organic source of phosphate.
Chase Organics	Sterilised bonemeal	3.5–20–0	Slow release organic fertilizer.
Gem	Fish, blood & bone	6–6–6	General-purpose organic fertilizer.
Greenvale	Organic plant food	5–3–3	Slow-release organic fertilizer.
Groworganic	Pelleted poultry manure	5–3.3–2.2	General-purpose organic fertilizer.
Miracle-grow	Long-lasting granular	10–11–18	Controlled release inorganic fertilizer.
Osmacote	Long-lasting granular feed	18–11–10	Controlled release inorganic fertilizer.
PBI Home & Garden	Phostrogen lawn food	38–5–5	Fast-acting inorganic lawn food.
PBI Home & Garden	Baby bio original	10.6– 4.4–1.7	All-purpose inorganic houseplant feed.
PBI Home & Garden	Organic liquid plant food	3–1–3.7	Multi-purpose organic fertilizer.
Vitax	Sterilized bone meal	5.5–22–0	Slow release organic fertilizer.
Vitax	Pelleted Q4	5.3–7.5–10	High-potash inorganic fertilizer.
Vitax	Dried blood	12–0–0	Fast-acting nitrogen-rich organic fertilizer.
Vitax	Organic rose food	5.2–5–8.5	Organic fertilizer.
Vitax	Sulphate of potash	0–0–49	Fast-acting inorganic fertilizer.

Solution 6 Make high-nutrition planting holes for annuals

Many annuals require fairly high nutrition. This isn't surprising when you consider that most grow quickly and bloom all season. If your soil is deficient in nutrients, amend the planting holes when you transplant.

Mix about a cup of a organic fertilizer into the top 15–20cm (6 inches) of a square foot area where the annual seedling is to go and transplant as usual. Be sure to use an organic fertilizer because using such a large amount of a synthetic one could burn the plant's roots. Watch the plant all season. If it begins to look weak, apply a foliar feed as described.

Solution 7 Choose plants that tolerate poor fertility

Some plants tolerate soils with low nutrient levels. While you are building your soil, you can depend on these plants to add interest to your garden. In general, plants that do well in dry sandy soil can tolerate lower than ideal nutrient levels, as can plants from the southern Mediterranean. You will be pleasantly surprised to discover how many plants you can grow.

PLANTS FOR LOW-FERTILITY SOILS

Annuals and perennials

Achillea spp. (yarrow)

Artemisia spp. (wormwood)

Asclepias tuberosa (butterfly weed)

Centaurea spp. (bachelor's button)

Cerastium tomentosum (snow-in-summer)

Convolvulus spp. (morning glory)

Coreopsis lanceolata (lance-leaved coreopsis)

Dianthus spp. (pinks)

Eschscholzia californica (California poppy)

Gaura lindheimeri (white gaura)

Geranium spp. (cranesbill)

Gypsophila spp.

Kniphofia uvaria (baby's breath, torch lily)

Limonium latifolium (sea lavender)

Monarda spp. (beebalm)

Oenothera spp. (evening primrose)

Papaver spp. (poppy)

Portulaca grandiflora (purslane, rose moss)

Salvia spp. (ornamental sage)

Tropaeolum spp. (nasturtium)

Verbena spp.

Yucca spp.

Shrubs

Berberis thunbergii (Thunberg's barberry)

Clethra alnifolia (sweet pepper bush)

Juniperus horizontalis (creeping juniper)

Ligustrum japonicum (Japanese privet)

Myrica spp. (bayberry, candleberry)

Santolina spp. (lavender cotton)

ABOVE *Santolina* spp. (lavender cotton)
FAR LEFT *Portulaca grandiflora* (rose moss)
BELOW *Eschscholzia californica* (California poppy)

problem
High soluble salt content in soil

Alkaline soils in dry areas often build up high levels of soluble salt. Technically, some of these soils are saline, meaning th[at] their pH is below 8.5 and the major salts contain calcium and magnesium; others are sodic, meaning that their pH is abo[ve] 8.5 and the major salts contain sodium. Either problem is serious. Plants don't grow well in these soils because th[ey] cannot get enough water. Even when the soil is moist enough, the salts in it hold the water, so plant roots just can't get [it].

Soluble salt problems arise in areas of low rainfall as a consequence of excessive surface evaporation from the soil; [if] the rainfall were heavier, the nutrient salts would wash away into the lower levels of the soil rather than remaining on [or] close to the surface. In areas near the ocean, salt spray may also contribute to the problem.

The most effective long-term ways to deal with excessive salt are to improve the drainage and increase the organ[ic] matter content of the soil. Other good solutions are outlined below.

solution 1 Test for available salts

The first sign that your soil might be salty is that plants look as if they are suffering from drought. If the soil is saline, you may also see a white crust or crystals on the soil surface. In sodic soils, you're more likely to see dark-colored material migrate to the top layer of soil. But no matter what clues you have that there is a salt problem, it's important to have your soil tested.

Take a soil sample (see page 74) and send it to a lab [in] your region. If the results show that the soil has a high sa[lt] content, you will have to modify your gardeni[ng] techniques to try to correct the problem and also preve[nt] it from becoming any worse.

solution 2 Change your fertilizer

Synthetic fertilizers tend to have high concentrations of immediately available soluble nutrient salts. No matter how badly your plants need the nutrients, they cannot take all of them up right away. Without a good rain or lots and lots of irrigation water, the salts will stay near the surface of the soil and eventually lead to problems.

Organic fertilizers, on the other hand, have much lower concentrations of available nutrient salts. Because these materials are composed primarily of compost and other materials that microbes must break down and transform before plants can use them, they don't leave the kind of residues that synthetic formulations do. If you are using synthetic fertilizers, switch to a compost-based organic brand. But even then, apply it only as needed. It's better to make several small applications during the year than a single huge one in the spring.

solution 3 Use transplants

Many plants that can tolerate some salts in the soil cann[ot] germinate in these conditions. For one thing, the seed mu[st] absorb an adequate amount of water to begin growing an[d] even if it does that, the tiny first root has to be able to ta[ke] in adequate water to continue growing quickly.

The simple way around this problem is to work wi[th] transplants. Grow all of your plants in pots until they are [at] least six weeks old. Before you transplant them into th[e] garden, improve the soil where they are to go by breaki[ng] up the subsoil with a spading fork and adding organic matte[r].

See also: **'The soil is poorly drained', page 90; 'The garden is by the sea', page 62; 'Build raised beds', page 52; 'Add organic matter', page 83; 'Mulch', page 54**

Solution 4 Choose tolerant plants and cultivars

Fortunately, some plants tolerate salty soils. Plants that grow by the seaside are often in this category, as are those that thrive in a desert.

But you needn't restrict yourself to these species. The plants listed below will tolerate fairly salty soils.

PLANTS FOR SALTY SOILS

Annuals and perennials

Armeria maritima (thrift)

Aster spp.

Campanula carpatica (Carpathian bellflower)

Cleome spinosa

Coreopsis spp. (tickseed)

Dianthus spp. (pinks)

Eschscholzia californica (California poppy)

Gaillardia spp. (blanket flower)

Geranium spp. (cranesbill)

Hemerocallis cvs. (daylily)

Heuchera spp. and cvs. (alumroot, coralbells)

Hosta spp. and cvs.

Limonium spp. (sea lavender, statice)

Lobularia maritima (sweet alyssum)

Papaver orientale (Oriental poppy)

Petunia hybrida

Phlox spp.

Portulaca grandiflora (rose moss)

Rosa rugosa (rugosa rose)

Sedum spp. (stonecrop)

Solidago sempervirens (goldenrod)

Tropaeolum spp. (nasturtium)

Verbena spp.

Shrubs

Clethra spp. (summersweet)

Juniperus horizontalis (creeping juniper)

Ligustrum spp. (privet)

Weigela spp.

LEFT *Ameria maritima* (thrift)

RIGHT *Rosa rugosa* (nugosa rose)

BELOW *Limonium* spp. (sea lavender)

chapter four

LAWN PROBLEMS

If your house is a jewel, the lawn is the setting. Just as a heavy, ill-formed setting can totally devalue the look of a delicate gem, an unattractive lawn can detract from the appearance (and value) of your home.

Lawns are paradoxical. Sometimes the best-looking lawns are those that get the least attention. If the soil under the grass has a good nutrient balance and is also well drained, if the area receives enough rainfall, and if the grass species in the lawn are well adapted to the climate in which they are growing, the best thing you can do for the lawn is mow it often enough to keep it looking tidy. Benign neglect does wonders in this situation.

Few of us are lucky enough to live in this kind of paradise, however, and we have to take care of the lawn. We have to fertilize it, see that it doesn't build up dangerous levels of thatch, keep it adequately watered, and prevent or solve problems with insect pests and diseases. If, as you go about your lawncare duties, you remember that your aim is to create a lawn that responds well to only a bit of care, you will do a better job of reaching this goal.

problem
Maintenance is too time-consuming

Large lawns require large efforts. It takes time and energy to mow them, fertilize them and care for their health. But eve
a small lawn can take entirely too much time to maintain. No matter how much you enjoy being able to play on the gras
have an impromptu picnic on the back lawn or set up a croquet game on your perfect turf, the pleasure can be spoiled b
having to spend too much time on lawn care.

Paving is a traditional way around the problem of extensive lawns. If you put in areas of paving stones or concrete, yc
will reduce the amount of time spent on maintenance. This strategy makes sense in some areas – extensions to a backyar
patio, for instance but most people want an area of grass at the entryway to their homes and also enjoy some lawn in th
areas where friends and family like to relax. If this is your situation, try some of the solutions described below to decreas
the time you spend on lawn care.

solution 1 Choose slow-growing grasses

Slow-growing and low-growing grasses can save you
enormous amounts of mowing time. They require the same
care in other respects – watering, fertilizing, dethatching,
and monitoring for pests and diseases – but they require
mowing much less frequently. You should, of course,
choose a grass appropriate to your climate. More varieties
of grass are becoming increasingly available.

Ψ ⚘ ◐ ▯

With the right grass species, good
soil, and consistent care, it's possible
to create a 'perfect lawn'.

See also: **'Decrease maintenance chores', page 20; 'Grow ground covers', page 64;
'Four-season ground covers', page 39**

LOW-GROWING GROUND COVER PLANTS

Ground covers can take the place of grass in many areas of your garden. Tuck them into corners and under trees. They will look as good or better than a well-maintained lawn, but they won't require much work at all. The following species are particularly well suited to substituting for grass because they are all low growing.

Ground cover	Average height (cm/in)
Ajuga reptans (bugleweed, carpet bugle)	15/6
Hedera helix (English ivy)	15–20/6–8
Nepeta hederacea (ground ivy)	15–20/6–8
Pachysandra terminalis (pachysandra)	15/6
Thymus serpyllum (creeping thyme)	8–15/3–6
Vinca minor (myrtle)	15/6
Viola cvs. (violet)	15–20/6–8

Pachysandra terminalis

INVASIVE GROUND COVER PLANTS

Ground covers are wonderful at covering soil where no other plant will grow and also giving you a low-maintenance area in the garden. However, some of them are just too good at their jobs when they are planted in a location that suits them. They can easily invade gardens and even the lawn. Protect your other plantings by enclosing the ground cover with an edging that keeps it from spreading. The following species can be invasive.

Aegopodium podagraria (ground elder)

Ajuga reptans (bugle)

Hedera helix (English ivy)

Lamium maculatum (spotted deadnettle)

Liriope spicata (lilyturf)

Lysimachia nummularia (creeping Jenny)

Vinca minor (lesser periwinkle)

Viola odorata (violet)

Viola odorata (violet)

solution 2 Straighten the edges

Mowing around curves takes much longer than mowing in a straight line. You can cut your maintenance time significantly by making all the edges of your lawns straight.

Follow the directions below to make straightening your edges an easy task.

1 Measure and then set stakes and strings to mark a straight line.

2 Use an edger or sharp spade to cut 15-cm (6-inches) deep along the line.

3 Holding the edge of the lawn in place, pull soil away from the cut.

4 Install a plastic edging strip the cut and backfill soil to secure

solution 3 Install mowing strips

Mowing strips also cut your maintenance time Rather than having to stop to lift plants that ar drooping over the lawn edge, you can simpl run the lawnmower wheel along the mowin strip. The blade will miss the plants and you wi be able to zip through the job.

The other advantage to mowing strips that they are attractive. They give a finishe look to a garden. For best results, choose material that will complement the house o other hardscaping elements in your garden.

Mowing strips allow you to mow along a bed without cutting off blooms and stems.

Solution 4 Create tree islands

Tree islands not only make a large garden seem smaller, they also decrease mowing time. Plant easy-to-care for trees and perennials that tolerate partial shade to make life, and garden chores, even easier.

problem
The lawn goes brown

Brown lawns just aren't attractive, especially if the surrounding by lawns are green and lush. Some lawns brown o▪ because the grasses are too dry, others because they are hosting a high population of grubs, and others because the typ of grass is not really suited to the climate. If you have a lawn that does this, your first job will be diagnosis.

Drought is easy to identify. You will know if moisture levels are too low to sustain good lawn growth. Undergroun grubs, on the other hand, can be a little mysterious. Fortunately, they usually leave an important clue: it's rare that an enti▪ lawn will be equally infested with grubs, and they tend to cause spotty rather than uniformly browned-out areas. The thi▪ cause is a grass that will survive your climate but doesn't thrive in it – it will get brown, uniformly, in late summer rath▪ than fall.

solution 1   Choose drought-tolerant grasses

Summer drought is a fact of life in many climates. In some areas, the problem is becoming more frequent. With global warming, droughts may happen more frequently in the future. If you live in an area that is becoming prone to drought, you may want to reseed with one of the drought-tolerant that are now being developed. Ask at the garden centre whether these are available in your area and whether they will be suitable for your local conditions.

Brown lawns can seriously detract from your home's good looks.

See also: 'Make compost', page 95

Solution 2 Choose grasses suited to your climate

Some grasses brown because they aren't suited to the climate where they are growing, not because of drought. If you don't know what your lawn grasses require, you could be watering them when more moisture is the last thing they need. Zoysia, grown in the United States, is a good example of this. Although it easily survives as far north as northern New Jersey and southern New York, it grows better in warmer climates.

As a result, it is slow to green in the spring and goes brown as soon as the weather begins to cool in the early fall.

Spend some time learning about the grasses in your garden. If you don't know what they are, take samples to a local garden centre for identification. Should they be inappropriate, ask for recommendations for grasses that are suited to your area.

Solution 3 Replace brown patches

If only a small area of the lawn is affected by drought a simple way of remedying the problem is to remove the areas that look particularly bad and sow new grass seed.

This is explained in the photos below. If the area is larger, new pieces of turf may be used instead of grass seed.

If only a small portion of the lawn has gone brown, solve the problem and then patch it with some sod or plant some new seed.

2 Using a spade, cut around the area you want to patch. Sever the roots of the old grass and lift out the piece.

3 Add 2.5–7.5cm (1–3 inches) of good quality compost to the spot and mix it into the top few inches of the soil.

4 Sew the seeds or set the sod piece in place, pressing down to eliminate air spaces around the roots. Water thoroughly.

Solution 4 Add organic matter

Organic matter is the best drought-preventive remedy available. Humus, the by-product of decomposed organic matter, can absorb and hold six times its weight in water. Any natural mulch you apply will eventually become humus, but it's much easier and more efficient to add compost.

Compost is the product of the decomposition of a variety of organic materials. You can make it yourself or buy it by the bag or truckload. Most lawns require a 13-mm (½-inch) application every two or three years.

However, if your lawn has been browning out because of moisture stress, it's worth it to apply this much annually until the problem has been solved.

You can simply scatter compost over the lawn in the early spring. Rain and irrigation water will leach the soluble portions into the soil while earthworms and other soil animals will mix it into the top layers.

solution 5 Reseed your lawn

If you decide that your lawn is going brown because the grasses in it are inappropriate to your climate, you can either lay new turf or reseed the area. Both techniques require that you kill the existing grasses as a first step, and correct the soil with fertilizers, topsoil and compost. Laying turf is relatively straightforward; you lay it down as you set bricks in a wall, so that the seam lines are not adjacent to each other. Reseeding is a more practical option in many cases because the choice of grasses is larger, the time commitment less and the cost lower. Follow the illustrations on this page to reseed your lawn.

1 After removing the turf layer from the area you want to reseed, spread compost, topsoil, and other necessary additives over it.

2 Work the compost and additives into the top few centimetres (inches) of the soil with a rake or by using a rotivator at a shallow setting.

3 Calculate the recommended amount of seed to use over the area, weigh it out and scatter it by hand, as evenly as possible.

4 Rake shallowly to barely cover the light-loving seed. If it's hot and/or dry, lightly cover with straw to keep in moisture.

5 Water immediately, to a depth of 8-cm (3-inches), as well as every evening after that until the grass is well-established.

Solution 6 Fertilize carefully

Far too many people fertilize their lawns too often. In addition to simply wasting time, money, and fertilizer – because as much as half of it will wash away without affecting the grass at all – excess nutrients can also lead to insect pests and diseases.

The type of fertilizer you use is just as important as the quantity. Bagged soluble fertilizers that you are likely to find at the garden centre are especially prone to being leached out of the soil. Other problems are common, too.

The soil is likely to become compacted because the nutrients are at the surface, and roots don't need to grow down into the soil to find them. This mean that growing roots won't aerate the soil and that the grass will be more susceptible to moisture-stress because the roots will all be near the soil surface where it is dry.

Fertilizers such as compost, liquid seaweed, and fish emulsion act differently in that a portion of them isn't immediately available to plants. Instead, soil micro-organisms and animals have to break them down and transform them into forms that plants can use. This doesn't happen with bagged soluble fertilizers, so many beneficial micro-organisms die because they have no food. Troublesome micro-organisms such as those that cause various grass diseases can take over the niches left behind by the beneficial organisms, too.

Time fertilizing according to your climate. In cooler areas, add compost in the late summer or early autumn. If the lawn is quite weak, repeat this in the early spring. In warmer climates, the best time to feed a lawn is early spring. You can repeat this in late summer, but don't feed in the autumn.

This simple tool allows you to fertilize a large area quickly. Once you learn how to tilt it, you can also be precise in your application.

Solution 7 Water wisely

Grasses are healthiest when they receive just enough, but not too much, water. So before you water, use the finger test. Stick a finger down into the soil about 8cm (3 inches). The bulk of the roots are growing at or above this depth. Wait to water until the soil is no longer moist.

If your lawn is disease-free, water in the evening. But move to a morning watering schedule if any diseases, particularly those caused by fungi, are present. When you water, water thoroughly. Keep the sprinkler going until the top 8cm (3 inches) of soil are moist. Set out a rain gauge where the sprinkler water will fall into it, and use this to check that the grasses are getting at least 2.5cm (1 inch) of water a week, whether from rain or irrigation. When conditions are quite warm and rains have lasted for only a short time, you may need to increase watering quantities to keep the top 8cm (3 inches) of soil moist.

Remember to sprinkle early in the morning, before the sun is high, if your grass shows any disease. Otherwise, it's fine to sprinkle in the evening.

problem
Thatch has built up

Thatch is organic matter, mostly roots, stolons, and rhizomes, at the base of the grass that has not decompose
A thin layer, 13mm (¼ inch) deep or less, can be beneficial because it acts like a mulch. But if the thatch is deeper, it ca
interfere with good lawn growth. A thick layer prevents rain from penetrating to the soil below and provides a habitat f
many insect pests. Depending on environmental conditions, it can also lead to a number of diseases because the wat
trapped in the thatch layer keeps the grass stems and lower leaves consistently damp. Areas of thatch can also interfe
with mowing and give a bumpy look to the yard.

solution 1 Aerate mechanically

One of the reasons that thatch builds up is a lack of oxygen in the soil. You may use the lawn so much that you compact it, forcing air out of it. If the problem is only slight, you might be able to solve it by raking it with a metal rake twice a year. But this won't work if the problem is serious. In that case, you will have to aerate it.

If the area is small, you can think about aerating it with something as simple and easy to use as specially built spiked shoes you see advertised in some gardening catalogs. But uniformity is important if you use the shoes. You will have to walk up and down the lawn in a regimented fashion to make certain that the spikes have penetrated the thatch all over the lawn.

Rental companies usually have a collection of power aerators. Look at them all before deciding which to rent. If possible, get one that removes cores of soil from th ground. The holes it leaves behind are adequate to aera even the most compacted lawn.

Aerate just after a rain or irrigation, preferably in th early spring and then again in the early fall. Once the law has recovered, you need do this only once every oth springtime.

A manual aerating tool is useful in a small garden. It's more effective than a fork because it removes slender cores of soil rather than simply piercing through the turf layer. But like a fork, it works best if you use it at close intervals and travel in at least two, but preferably three, directions across the lawn.

See also: **'Add organic matter', page 83**

olution 2 Don't kill the worms

Worms are a great defence against thatch. They travel up and down in the soil, creating huge pores for air and water to penetrate. They also eat dead organic matter; they are as appy to dine on grass clippings as on dead flowers. But worms can't live just anywhere. The pH in the area has to e slightly acid, a great deal of organic matter on the soil urface must be available for them to eat, and there should lready be pore spaces in the soil.

Once again, compost is your best ally. Spread a layer bout 13mm (½ inch) thick over the entire garden in the arly spring and then again, if necessary, in early fall. The ompost may contain worm eggs, or even worms if it has cured for any length of time. Compost also brings in micro-organisms that provide part of a balanced diet for the worms, so it serves two purposes.

Many herbicides and fertilizers kill worms. In general, stay away from synthetically derived materials because they are likely to fall into this category. Of substances used by organic gardeners, rotenone, copper, sulfur, and any formulation of *Bacillus thuringiensis* (Bt) can also be lethal to worms in high concentrations, so avoid them if you can.

olution 3 Choose low thatch-producing grasses

ome grasses are more apt to produce hatch than others are. Those that eproduce by stolons that travel along n top or just under the soil surface end to create the most thatch. In ontrast, other grasses rarely produce hatch. If thatch is a problem in your ard, practice prevention by applying ompost and avoiding harsh pesticides nd herbicides. If that doesn't work, onsider reseeding the area with a hatch-resistant grass. To find out vhether any particular strain of grass s available to you that will fulful hese requirements ask at your local arden centre.

In the United States, new grasses ire being developed that are suited to he more extreme climate changes hat are experienced there. In many ases, conditions are not so extreme in Europe and the problems that have ed to the development of these new grasses do not exist. However, it is vorth looking on the internet or hecking with your garden centre vhether there are any grasses available hat will produce less thatch.

Pull grass leaves aside to look for a layer of thatch, or undecomposed grass residues.

Thatch is easy to recognize; it looks like a mat of dried out grass leaves and stolons.

problem
A path has been worn in the lawn

Everyone likes to take the shortest possible path to get where they are going. This is particularly true of children, of cours
but adults can be just as guilty of crossing a lawn or jumping over a flower bed if it's in their way.

It doesn't take long before the grass under the pathway looks worn. Once the soil starts to be heavily compacte
and grass blades are broken off, bare ground will start to show. Before long, weeds that like compacted soil will beg
invading the area and what was once a lovely lawn will look terrible. Try to fix the problem before it gets to this point,
only to keep the weeds from spreading.

solution 1 Create a stepping-stone path

Many materials are appropriate for paths in lawns, but some are not. Gravel, for example, has a tendency to migrate into the lawn, even if you enclose it with an edging. Once there, the lawnmower can pick it up and throw it in any direction. Instead, use something solid and immovable, such as bricks, or, as illustrated at right, flagstones.

1 Experiment with stone placement before you begin laying a path. Once satisfied, measure carefully so stones are in alignment.

2 Use an edging tool to cut around eac stone and through the entire turf layer. Kee measuring to make sure you aren't moving th stones as you cut

3 Use a flat, sharp, spade to remove the turf from the area where the stone will go. Work deeply enough to remove all the roots from the area.

4 Rough up the area for drainage. In poorly drained soils, remove enough soil to add 5–6cm (2–3 inches) of sand and then check level or the desired slope.

5 Set the stone, pressing and moving it aroun until it is level or at a slope that conforms t the yard. Set it deeply enough so that mowe blades miss it.

Solution 2 Put up a fence

The path in your garden may have nothing to do with the people in your house. Neighbourhood kids could be the culprits. If they are ignoring your requests that they take a different route, you may have to come up with an alternate solution.

A barrier may be the only way to keep unwelcome visitors off your lawn. A hedge might sound like a good idea in principle, but unless you put in fairly large and expensive shrubs it won't slow them down a bit. A fence, on the other hand, will, especially if it is a tall stockade fence that requires some ingenuity to climb.

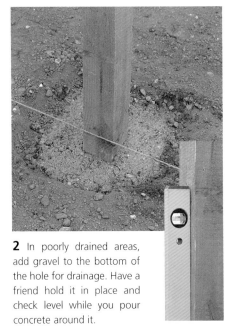

1 Measure the line of your fence and then set stakes and string to mark it. Remove the string long enough to dig post holes but set it up again before installing the posts.

2 In poorly drained areas, add gravel to the bottom of the hole for drainage. Have a friend hold it in place and check level while you pour concrete around it.

Solution 3 Renovate the pathway

If you do put up a fence, you might be able to reclaim the pathway as a part of the lawn. Because the soil under the pathway is compacted from all the foot traffic, you can't just reseed the area. It's far better to aerate it as your first step towards renovation, using a fork at fairly close intervals or a mechanical aerator. Spread 13 mm (½ inch) of compost and 13 mm (½ inch) of good topsoil over the area and seed. Rake it to cover the seed and then water. If it is later than early spring, cover the area with chopped straw to keep the moisture from evaporating.

Putting up a fence in your yard may allow you to reclaim areas you had not been using effectively.

Solution 4 Choose a tough grass

Some lawns take a great deal of punishment on a regular basis. If you and your children routinely play on the grass, it may suffer. However, some grasses can withstand this treatment and still look good. Find out about different varieties of grass available in your area and their properties from your local garden centre.

The lawn is unattractive

It's easy to take your lawn for granted. Aside from regular mowing, you probably don't give it much thought. However, t[l] lawn is a truly integral part of your garden. When it looks good, it helps to make your house look good; when it looks ba[l] it diminishes the appearance of your home and garden.

Subtle things can make your lawn attractive or unattractive. Hollows and bumps can lead to irregular grass heights, they are small, or give an unkempt appearance if they are large. Ragged edges look untidy; cleaning them up goes a lor[l] way to improving the lawn's appearance.

solution 1   Level a small hollow

Small hollows in the lawn can be annoying. If the lawn-mower dips down to cut the grass to the same height as the surrounding plants, the hollow will be quite visible. However, if it rolls right over the hollow, the grasses growing there may be able to grow tall enough to form seed-heads.

To fix a hollow, first cut an X through the sod and roots of the grasses growing in the hollow. Starting at the center, pull back each triangular-shaped piece of sod and roots to expose the soil below. The depression will be obvious. Fill it with compost, tamp it down, water it well, and roll the sod back over it. Peg the sod in place with pieces of bent

9- or 10-gauge wire. Water again and leave the pegs in unt[l] the seams of the X have grown back together.

Level a bump

Bumps can also cause problems. A lawnmower is likely t[l] cut the grass so low that it's unhealthy. To correct a bum[l] begin by making an X incision, as described above. Aft[l] you've pulled back the sod, gently remove the soil that [l] creating the bump.

1 Water the grass first as this will make the task easier. Cut a cross in the turf using a sharp-edged shovel as shown and peel back the edges. Be careful to keep the turf intact.

2 Using a trowel, add, remove, or redistribute the soil under the turf to even out the bump or hollow. Then spike the soil using a hand fork to aerate the soil.

3 Replace the flaps of turf and tamp dow[l] using the back of a rake. This can be done at ar[l] time between spring and fall. Water the are[l] and avoid walking on it for a couple of days.

See also: **'The garden is in an urban area', page 66; 'Low fertility soil', page 94; 'Plants won't bloom', page 130**

ADD OLD TYRES FOR RESILIENCY

Some hollows occur in locations where there is a lot of heavy traffic. If you are filling such[l] a hollow, you can prevent the soil from compacting again. After you have made your X and pulled back the sod, add a layer of chipped automobile tyres to the soil. Add at least 5cm (a couple of inches) of compost over the tyre chips, shaking the chips to let the[l] compost fall into the spaces between them. The grass roots will find the compost and the[l] old tyres will add some resilience to the area.

solution 2 Repair ragged edges

Lawn grasses can migrate into garden beds and overlap paths and driveways. In some landscapes, this gives a natural, informal appearance that adds to the ambience of the garden. But it looks out of place in more formal areas. Here, the edges of the lawn look best when they are as crisp and clean as the other lines in the planting design.

To make the edging straight, set up stakes at intervals along the edge. Tie a string to the stakes for a guide. With a sharp, flat-bladed spade or edging tool, cut through the grass and root area all along the string. Remove the extra grass, making certain to include the roots. The first time you do this, it may take some time and energy to accomplish. However, if you recut the edge at least once a month your lawn will always look impeccably trimmed.

Take the time to get rid of unsightly bumps and hollows, repair ragged edges and reseed bare patches to make your lawn attractive.

solution 3 Fix bare patches

Bare patches in the lawn may indicate that man's best friend has been visiting the area, soil-dwelling beetle grubs are at work or a disease has taken over. Your best course of action is to returf or reseed the area.

Reseed a small area. With larger areas, you should repair the bare patches in the following way.

Remove the top layer of soil and grass. If you are planning to lay turf, cut through the grasses, including the root zone, in one or more rectangles that are the same size as the turf you will add. Scratch the surface of the remaining soil to make it rough and add enough good quality compost to bring the new turf piece level with the rest of the lawn. Roll out the turf and press it into place. Water well and refrain from walking on it until the seams have grown into the surrounding grass.

If you are reseeding, you can cut an irregularly shaped area out of the old lawn. Remove soil from the old root zone, scratch the surface of the remaining soil, and add enough compost to make the area level. Water well and seed it by throwing seed to land at roughly 13mm (½-inch) intervals on the soil surface. Apply a 3–13mm (⅛–½-inch) layer of peat moss over the soil surface. Either roller over the are or press a board over the seeds.

1 Rake the soil to remove dead grass, pull up any weeds, and loosen the surface of the bare patch with a hand fork to create an area of fine soil.

2 Water the soil but don't soak it. Carefully scatter the grass seeds over the bare patch, taking care to distribute the seed as evenly as you can.

3 Speed up germination and protect the patch from birds by covering it with a sheet of pierced clear plastic, pegged down to create a mini greenhouse. Remove it when the seedlings are about 2.5cm (1 inch) high.

problem

Grass won't grow under the trees

We sometimes think of grass as a plant that is happy to grow well under trees and shrubs. However, most species requi[re] some sunlight. Without it, they become weak and spindly.

Trees such as Norway maples (*Acer platanoides*) cast such deep shade that no grass will grow under them. Howeve[r] when trees with small, fluttering leaves such as birches, larches, and gingkos, set widely apart, they cast filtered light o[r] partial shade, fortunately there are some grasses that grow well in filtered light or partial shade. You local garden centr[e] may be able to recommend a grass that grows well in your area.

solution 1 Create a refuge

What could be lovelier than a sitting area under a tree? On hot summer days, the shade cast by the tree will be a welcome refuge, but even on the cooler spring and fall days, you will have a lovely spot where you can watch the world go by.

Create this area by adding a layer of mulch, up to 2.5cm (1 inch) thick, all around the tree. Remember that trees suffer if their roots are covered by more than 2.5cm

(1 inch) of extra soil or mulch; their roots push up to th[e] correct level and it's important not to alter this. If thi[s] shallow layer doesn't give you a level enough spot to kee[p] tables and chairs on it from rocking, use wedges under th[e] legs to make them even. This will save the tree and sti[ll] give you garden furniture that doesn't rock.

solution 2 Choose shade-tolerant ground covers

Many ground cover plants prosper in the same conditions that grass does – that is, high levels of moisture and nutrient levels and about six hours a day of sunlight. Obviously, these plants are not a good choice for growing under a tree that casts much shade. But don't despair; there are plenty of plants that will not only grow in that area but

will also prosper, giving it a lovely, lush look. Within just [a] season or two, no one will ever guess that the areas unde[r] your trees were once 'problem spots'.

SHADE-TOLERANT PLANTS FOR UNDER TREES

Asarum caudatum (wild ginger)
Ceratostigma plumbaginoides (blue
  plumbago, leadwort)
Chrysogonum virginianum (green
  and gold)
Convallaria majalis (lily of the valley)
Cornus canadensis (bunchberry)
Galium odoratum (sweet woodruff)
Gaultheria procumbens (creeping
  wintergreen)
Lamium spp. (deadnettle)
Tiarella cordifolia (foam flower)

LEFT *Lamium spp.* (deadnettle)
RIGHT *Tiarella cordifolia* (foam flower)

olution 3 Grow woodland wildflowers

Many wildflowers have evolved to live under a tree canopy and grow well with the shifting patterns of light and dark. Most of these species flower in the early spring, before the trees have completely come into leaf. Some go dormant immediately afterward, but others retain their leaves throughout the season and grow slowly during that time. Do some research before you buy; it's important to choose a plant with leaves that you like because you will see them for much longer than you will see the flowers. The species listed below are worth considering for areas under your trees.

PLANTS FOR A WOODLAND GARDEN

Anemone nemorosa (wood anemone)

Arisaema triphyllum (Jack-in-the-pulpit)

Asarum caudatum (wild ginger)

Clintonia umbellulata (speckled wood lily)

Cornus canadensis (creeping dogwood)

Cyclamen hederifolium f. *albiflorum* (hardy cyclamen, sowbread)

Erythronium americanum (trout lily)

Gaultheria hispidula (creeping snowberry); *G. procumbens* (checkerberry, creeping wintergreen)

Hepatica americana (round-lobed liverwort)

Linnaea borealis (twin flower)

Mertensia virginica (Virginia bluebell)

Oxalis oregana (redwood sorrel)

Podophyllum peltatum (mayapple)

Polygonatum spp. (Solomon's seal)

Sanguinaria canadensis (bloodroot, red puccoon)

Smilacina spp. (false spikenard)

Tradescantia spp. (spiderwort, trinity flower)

Trillium spp. (wake robin)

Gaultheria procumbens (creeping wintergreen)

Podophyllum peltatum (mayapple)

problem
Insects are eating the grass

Grass is like any other kind of plant in that it sometimes hosts insect pests. If the damage is slight, you can often ignore the problem, but if the pest is one that increases under a regime of neglect you might want to control it right away.

Prevention is the first line of attack. Make sure that you are watering enough, but not too much, and that the nutrient supply is balanced and adequate without being excessive.

In most cases, there really isn't any need to spray noxious chemicals. After all, your kids and pets play on the lawn, and it just doesn't make sense to expose them to pesticides. The solutions below offer effective ways to handle all but epidemic populations of the pests in question.

solution 1   Eliminate grubs from Japanese beetle grubs and other species

Adult Japanese beetles will never eat the grasses in your lawn. But they will lay eggs that develop into root-eating grubs. The grubs of May beetles (called June beetles in the North) and several other species of large beetles are also to blame.

A small population of grubs won't do much damage, but this is a problem that can grow over the years, so if you see some grub damage it's wise to control it right away.

Symptoms of grubs are areas of brown, dead grass at a time when the rest of the lawn looks green and healthy. The other telltale sign of grubs is mole runs. Moles won't eat the grass roots, but they love the grubs. If you see a sudden increase in mole tunnels, you can be sure that you have a grub problem.

There are two good remedies. The first is a commercially available bacterium called milky spore disease (*Bacillus popilliae*). Apply it at a rate recommended on the bottle in mid- to late summer. It will affect populations for many years to come, eventually eliminating them.

Beneficial nematodes are the second solution. Water them in as directed on the package in early summer. They rarely overwinter in cold soils, but if you do it early enough they will search out and kill the grubs in your yard.

ABOVE Japanese beetle grubs.
LEFT Damage caused by Japanese beetle grubs.

Solution 2 Eliminate billbugs

Billbugs are similar to Japanese beetles in that the adults don't cause problems for lawns. However, the larvae of the billbug weevils can be disastrous. The adults lay eggs on the stems of grasses in late spring or early summer. The larvae are white with yellow-brown heads, and they have been compared to puffed rice in appearance. They eat the stems of the grass while the weather is cool. Affected grass turns brown and dies. When the weather begins to warm, the caterpillars burrow down into the cool earth. There, they eat grass roots and rhizomes.

You sometimes see the adult billbugs on sidewalks in spring, just about the time they are laying eggs. They are small – 6–13 cm (¼–½ inch) long – and are brown or gray. Their defining characteristic is the pair of mandibles at their snout that declares them weevils.

You can prevent infestation with good lawn care practices. Billbugs thrive on dry, stressed lawns. Aerate the soil and remove thatch to allow moisture to penetrate, add organic matter to feed beneficial organisms, and water deeply, particularly in the spring.

If the problem is severe and you can't control the billbugs with these techniques, apply beneficial nematodes. You can also reseed the lawn with a pest-resistant grass.

PEST-RESISTANT GRASSES

The following grasses, only available in the United States at present, are somewhat resistant to attack from billbugs, armyworms, cutworms, and sod webworms:

'Apache' tall fescue

'Citation II' perennial ryegrass

'Pennant' perennial ryegrass

'Repell' perennial ryegrass

'Sunrise' perennial ryegrass

Solution 3 Eliminate armyworms and cutworms

Armyworms and cutworms actually eat grass. A stray cutworm here or there isn't likely to damage the lawn much, but armyworms are named because they travel in huge groups, eating their way through lawns as they go.

Mother armyworm moths lay as many as 180 eggs at a go. They cover up the eggs with a fuzzy material, but the egg mass and fuzz are small enough so that you might miss them. The larvae, or armyworm caterpillars, hatch out of the eggs as tiny white caterpillars with black heads. They stay above ground, eating for about a month before they pupate and become moths. There can be as many as six generations in a year in warm parts of the country.

Endophytic grasses are one of the best controls because they kill the caterpillars soon after they begin feeding, but if you don't have one of these grasses, you can control them by applying *Bacillus thuringiensis* var. *berliner* or beneficial nematodes. The botanical pesticide sabadilla dust kills them too, without hurting mammals or birds.

solution 4 Eliminate cinch bugs

Cinch bugs are small, but the damage they cause can be extensive. The key is population, of course. If you have only a few cinch bugs, the lawn won't suffer much, but, if there is a large population, areas of your lawn are likely to turn yellow and then brown before dying.

Both adults and nymphs feed on grasses. The adults can be any color from a rusty brown to black, but they have white wings. They are only about 4cm (⅙ inch) long. The nymphs are so tiny when they first hatch that you can barely see the small red insects with a white band across the back.

You will know you have a problem with cinch bugs if you see dead areas of your lawn, and you can also smell an unpleasant odour when you walk in areas close to the dead spots. Cinch bugs smell dreadful; you aren't likely to see a lot of damage unless populations are high, but once they are you will kill so many when you walk on them that the odor will be noticeable.

Prevention is a matter of keeping the lawn moist. Water as necessary and add organic matter to improve the water-holding capacity of the soil.

A commercially available fungus (*Beauvaria bassianna*) kills cinch bugs, as does sabadilla dust. Endophytic grasses also kill them, so, if you can't get rid of them any other way, reseed the lawn.

solution 5 Eliminate sod webworms

Mother moths of sod webworms are the light tan–colored moths that fly over the lawn in irregular patterns after the weather has settled in spring. The moths are laying eggs as they fly. The larvae that hatch from the eggs have dark coloured heads and spots over their bodies. They feed on grass leaves and stems after dark. Their feeding eventually leads to dead patches in the lawn.

Several generations of moths will be produced during the season, but only the larvae overwinter. They create cozy winter quarters by burrowing down into the thatch layer and spinning a thick, silklike web to line the burrow. They pupate in the spring and emerge as egg-laying moths.

If you see a great many tan moths flying over your lawn in late spring, you can be pretty sure that you have sod webworms. Dethatch the lawn to prevent problems; you will be removing their overwintering site. If you need to control them, use *Bacillus thuringiensis* var. *berliner*. Endophytic grasses are also effective, so you might consider reseeding if your problems are severe.

CHOOSE A GRASS WITH ENDOPHYTES

Endophytes are fungi that live on some grasses. They secrete substances that are toxic to many pest insects and can even cause problems to cattle. They won't hurt your children or pets, however, so they are a wonderful addition to a lawn mixture. The following grasses all host endophytes. These grasses are not currently available in the UK, but new strains of grass with properties suited to different problems are being developed. Enquire at your local garden centre or check the internet to find out what is available to you.

'All Star' ryegrass

'Apache' fescue

'Citation II' ryegrass

'Repell' ryegrass

problem
The lawn has a disease

Diseases can be more frequent than insect pests in lawns, especially in lawns that are treated with a number of synthetic fertilizers and pesticides. This is one area where a little benign neglect can pay off. As long as the lawn gets the right amount of water and soil nutrition, grasses tend to be healthy. They become susceptible to diseases when they are over-fertilized, particularly with high nitrogen materials, or when nutrients are unavailable. Overwatering and underwatering can both cause diseases, too, as can soil compaction.

Prevention is really the best cure. Apply balanced fertilizers, such as compost, or a liquid feed of diluted fish emulsion and seaweed to the soil. Water to keep the soil moist but not saturated. Aerate it when thatch threatens to build up.

solution 1 Prevent brown patch

If there ever was a ubiquitous lawn disease, it's brown patch (*Rhizoctonia solani Kuhn*). The fungus is widespread, too; chances are that your lawn is hosting some of it even if it hasn't become prevalent enough to become a disease problem. It shows up in humid weather when temperatures are between 6 and 30°C (80°–85°F), and its favourite hosts are grasses that have been given excessive amounts of nitrogen fertilizer.

Like so many other diseases, brown patch shows up as areas where the grass darkens and then browns and dies.

To prevent brown patch, cut back on fertilizers containing nitrogen and check the drainage in the lawn. If you can improve it by putting in a ditch, do so. Otherwise, rely on additions of compost to help build a soil structure that allows fast drainage.

Brown patch shown up in humid weather conditions.

solution 2 Prevent dollar spot

Dollar spot (*Sclerotinia homeocarpa*) causes round, white spots about the size of a silver dollar, hence the name. The margins of the spot are sometimes a dark brown, but this is not always the case. The fungus itself is visible, too. Look closely for white, almost fluffy-looking material on the grass. You may also see tan spots on the tops of the leaves. This disease usually occurs in early and late summer because it prefers moderate temperatures, from 15–26°C (60°–80°F). The grasses most susceptible to dollar spot include annual ryegrass, bent grass, Bermuda grass, bluegrass, red fescue, and zoysia.

Prevent dollar spot by keeping the grass moist and by making certain that nitrogen levels are adequate; the disease is most likely to strike when both water and nitrogen levels are low. Mow high to cut off the infected areas and bag the cuttings so you can remove them. Top-dress the lawn with high quality compost in the early spring and apply a dilution of liquid seaweed and fish emulsion early on a midsummer morning.

solution 4 Prevent fairy ring

You might not notice fairy ring (*Marasmius oreades*) until a ring of mushrooms appears in the lawn one day. But even if you hadn't seen it, the fungus was present. The first sign that fairy ring has infected your grass is a circle of dark green grass. This grass turns a rich green colour because the mycelium of the fairy circle fungus breaks down organic matter, releasing nitrogen, as it feeds. So you have a spot of grass with symptoms of excess nitrogen. But it isn't long before the fungus moves on to feed on the roots of the grasses, killing it. The mushrooms are the fruiting bodies of the fungus and grow only on the circumference.

The fungus grows only in areas with high rainfall. It most often attacks red fescue, bent grasses, and bluegrasses.

Some people suggest that you can kill it by drowning –

saturating the soil to a depth of 60cm (2 feet) every fe[w] days – but that solution could cause other problem[s] including brown patch, red thread, and some of the le[af] spot diseases. You can try to dig out the fungus when yo[u] first spot the darkened circle of grass, but you will need t[o] dig down about 60cm (2ft). If you don't notice a proble[m] until the ring of mushrooms appears, pick them off th[e] lawn immediately, and put them in a plastic bag. Throw th[e] closed bag in trash destined for the landfill; don't take [a] chance of killing the spores in the compost pile.

Fairy rings usually delight children because they spring up as if by magic. However, their parents are usually less than enchanted with these miserable fungi.

Solution 5 Prevent leaf spot

The diseases that affect grass are similar to the leaf spot diseases that attack vegetable crops. A number of different organisms cause a number of different leaf spot diseases but most are caused by one or another species of *Drechslera* spp. Common names for these diseases include brown blight, leaf blotch, and melting out. In western Canada *Ascochyta phleina* is the usual culprit.

Melting out strikes when the weather is cool and moist. Light tan-coloured spots with darker borders darken as they 'melt out', or rot. This is one disease that responds favorably to nitrogen fertilizers, which should be applied when the weather gets hot in summer. Mow high and remove clippings and make certain to keep thatch from accumulating.

Other leaf spot diseases attack bent grass and Bermuda grass, primarily in the Midwest of America and coastal area in Virginia and North Carolina. The spots are light brown or purplish. Eventually the spots die. If they cover a great deal of the leaf area, the entire blade will die. Control these diseases as you do melting out – by applying nitrogen fertilizers, removing thatch, and taking clippings when you mow.

Solution 3 Prevent fusarium blight

Fusarium blight (*Fusarium tricinctum*) shows itself as small, discolored patches in the lawn, only 5–15cm (2–6 inches) wide, that look reddish brown in colour. As the disease processes, the spots turn yellow. If you examine the rotting crowns of the plants, you may see the pink fungal body. The disease can spread rapidly in hot humid conditions because it thrives in night temperatures of 21°C (70°F) and daytime temperatures of (30°C (85°F) or above.

Fusarium blight attacks lawns in the US. It also has defined tastes; over-fertilized Kentucky bluegrasses are its preferred hosts, but it also strikes nitrogen-rich bent grasses and fescues.

Prevent fusarium blight by keeping nutrient levels balanced. Don't add nitrogen-containing fertilizers after early spring. Water early in the day to reduce night-time humidity levels. Mow high to avoid stressing the plants and remove the clippings rather than leaving them on the grass. If your grass has a thatch problem, remove what you can and aerate to discourage it.

Solution 6 Prevent pythium blight

Pythium blight (*Pythium aphanidermatum*) occurs only when daytime temperatures have been 31°C (86°F) or higher, the following night temperature was at least 20°C (68°F), and relative humidity levels were 90 percent or more for at least 14 hours during this time. Although these conditions seem unlikely, particularly in northern areas where the disease strikes most frequently, they happen often enough to make pythium a fairly common disease.

The disease looks like what it is – patches of rotting grass. It spreads quickly, so prevention is the best recourse.

Watch pH and calcium levels in the soil and add lime whenever there is a deficiency of calcium or the pH falls below 6.0. Water only in the morning and don't let thatch accumulate.

solution 7 Prevent red thread

Red thread (*Laetisaria fuciforme*) grows best in cool, moist condition. Bluegrasses, Bermuda grass, bent grasses, perennial ryegrass, and red fescue are all susceptible to red thread and, to date, no cultivars are resistant.

The red thread fungus grows on the grass surfaces and gets its name because you can see red threads of the fungus growing beyond the leaf tips. Mowing with a box attached often keeps the disease from spreading extensively. Preventive treatments include keeping nitrogen levels adequate for good growth and watering deeply and frequently without keeping the soil saturated.

solution 8 Prevent rust

Rust (*Puccinia* spp.) can strike in any part of the country and at any time of the year. The symptoms of this disease are rusty- to yellow-looking patches on individual leaf blades. You can rub off the coloured spores if you try.

The disease is most common on damp areas of lawn in the shade. Take a tip from this and remember to water only in the morning so the grass can dry by nightfall. If drainage is a problem, try to improve it, and keep grass growing well with adequate, but not excessive, nutrient levels.

Leaf rust can affect the lawn as well as plants like this.

solution 9 Prevent snow mould

Snow mould (*Fusarium nivale*) gets its name because it often becomes apparent as the snow melts in the spring. It was present the previous fall, but because it got covered up, it was unnoticeable. The first symptoms are 2.5 to 5-cm- (1–2 inch-) wide circles of grass with dark coloured, wet-looking spots. As the disease progresses, the spots change to a tan and then a white colour. You can sometimes see the mould itself, too. It looks pink in bright light.

Prevent this disease by fertilizing and liming only in the early spring – never in the fall. Don't let thatch build up and improve drainage if it's a problem.

Adding lime to the lawn will help to prevent snow mould.

roblem

Moles are digging up the lawn

ole tunnels can be distressing. If you want a smooth, unbroken look to your lawn, a lumpy mole tunnel can make you urderous. But before you decide to run to the local garden centre to research poisons to kill the monsters sponsible for creating these lumps in your grass, think about it.

Moles don't eat grass roots. They don't eat any plant products. They live entirely on meat – grubs are their favourite re. This is a case when you will get better results by tackling the problem of a high grub population, rather than the mptom – moles in your garden.

olution 1 Reseed the tunnels

bandoned mole tunnels sometimes look a bit ragged, pecially at the doors. Gently tread over the area to make level with the rest of the lawn and then reseed it as escribed in 'Fix bare patches' (page 115). It won't be long before the new grass takes the place of the old and you will be barely able to tell where the mole was living.

olution 2 Use cat box filler

ats kill moles, and moles know it. So the last thing they ant to smell in their homes is evidence of a cat. You can ake use of this not only to get rid of moles in your yard, it also to discourage the other rodents that sometimes ove into their runs after they have abandoned them.

Aside from their exit runs, moles generally use a tunnel ily once. They continually tunnel on to find new grub supplies. Watch to see which runs look active, and when you think you have found an active one, dig into it and put some well-used cat box filler in the spot. You can also put a shovel full of used litter in any entrances to mole tunnels that you see.

olution 3 Use whirligigs and bottle music

Ioles don't like music in their unnels. They want a calm, quiet vironment so that they can hear a redator coming their way. Vibrations the soil are a guaranteed way to pel them.

You can buy devices that make he ground vibrate, but it's just as ffective to make your own. A child's hirligig makes a fair amount of nderground noise. Set the sticks of everal of them along the run. ncapped glass soda or wine bottles ake so much noise that you can even hear them. Partially bury a group of bottles in a mole tunnel. Set the bottles at different depths, for different tones, and make certain that they are upright so that wind rushing across their openings will produce a vibration. It won't take more than a day for the mole to move to a better and quieter neighbourhood.

Glass bottles in the lawn can be a decorative element. Search for bottles of different shapes and sizes and arrange them as you would a still-life.

See also: **'Japanese beetle', page 162**

chapter five

PLANT PERFORMANCE

Trying to decide what's wrong with a plant can be frustrating. Sometimes a plant won't bloom or you can't get it to grow more than a few weeks in your garden. Perhaps one or two types of seeds just will not germinate for you, or you don't know what to do when mail-order plants arrive when there's still a layer of snow on the ground. And if you grow plants in containers, you're likely to have trouble keeping them looking good all through the season. These problems, and others, happen in the best of gardens.

When you're faced with a problem like this, the first thing to explore is the plant's environment – soil conditions, exposure to sunlight and wind, relative humidity levels, soil moisture and consistency, and finally, both day and night temperatures. Next, check for pests and diseases (which are covered in chapters six and seven).

Most plant ills can be traced to problems in one or another of these areas. But what happens when the soil seems fine, the exposure is correct, the temperature is reasonable, but the plant still looks sickly or won't bloom? The plant could require something that isn't immediately apparent. The advice in this chapter will help to identify what might be wrong and solve the problem.

problem

The mail-order plants arrived too early

Plant suppliers work hard to deliver plants at just the right time to transplant them, no matter what the climate is like whe[re] you live. However, the weather doesn't always follow the expected schedule, which is, after all, an average. When th[is] happens, many gardeners panic. The written material that comes with the plant will direct you to open it immediately [on] receipt to check that there is enough moisture in the packing material. Do you do this when you have got a couple of wee[ks] to a month before you can plant? And if you do, what do you do next? The following solutions will guide you through th[is] annoying problem.

solution 1 Try heeling-in

Heeling-in is an old-fashioned technique that works as well today as it did in your grandparents' time. Essentially, it involves storing plants in the soil until it's time to plant them. The idea is that you make a trench, stand the still-wrapped plants in it at about a 45-degree angle, and heap soil over the roots and the bottom of the stem. Then, when conditions are right for planting, you uncover the heeled-in plants and plant them where they are to go.

What happens when the temperature falls and the soil is rock solid? Not even a backhoe can dig a trench in those conditions. However, there is a way around this.

Often, you will have ordered the plants the previous autumn, long before the ground was frozen solid. If you live where winters are long or unpredictable, it's best to dig the trench as soon as you order the plants.

It doesn't have to be long because you can place the root balls right up against each other when you're heeling-in. If possible, load the soil from the trench into strong feed or plastic bags and store them where the soil won't freeze, such as in an attached and slightly heated garage or cellar. You will want to be able to dump the soil on top of the plants after you set them in the trench But if you don't have a storage spot, plan to buy lots of bagged topsoil when you need to cover the plants in the spring.

To protect heeled-in plant roots from freezing, it's wise to cover the soil you have heaped over them with a thick layer of mulch. Straw bales are the best choice for this job, but any deep organic mulch will work.

After covering the roots with soil, tamp it down well to exclude air pockets. Soil is a goo[d] insulator, but air is not, so this step is crucial.

solution 2 Use the crisper

If you have only a few comparatively small plants and bulbs, unwrap them as usual to check and adjust moisture levels around the roots, rewrap, and put them in the vegetable crisper of your refridgerator. The temperature and humidity levels are just right to keep the plants in goo[d] condition until the weather outside says that it's tim[e] to plant.

Solution 3 Check moisture levels

Follow the directions to open the plants as soon as you get them. Most of the plants you get in early spring are bare-root, meaning that the supplier dug them up or took them out of a pot and washed their roots. The roots were then wrapped in damp peat moss and encased in plastic sheeting, maybe vented but maybe not.

Inspect the roots and the peat moss. Check to make sure there's no fungus – you would be able to see a light-coloured growth or a dark-looking rot on the roots if there were. If you see anything like that, wrap up the plant and send it back to the supplier. Next, check the moisture level of the peat moss. Wrap the plant back up if the moisture level is good. However, if the peat moss feels dry, sprinkle it with water before rewrapping. 'Sprinkle' is the operative word – soggy wet roots are susceptible to fungal diseases. It's better to sprinkle the peat moss every week than to get it too wet. Store the plant in cool, dark conditions.

Solution 4 Set the plant in a bucket of muck

When you are planting woody perennials, such as shrubs, trees or vines, you can help to prevent trans-plant shock by setting the unwrapped root balls in a bucket containing a slurry of soil and compost for between 8 and 24 hours. Not only will the roots be rehydrated when they go into the soil, but small particles of this mixture will also adhere to them, making the transition easier.

You can use the same technique if you are waiting only a short time – a week to two weeks – before you plant. Unwrap the root ball and set it into a mixture of soil, compost and water. Place this in a cool spot so you don't encourage much growth. Don't worry if buds begin to plump up a bit before you plant, but don't store the plants for long enough or where it is warm enough so buds begin to open. If it looks as if that is going to happen, move the plant to a cooler spot or dig a hole in the garden and heel it in until you're ready to plant.

Keep the plant's crown above water.

Solution 5 Store in a cool area

The goal of storing plants before planting them is to keep them alive. It's also best to keep them in a dormant state.

Freezing temperatures kill unprotected roots of even the hardiest species. The soil is a wonderful insulator, after all, and plants in the ground can prepare for winter. Decreasing photoperiods in combination with lowering temperatures tells them to get ready for the long, frozen months. But roots coming from a cooler – where most of the spring-shipped plants spend the winter – aren't ready for freezing temperatures.

Temperatures of 3–4°C (38°–40°F) and higher stimulate growth. But if plants start growing before they are planted, they may need nutrients and sunlight that just aren't available. At best, they will become stressed. At worst, they will die once you do transplant them because their new, tender growth won't be able to withstand early spring conditions.

If you get plants only a week or two before you expect to plant, don't heal them in. Instead, store them in a cool but not freezing area. Basements and attached garages are often just right. If the area seems just a bit cool, put a sheet of plastic on the floor and put a 30cm (1-foot) layer of peat moss or straw in the centre of it. Set plants on this 'mulch' and add more mulch around the root balls. Tie the plastic around the stems to enclose the mulched root balls.

problem
The plants won't flower

Flowering plants don't always bloom, and this can be extremely frustrating. You buy a beautiful perennial at considerab[le] expense, plant it, and wait for the flowers – and wait and wait and wait. You can't ask for your money back, because th[e] plant is obviously growing well. You check the soil to make certain that it drains well, that there are adequate nutrients [in] it, and that the pH is within an acceptable range. You look for pests and diseases but don't find any. So what's wron[g?] Why won't your plant bloom?

The reasons tend to be different for each species, but there are a few causes that account for most problems. The advi[ce] below covers the plants that are typically problematic when it comes to blooming as expected.

solution 1 Take all-purpose action

A few solutions fit all plants, so they are the first things to explore. Age is a major factor; plants need to be at a certain stage of maturity before they can bloom. Because the age varies according to the species and sometimes even the cultivar, ask the supplier about this when you buy the plant. If that is impossible, call local nurseries and ask.

Pruning time is also important. You may be pruning off the flower buds by pruning at the wrong time of year. Prune spring-flowering plants just after they bloom because they bloom on last year's growth, and summer-flowering plants in late winter because they bloom on the current season's growth.

Lack of winter cold could be to blame. Many plants mu[st] experience a certain number of hours at temperatur[es] lower than 4°C (40°F) to flower, and some need it to brea[k] dormancy. Check the plant's 'chilling requirements' whe[n] you buy it; certain cultivars are bred for warm climes an[d] some are not.

Excess soil nitrogen can inhibit flowering in som[e] species. Nasturtiums and wallflowers are notorious for th[is] quality, but other plants, particularly those that live well [in] sandy soils, such as thrift (*Armeria* spp.), also react this wa[y.]

solution 2 Prune lilacs

Lilacs usually flower a few years after they are planted. Each year, the number of flowers increases, until the bush is a fine specimen every spring. However, if the shrub is not treated correctly, flowers will begin to decline. Springs will come when only half the normal number of flowers form.

The reason is that the plant has put too much energy into making seeds. The solution is simple. Immediately after blooms fade, cut off every cluster. Timing is important because lilacs make new buds in early to mid-summer. This may mean climbing a ladder, but it's worth the effort. And while you're at it, head back overly long shoots, cut out dead-wood, and prune out old or crowded branches. Your lilacs will be glorious the following year.

Prune off clusters as they fade, but use them a[s] indicators. Frosts are finished when half the blooms have browned.

See also: **'The plants are slow to flower', page 134; 'The plants have stopped blooming', page 136**

olution 3 Examine peonies

eonies must become established in your garden and grow
or a few years before they bloom. But if your plant is more
han three years old and hasn't flowered yet, you might
want to examine its planting depth. In order to flower well,
he crown and buds of the plant must be no deeper than
5–8cm (2–3 inches) below the soil surface. If they are
deeper than this, clear away some of the soil on top of
them and do not allow it to fill back in.

Peonies bloom well for 25 to 30 years.

solution 4 Prune roses

Although not all roses are remontant (repeat-flowerers), many of the newer cultivars are. Check with the supplier or read the cultivar description before you buy a rose to find out if it is supposed to bloom only once, fairly continuously through the summer, or if it will bloom once in the spring and then again in late summer. You need to prune according to these characteristics.

If the rose flowers on new wood – that is, on the current season's growth – prune it in late winter. If it blooms on both old wood – last year's growth – and new wood, you also prune in late winter. But if it blooms on old wood only, you prune after it has bloomed.

Don't be confused by climbing roses. Most modern climbers are remontant and flower on new wood, so you will need to prune them in late winter to get them to rebloom. In contrast, most old ramblers bloom only once, on old wood. Prune them no later than a month after they have bloomed to give them a chance to make new buds.

Prune roses by cutting the flower stem just above the first group of five, rather than three, leaflets.

solution 5 Prune wisteria

Wisteria can be a difficult plant, especially when it comes to flowering. Firstly, the plant must be the right age, which will vary with species and cultivar. Secondly, it must grow in the right kind of soil. Finally and most importantly, you must prune it correctly.

Provide a well-drained soil of average fertility that is not too rich and not too lean. Once the plant starts flowering abundantly you can give it yearly applications of finished compost, laid to a depth of about 2.5cm (1 inch) over the entire root area. Until then hold back on all fertilizers unless the soil is low in organic matter and nutrients.

Wisteria blooms on short spurs that form on old wood. You must prune them in two stages, once in the summer

and again in winter. In summer, cut back shoots to about the seventh leaf. Wait until winter to shorten them again. Look for flower buds – they will be plump and obviously ready to turn into blooms. Shorten the shoots to within 2.5–8cm (1–3 inches) of the base without pruning out any flower buds.

If you have a wisteria on which flowers are gradually decreasing, you may have to do emergency root pruning and feeding during the summer. Follow the illustrations below to do this correctly.

1 In summer, root-prune wisteria plants by using a sharp spade to cut a circle around the plant, about 30cm (1ft) from the stem, 20–25cm (8–10in) deep, and 8–10cm (3–4in) wide.

2 Pour a mixture of 2 parts bonemeal and 1 part compost into the trench. Gently pack it down and water at the halfway point and when filled to eliminate air pockets.

3 After filling and tamping the trench, take the time to prune off the oldest and longest stems. The fresh nutrients and pruning will stimulate more spring blooms.

olution 6 Prune clematis

runing time is almost always the cause of flowering roblems with clematis, and it varies according to the roup into which the clematis falls. As with roses and other owering shrubs, however, it's easy to work out when lematis should be pruned, even if you do not know the lass the plant falls in. If it blooms on old wood, prune after it blooms in spring or early summer. If it blooms on new wood, prune in late winter. If it has never bloomed to let you know its habit, don't prune at all for a year. You will soon see how it works.

Clematis bloom lavishly.

BLOSSOM DROPS WITHOUT OPENING

Plants as varied as peppers and peonies drop unopened flowers if they are suffering stress. The reason is simple: because the plant doesn't know you're going to deadhead the bloom as soon as it fades, it is conserving precious resources by making certain that it doesn't have to put any energy or nutrients into making seeds. If you remove the stress, you will eliminate the problem.

Check soil and exposure conditions to see that they are appropriate.
After that, try:
- increasing the humidity around the plants
- mulching to provide consistent soil moisture
- shading plants during hot afternoons.

problem
The plants are slow to flower

Long before you decide that a plant simply will not bloom for you, you might describe it as being slow to flower. Fo
example, you may have purchased a bare-root plant from a mail-order supplier. According to the information you can fin
in books and on the Internet, you expect it to come into flower in the second or, at the least, the third year. But it doesn'
You probably bought the plant because you liked the flower or its fragrance, and it's difficult to wait, so you begin t
explore the possible causes for the delay in blooming. The solutions below and in the other related problem areas may giv
you the clue you need to speed up things.

solution 1 Use Epsom salts

When perennial plants are slow to bloom it is often because magnesium is deficient. Fortunately, there is a fast, inexpensive, and easy way to supply this element. Use Epsom salts, the same kind you'd use to ease your aching feet in a footbath.

Make a liquid root drench by dissolving 28g (1oz) of Epsom salts in a cup of boiling water and stirring thoroughly. When the mixture is cool, add enough water to make 3.7 litres (1 gallon) of solution. Use this mixture to water the plant. Repeat in a month if the plant still hasn't flowered, but after that, wait until the following year and begin the treatment early in the season.

Use boiling water and stir well to thoroughly dissolve the Epsom salts. Add more boiling water if you don't succeed the first time.

solution 2 Increase light levels

Slice more deeply every month. Cut under the plant at 1–1½ft (30–45cm) deep to form the rootball.

Shade slows growth and flowering in many plants. The obvious remedy – to get rid of the shade – is usually easier said than done. You can sometimes remove an unattractive tree or prune others (see page 48), but these solutions aren't always practicable, desirable, or, if the tree is in someone else's yard, possible.

The solution in these cases is to move the plant. If the sun can't come to it, it must go to the sun. Choose the new spot carefully; look at it at all times of day and during the entire growing season. If it's sunny in spring but shady in summer, for example moving the plant to that spot may no be effective. Once you know that you have found the right place, move the plant in the spring in the colder area and in the autumn in warmer places.

If the plant seems too large to move, try a nurseryman's trick. With sharp spade, slice into the soil al around the plant. Begin in the sprin if possible, and repeat this actior every month thereafter. By the following spring or fall, the plant wil have formed enough fibrous root within the spaded circle so that it car withstand the move.

See also: 'The plants won't flower', page 130; 'The plants have stopped flowering', page 136; 'Prune nearby trees', page 48

Solution 3 Increase temperatures

A warm-weather plant may be too cool to flower well. If this is the case, there are several possible remedies.

Begin by increasing soil temperatures. Lay a black plastic mulch over the entire root area, making certain that it doesn't cover the plant's crown. Hold it in place with ground staples – homemade or store-bought – because you can't cover the plastic a light-reflecting mulch.

Next, increase air temperatures around the plant. If possible, set up stakes around it and wrap a piece of construction-grade polyethylene around the stakes. Tape the polyethylene in place, leaving the top of the structure open so that plants don't die from roasting. Once the plant is in bloom, you can remove the plastic altogether if the weather is warmer, or, if not, cut some slits into the sides of the polyethylene to vent it.

Clear plastic enclosures heat the air inside them by letting in light waves but inhibiting the longer heat wavelengths from escaping.

Vivid *Clarkia* blooms best in heat.

problem
The plants have stopped flowering

Plants may stop blooming long before you think they should. This is particularly true of annuals, although perennials ca[n] also behave this way. This can be particularly annoying if you have gone to the trouble of planning a border with [a] complicated colour scheme and a tone is now missing from the palette.

The fastest and easiest solution to this problem is to try to find replacement plants in the same colour, shape and size[.] If you find these plants but it's too hot to count on their being able to establish themselves in the garden, you can simpl[y] set their pots in the correct positions in the border until it's safe to transplant them. If their pots are too small, you coul[d] transplant them to larger containers to set among the other plants.

Even if this gives you a quick fix to the current problem, it is still a good idea to find out why your plants stoppe[d] flowering prematurely so you can prevent it from happening in future years.

solution 1   Remove the flowers

As far as a plant is concerned, the purpose of life is to reproduce. If the plant is a perennial, it probably counts more on its ability to propagate vegetatively – by sending out runners, growing offsets, developing multiple crowns, or rooting at stems that touch the ground – than it does on making seeds. However, some perennials reproduce more freely and generously from seeds than they do from any other mechanism, and most annual plants depend almost entirely on their seeds.

Once seeds have set and matured, a perennial plant and many annuals lose the ability to make flowers. Some annuals, in fact, can no longer live but die right away. So deadheading, or removing the flowers as soon as they have faded, is imperative to keep plants both alive and blooming. Don't give them time to develop seeds or the deadheading will not be effective.

To keep plants looking their best, cut off the whole flowering stem when possible. Plants such as black-eyed Susan (*Rudbeckia hirta*) and zinnias allow this treatment. If plants produce multiple blooms on the same stem – petunias, for example – snap off the spent bloom below the enlarged area at the base of the flower.

Deadhead every morning when you check plants for watering. With this routine, you won't fall behind.

See also: **'The plants won't flower', page 130; 'The plants are slow to bloom', page 134; 'Cut back annuals', page 148; 'Apply foliar feed', page 95; 'Apply liquid fertilizers', page 152; 'Low fertility soil', page 94; 'Prune your trees', page 48**

Solution 2 Fertilize

When a perennial plant runs out of vital nutrients during the season, the first thing it does is slow or stop flowering. It has other ways to reproduce, after all. Nutrient-deficient annual plants put all their available energy into maturing a few flowers and seeds, so they often stop growing new branches or top growth. But long before things get this serious, most plants make fewer flowers than usual, and the flowers that they do make are often smaller than normal.

As soon as you notice that the plants look nutrient deficient, take action. If you begin by foliar feeding right away and then follow it up with liquid fertilizers as a root drench, and a top-dressing of compost, you can stop the damage before it affects flowering.

Mulch with nutrient-rich compost in early and mid-summer – at least a month before frost.

Solution 3 Provide shade

Many cool-loving perennials will not flower properly if they get overheated, and some annuals drop blossoms when temperatures are too warm. The best way to keep plants cool enough to bloom is to give them some afternoon shade.

If possible, grow these plants to the east of other, taller plants, a hedge or a wall. When you can't do that, set up a temporary shading device. A trellis that you buy from a home and garden supply store can serve as the framework. Hang brightly coloured fabric or natural-looking canvas from it and set it up so it shades the plants in question. You will be amazed at the difference just this little bit of shading can make to sensitive plants.

Solution 4 Provide light

A certain number of hours a day of sunlight is essential for some plants. If they don't get it, they may be able to live but they probably will not flower.

It's important to know how the light patterns in your garden work, because a spot that is brightly lit on spring mornings or afternoons could be shaded during midsummer. If your plant requires a full six hours of unobstructed light in order to bloom well, this shade pattern could cause a problem.

The obvious remedy is to remove whatever it is that casts shade on your plants. This is rarely an easy solution, however, so you may need to move the plant to an area where it does get the required amount of light.

If you can't transplant it to an appropriate location, set up some screens to reflect light onto it. These screens can solve minor light problems. Install a white woven screen made of wicker or wood so that the light bounces from it to the plants that require it. It may take you a few days of positioning to find just the right place for this screen, but once you do your plants are likely to respond well. Remember to make this screen penetrable to wind, otherwise it could create turbulence that would be harmful to the plants just beyond it.

problem
The plants won't bear fruit

Fruiting plants usually crop on schedule. If your supplier tells you that a particular tree will bear fruit in four to five year you can be sure it will. Brambles fruit in their second year; blueberries usually begin yielding in their third or fourth yea strawberry plants produce berries anytime from a few weeks after you plant them until the next spring.

When a plant doesn't fruit as promised, you need to search out the cause. It could be as simple as a lack of chillin hours or not enough hours under bright light every day. Sometimes a late frost will kill the blossoms, resulting in a ye without fruit. Occasionally, it's because the soil is too wet or lacks adequate nutrients for the plant. But if none of the factors is to blame, you will need to look elsewhere for the problem. The solutions described below should help you to g fruit from your plants.

solution — Grow compatible pollinators

The flowers of many fruiting plants are unable to pollinate flowers of the same cultivar. For example, while most European apricots (*Prunus armeniaca*) are self-fruitful, meaning that they can pollinate themselves, most Manchurian apricots (*P. mandschurica*) require a pollinator. But rather than another apricot, they perform best if a Nanking cherry (*P. tomentosa*) pollinates them, and as a matter of fact European apricots also bear better if they are pollinated by a Nanking cherry.

As the above example so clearly shows, it's hard to guess about pollinators. You must ask your supplier if the plant you are buying needs a pollinator and, if so, what species are most appropriate. Not only does the pollen have to be compatible, but the flowering times have to be similar so that bees, other insects, or the wind can move the pollen from one plant to the next. Look at the list opposite to check if the plant you want to grow requires a pollinator.

Once you know whether the plant needs a pollinator and what other species or cultivars make good pollinators for it, you have to decide where to grow the pollinator. If your garden is small, the thought of two trees might be enough to discourage you from trying to grow fruit. But there are space-saving ways around this problem. Explore whether you can find the cultivars you want grafted to dwarfing or semidwarfing rootstocks. If so, plant them. You will be getting fruit from two trees rather than one, so you will not be losing much by growing dwarfs or semidwarfs.

If you can't find room for two trees, two strategies will accomplish the same purpose. The first requires some skill, although you can probably find someone to help you do it. Buy some scion wood, or young branches, of the pollinator species from a nursery and graft them onto your tree i place of some of its branches. Remember not to cut then off when you are doing your annual pruning.

The second solution is much easier. Look for container-sized cultivar that can pollinate your tree. Set th container near the tree you want to pollinate through th bloom season. After that, you can move the container t any convenient spot in the yard. In cold climates, it's bes to sink the container into the soil for the winter so that th roots don't freeze.

These trees have been planted to encourage cross-pollination.

See also: **'The plants won't bloom', page 130**

FRUITS THAT NEED POLLINATORS

Apples	Required by most cultivars
Apricots	Required by Manchurian and Siberian cultivars; increases fruiting for European cultivars
Blueberries	Required by all cultivars, plant at least 3 cultivars
Cherries, sweet,	Required by most cultivars
Currants, black	Required by most cultivars
Currants, red and white	Not essential but will increase fruiting
Dewberries	Not required by most cultivars; 'Flordagrand' requires pollination
Elderberries	Required by all cultivars; plant two types
Gooseberries	Not essential but will increase fruiting
Grapes, muscadine	Required by many cultivars
Jostaberries	Not essential but will increase fruiting
Kiwifruit	Male plants of the same cultivar are required
Pawpaws	Required by most cultivars; hand-pollinate
Pears	Required by all cultivars
Pears, Asian	Required by all cultivars
Persimmons	Required by most American and many Oriental cultivars
Plums	Required by most Japanese and many European cultivars

WHEN TO PRUNE

Almost all fruiting plants require some pruning. But just as you can prune flowers off ornamental plants if you prune them at the wrong time, you can also prune them off fruiting plants. Use the following chart to check when to prune your fruiting plants.

Fruit	Pruning time
Apple	Late winter to early spring; head back shoots in summer
Apricot	After blooms have dropped
Blackberries	Head back primocanes (new growth) to 75cm (30 inches) in midsummer; prune out fruiting canes after harvest; head back laterals on floricanes (second year canes) in late spring
Blueberries	Late winter to early spring; remove laterals that fruited once the plant is dormant in winter
Boysenberries	See blackberries
Cherries, sour and sweet	Late winter to early spring
Citrus	After harvest; remove only dead, weak, or crowded growth
Currants	Late winter to early spring
Dewberries	See blackberries
Elderberries	Late winter to early spring; prune out 4-year-old canes and weak or crowded growth
Figs	During dormancy but only as needed; check with supplier
Grapes	Spring

Fruit	Pruning time
Kiwifruit	During dormancy
Loganberries	See blackberries
Nectarines	After blooms have dropped
Pawpaws	During dormancy
Peaches	After blooms have dropped
Pears	Late winter to early spring
Pears, Asian	During dormancy
Persimmons	During dormancy
Plums	Early to midspring
Quinces	Late winter to early spring
Raspberries, summer bearers	See blackberries
Raspberries, autumn bearers	Midsummer; prune out second-year canes or, if plants are diseased, mow plants in autumn to a few inches above the soil surface

Malus spp. (crab apple)

problem
Plants have difficulty getting established in the soil

Some soils are so difficult that plants have a terrible time getting established in them. Once an appropriate plant does g[et] established, it grows well, but often it dies before its roots manage to work their way into the surrounding soil.

If you have a soil like this, confine your selection of plants to those that tolerate the particular condition that mak[es] your soil so difficult. These plants have the best chance of growing and eventually thriving. Next, work to improve the so[il] in every way possible. Check the appropriate sections in Chapter 2 (Site Problems) and Chapter 3 (Soil Problems) f[or] suggestions. But while you are working to improve the soil, try some of the following solutions to help plants g[et] established right away.

solution 1 Split the root ball

One of the best ways to encourage a plant to become established is to give it no choice. You can cut about halfway up into the center of the root ball of a plant with fibrous roots. Make a mound of soil in the planting hole that you prepare for the plant. When you transplant, spread the two halves of the root ball over the mound, making certain that all parts of the root ball are in good contact with the soil. Heap soil over the whole root ball and water well to settle the plant.

If your plant has a taproot, you'd injure it by splittin[g] it in half. Instead, make cuts along the outside of the roo[t] ball without hurting the central root. When you transplan[t] push some garden soil into the spaces that form where yo[u] made the cuts.

solution 2 Use organic matter to make a planting hole

Organic matter is the best remedy for difficult soils. But even with copious amounts of the best compost, it's impossible to rebuild a really difficult soil in anything less than five years and often up to ten years. Fortunately, you don't have to wait that long. Just as you can build a raised bed filled with a mixture of good topsoil and compost, you can also create a deep planting hole filled with this mix.

Ordinarily, gardeners are advised to plant perennials so that they will adjust to the soil that is already on the site. This advice assumes that the plant will be able to grow in that soil, but if the plant can't even get established you will have to make an exception to the general advice.

When you dig the hole, remove as much soil from the area as you can. You will want the area to be at least 30cm (1 foot) deep and 60cm (2 feet) wide. Fill this hole with a mixture of purchased topsoil and compost. A hole of this size will guarantee your plant a few years of good growth before it hits the native, less friendly soil. But look ahead and continue to dig in compost around the perimeter of the original planting hole while the plant is small. It could be that you will improve the surrounding soil by the time the plant grows into it.

Compost contains a long-term supply of nutrients and also holds moisture and supplemental nutrients while increasing soil aeration.

See also: 'Plants tolerant of clay soils', page 87; 'Rock-garden plants', page 69; 'Plants for sandy soils', page 89; 'Build raised beds', page 52

Solution 3 Time planting properly

Plants sometimes have difficulty getting established simply because they are planted at the wrong time of year. This is particularly true when you are working with bare-root plants because they are the most delicate. If you plant them after the weather has begun to warm in spring, they may not be able to live. Higher temperatures demand that the roots take up water, but if they haven't had time to grow into the surrounding soil they will not be able to do that.

In contrast, balled-and-sacked plants and those in containers are able to withstand warm soil for a little while if you keep them well watered, because their roots will keep growing in the soil they were planted with. However, even these plants can fare poorly if you plant in hot weather. Their root balls may be too small to provide adequate amounts of water or nutrients, and the surrounding soil may be too dry. As a consequence, the roots of these plants sometimes don't grow beyond the confines of their original container. Even if they don't become drought- or nutrient-stressed, they will eventually suffer. When winter comes, they will not be well enough anchored to withstand high winds or snowdrifts.

Just as it's best to plant in early spring in cooler regions, it's best to plant in the autumn in warm regions where the weather becomes warm quickly and the plants don't have time to establish themselves before facing high water demands. In addition, it's more likely to rain frequently in the autumn than in the late spring and early summer, so roots have an easier time penetrating the surrounding soil. Don't plant too late, especially if you live in a marginal area where winters can bring freezes, because it's important to give plants time to grow roots before winter strikes.

All plants, even those that thrive in dry soils, require extra water while they are getting established. As a general rule, provide at least 7.5 litres (2 gallons) of water for every 0.1 metre square (square foot) of root area every week. Increase this amount for moisture lovers if the weather is hot.

problem
The seeds germinate poorly

Growing your own plants from seed is one of the most exciting parts of gardening. Most annuals, vegetables and her are relatively easy to grow from seed, but a few can cause problems unless you know what they require and cater to the

Nature designs seeds to ensure the survival of the particular species. Consequently, some seeds have built-in mech nisms that prevent them from germinating when environmental conditions will not support their growth. If the seed buried too deeply in the soil, for example, it will die if it germinates because the tiny hypocotyl (first stem) isn't long enou to push the cotyledons (seed leaves) above the soil surface and into the light. Seeds 'know' where they are in the soil the proportion of carbon dioxide to oxygen that surrounds them; if they are close enough to the soil surface to push th seed leaves into the light, the oxygen levels are high enough to trigger germination.

A seed's requirements for germination – light level, temperature, rainfall and freeze-thaw cycle – are designed to ma sure that the seed germinates only when it can grow well. As the following solutions show, however, you can learn ho to simulate these conditions and germinate seed for just about any plant you want to grow.

solution 1 Provide the correct temperatures

Most seeds germinate at soil temperatures close to the same air temperatures that favour them or about 10 Celsius higher. This means that a plant that thrives at 15°C (60°F) will germinate well at soil temperatures between 13–21°C (55°–70°F), and one that grows best at 26°C (80°F) will germinate well at temperatures between 24–32°C (75°–90°F). If you use this as a basic rule, you will rarely go wrong.

Some plants require alternating day and night temperatures, however, and they simply will not germinate if the soil temperature is consistent

from day to night. If you are germinating seed trays on a windowsill or in a cold frame, this requirement will be met automatically as night temperatures are cooler. However, if you are growing seeds on a soil-heating mat, you will have to lower the temperature at night. If the heating mat has a thermostat, lower it to an appropriate temperature; if not, take the tray off the heating mat in the evening and put it back on in the morning.

Use a small soil thermometer to check the temperature of the medium.

TEMPERATURE REQUIREMENTS FOR GERMINATING COMMON PLANTS			
Plant	Temperature	Plant	Temperature
FAmmi majus (bishop's flower)	26°C day/18°C night	Matthiola incana (stock)	15°C but hold seedlings
Aquilegia spp. (columbine)	26°C day/21°C night	at 5°C for 14 days after second leaves form	
Bracteantha bracteatum (strawflower)	26°C day/21°C night	Monarda spp. (beebalm)	21°C day/10°C night
Consolida spp. (larkspur)	13°C day/7–10°C night	Physostegia spp. (obedient plant)	24°C day/13°C night
Delphinium elatum	26°C day/21°C night	Salvia spp. (ornamental sage)	21°C day/15°C night
Euphorbia griffithii (spurge)	30°C day/21°C night	Stachys spp. (lamb's ear)	21°C day/15°C night
Gaillardia grandiflora (blanket flower)	26°C day/21°C night	Verbena bonariensis (butterfly verbena)	24°C day/15°C night
Geum spp. (avens)	26°C day/21°C night		
Kniphofia spp. (red–hot poker)	30°C day/21°C night	Conversion: 30°C=85°F; 26°C=80°F; 24°C=75°F; 21°C=70°F;	
Lunaria annua (honesty)	18°C day/13°C night	18°C=65°F; 15°C=60°F; 13°C=55°F; 10°C=50°F; 7°C=45°F	

olution 2 Light seeds correctly

f you have been having trouble germinating a particular eed, find out whether it requires light or darkness to erminate. Many seeds will germinate no matter how nuch light they receive, but others are more particular. he list below indicates the requirements for many ommon plants, but it certainly doesn't cover them all. If he plant you are trying to grow is not on the list, you can ften guess its requirements. Usually, small seeds require ght while larger seeds require dark. You can also run an xperiment. Sow seed into two trays and germinate one in ght but cover the other with newspaper and black plastic heeting to give it dark conditions. You will quickly see vhich conditions are required.

A thick layer of newspaper usually creates enough darkness, but add a piece of cardboard or put the tray in a dark place to be certain.

LIGHT REQUIREMENTS FOR COMMON PLANTS

Plant	Light/dark requirement for seed germination	Plant	Light/dark requirement for seed germination
Achillea spp. (yarrow)	Light	*Impatiens* spp. (busy lizzie)	Light
Ammi majus (bishop's flower)	Light	*Lathyrus odoratus* (sweet pea)	Dark
Antirrhinum majus (snapdragon)	Light	*Limonium sinuatum* (statice)	Light
Aquilegia spp. (columbine)	Light	*Lobelia* spp.	Light
Arisaema triphyllum (Jack-in-the-pulpit)	Light	*Lupinus* spp. (lupin)	Dark
Armeria spp. (thrift)	Dark	*Lychnis coronaria* (dusty miller)	Light
Artemisia spp. (wormwood)	Light	*Matthiola incana* (stocks)	Light
Asclepias tuberosa (butterfly weed)	Light	*Molucella laevis* (bells of Ireland)	Light
Begonia spp.	Light	*Nicotiana* spp (tobacco plant)	Light
Bracteantha bracteatum (strawflower)	Light	*Oenothera* spp. (evening primrose, Ozarks sundrops)	Dark
Browallia spp. (bush violet)	Light	*Penstemon* spp.	Light
Calendula spp. (pot marigold)	Dark	*Pentas lanceolata* (star cluster)	Light
Catharanthus rosea (rose periwinkle)	Dark	*Petunia* cvs.	Light
Celosia spp.	Light	*Phlox* spp.	Dark
Consolida spp. (larkspur)	Dark	*Physalis alkekengi* (Chinese lantern)	Light
Delphinium elatum	Dark	*Platycodon* spp. (balloon flower)	Light
Digitalis spp. (foxglove)	Light	*Portulaca* spp. (purslane, rose moss)	Light
Echinacea spp. (coneflower)	Light	*Primula* spp. (primrose)	Light
Gaillardia grandiflora (blanket flower)	Light	*Salpiglossis sinuata*	Dark
Gomphrena globosa (globe amaranth)	Dark	*Scabiosa* spp. (scabious)	Light
Goniolimon tataricum (statice)	Dark	*Tithonia* spp. (Mexican sunflower)	Dark
Gypsophila elegans (baby's breath)	Light	*Tropaeolum majus* (nasturtium)	Dark
Helenium autumnale (sneezeweed)	Light	*Verbena hybrida*	Dark
Heuchera spp. and cvs. (geranium)	Light		
Hibiscus moscheutos (rose mallow)	Dark		

solution 3 Treat with water

Some seeds are protected from germinating too early in the spring by a natural substance that covers their seed coats. This coating inhibits germination, even if the temperature, lighting, and oxygen levels are perfect. In nature, these seeds sit in the soil until enough rain or running snowmelt has passed over them to wash away the inhibiting substance. Parsley and carrots are both this category, as are some ornamentals. If you are having trouble germinating a seed that is supposed to take 20 days or longer to germinate and that also requires cool germination temperatures, it certainly doesn't hurt to try this technique before you plant it. It often hastens germination by as much as two weeks.

Start by soaking the seeds in warm water for 24 hours and then drain them in a sieve that they cannot fall through. Leave them in the sieve and set it on top of a jar to keep it steady. Each time you pass, run warm water through the sieve. At night, put the sieve in a closed plastic bag, along with a couple of wet cotton balls. This should prevent the seeds from drying, which would kill them. Repeat this washing routine for a few days and then plant the seeds as usual. More often than not, they'll be up long before the time allotted to them.

Don't let the seeds soak for more than 24 hours before beginning the draining and rinsing step because it could make your seeds rot.

SOAKING SEEDS

Some seeds benefit from soaking for a period before you plant them. They don't necessarily require the same kind of washing that parsley and carrots do, but they do germinate more successfully if you soak them for a while. Follow the suggestions for the plants below for outstanding germination success.

Plant	Treatment
Abelmoschus moschatus (musk mallow)	After scarifying (see page 146), soak in warm water for 1 hour
Armeria spp. (thrift)	Soak in warm water for 6 hours
Canna x *generalis* (canna lily)	After scarifying, soak for 48 hours, changing the water every 12 hours
Euphorbia griffithii (spurge)	After freezing, soak in water for 5 days, changing the water daily
Gomphrena globosa (globe amaranth)	Soak for 3 days, changing the water every 12 hours
Hemerocallis cvs. (daylily)	After freezing, soak for 5 days, changing the water daily
Hibiscus moscheutos (rose mallow)	Soak in hot water for 48 hours, changing the water every 12 hours
Lathyrus odoratus (sweet pea)	After chilling, soak in warm water for 48 hours, changing the water every 12 hours
Lupinus spp. and cvs. (lupin)	Soak for 5 to 7 days, changing the water every 12 hours
Molucella laevis (bells of Ireland)	After freezing, soak for 5 days, changing the water every 12 hours

olution 4 Stratify seeds

regions with cold winters, seeds that drop to the ground autumn automatically go through radical temperature hanges. They freeze and thaw repeatedly through the inter months unless they are buried so deeply that they ay frozen. Not surprisingly, many seeds have evolved to eed these conditions; without a period of fluctuating emperatures – or at least winter cold – they can't break ormancy and germinate in the spring.

If you are trying to germinate a seed that grows best in ool climates, it is wise to stratify it, or store it in the refrigrator or freezer for a period of time before planting it. You an store many seeds in the packets they come in; put the packet in a plastic bag or glass jar that you can seal tightly against moisture, and leave it in the refrigerator or freezer for the specified period.

A more consistently reliable method is to plant them in trays filled with moist peat moss and then cool or freeze them, either inside or out. Place the tray in a plastic bag, seal the bag, and place it in a cold frame, a safe spot in the garden, the refrigerator or the freezer. By the time spring comes, the seeds will be primed for germinating.

The box below gives stratification instructions for some common plants.

STRATIFICATION REQUIREMENTS FOR COMMON SEEDS

Plant	Seed requirements before planting
Aconitum carmichaelii (monkshood)	Refrigerate for 3 weeks
Antirrhinum majus (snapdragon)	Refrigerate for 4 to 6 weeks
Aquilegia spp. (columbine)	Refrigerate for 2 to 8 weeks
Bupleurum rotundifolium	Refrigerate for 4 weeks
Clematis spp.	Refrigerate for 3 months
Consolida spp (larkspur)	Refrigerate for 6 weeks
Delphinium elatum	Freeze for 4 to 6 weeks
Dianthus spp. (pinks)	Refrigerate for 4 to 8 weeks
Dicentra spectabilis (bleeding heart)	Refrigerate for 6 weeks
Dracocephalum spp. (dragon's head)	Refrigerate for 4 to 6 weeks
Echinacea spp. (coneflower)	Refrigerate for 2 to 3 weeks
Eryngium giganteum (sea holly)	Refrigerate for 6 weeks
Euphorbia griffithii (spurge)	Freeze for 2 weeks
Gentiana affinis (gentian)	Refrigerate for 2 to 4 weeks
Geranium sanguineum (cranesbill)	Refrigerate for 1 to 2 months
Heliopsis helianthoides (oxeye)	Refrigerate for 4 weeks
Helleborus niger (Christmas rose)	Freeze for 2 weeks
Hemerocallis cvs. (daylily)	Freeze for 2 weeks
Hypericum hirsutum (St.-John's-wort)	Refrigerate for 2 to 4 months
Lathyrus odoratus (sweet pea)	Refrigerate for 2 to 3 weeks
Lavandula spp. (lavender)	Refrigerate for 4 weeks
Liatris spp. (gayfeather)	Refrigerate for 4 weeks
Lobelia spp.	Refrigerate for 3 months
Lychnis spp. (dusty miller)	Refrigerate for 2 weeks
Mimulus spp. (monkey flower)	Refrigerate for 3 weeks
Molucella laevis (bells of Ireland)	Freeze for 5 days
Paeonia spp. and cvs. (peony)	Refrigerate for 2 months
Penstemon spp.	Refrigerate for 4 to 8 weeks
Polemonium boreale (Jacob's ladder)	Refrigerate for 2 months
Primula spp. (primrose)	Refrigerate for 4 weeks
Rosa spp. (rose)	Refrigerate for 5 months
Trollius spp. (globeflower)	Refrigerate for 1 month
Veronica longifolia (speedwell)	Refrigerate for 2 months
Viola spp. (pansy, violet)	Refrigerate for 4 weeks

Mimulus (Monkey flower)

Primula (primrose)

solution 5 Scarify seeds

Not all seeds drop to the ground and wait to germinate. Many are picked up by birds, some drop into running water, and a few are singed by fire. Fortunately for the plants involved, the seeds survive all but the worst of these encounters and go on to germinate. Because these events are common for some plants, the seeds have evolved hard seed coats. In some cases, these seed coats are so hard that the seeds will not germinate unless they are softened by soaking or damaged by physical injury.

If you are trying to germinate a plant with seeds that require scarification, or injury to the seed coat, there are a couple of ways to mimic nature. You can nick the seed coat with a sharp paring knife or rub the seed between two sheets of fine sandpaper.

The seeds of the plants listed below right germinate much more readily if you scarify them. In some cases, they profit from soaki.. afterward, too, so check the list c page 144 to learn if this is the case.

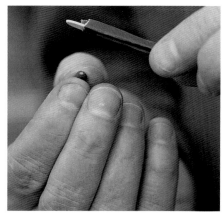
Just scratch the surface so water can penetrate.

SEEDS TO SCARIFY
Abelmoschus moschatus (musk mallow)
Alcea rosea (hollyhock)
Baptisia spp. (false indigo)
Brugmansia spp. (angel's trumpet)
Canna generalis (canna lily)
Doronicum spp. (leopard's bane)
Hibiscus spp.
Ipomoea spp. (morning glory, moon-flower, cardinal climber, cypress vine)

solution 6 Plant in vermiculite

Seeds must remain moist while they are germinating. This isn't difficult for a pea or nasturtium seed, which is big enough to stay under the moist soil for the time it takes it to sprout, but it can be a problem for seed that must stay close enough to the soil surface to see light while it is germinating or for seed that can take a few weeks to begin growing.

Fortunately, there is an easy way around this problem, and it works in the garden as well as it does in a seed tray.

If you are sowing in a garden bed and the seed requires light to germinate, make your furrow as usual. But don't plant the seed into it right away. Instead, add a layer of vermiculite, about 6mm (¼ inch) deep, and then plant. Use a gentle water-breaker or rose nozzle to water the furrow after you have planted; the gentle stream of water will move the seeds into niches in the vermiculite where they will stay moist while still receiving light. Make certain to water the area gently each morning until the seeds germinate. In midseason, when it may be so hot that the vermiculite dries out during the day, use floating row cover on top of the furrow to hold in some moisture.

You can use a variation of the same system in a seed tray. Make small furrows as usual and seed into them. Cover the seeds with 6mm (¼ inch) of vermiculite and use a misting nozzle or spray bottle to moisten it. If yo can, place the flat out of direct ligh and cover it with plastic wrap to hol in the moisture. A plastic coverin will heat the flat too much if it's i direct sunlight, so leave it uncovere if it's on a windowsill and check i frequently for moisture levels.

Mist the seeds gently so they stay relatively close to the spot you planted them.

Remove the plastic wrap when seeds germinate or if the trays are in bright light.

solution 7 Keep air circulation high

Their proximity to each other killed these seedlings! They released, and also trapped, so much water vapor that fungal diseases had an easy target.

Seedlings sometimes die from damping-off diseases (see page 182). These diseases are caused by a number of different fungi, many of which are almost always present in the soil and as spores in the air. The fungi attack plants as they are germinating and can kill seedlings not only before they have had a chance to emerge above the soil surface but also any time between the seed-leaf and the four-leaf stage of growth. If they attack after this, the problem is known as root rot, even though the organisms involved might be the same as those that caused damping-off diseases.

Starting media that contain no soil, generally composed of a half– and–half mixture of peat moss and vermiculite, can reduce the incidence of damping-off diseases simply because they do not carry the fungal spores. However, they will not eliminate them altogether because so many spores travel through the air at all times.

Compost-based starting media should not be discarded, however, because they contain many organisms that prey on the damping-off microbes. Again, they will not entirely eliminate problems.

Good drainage in the soil mix and, especially, good air circulation around the plants are the best preventive measures. If the starting mix does not contain damping-off diseases to begin with, good air circulation can keep these humidity-loving fungi from attacking. Seedling leaves will dry almost immediately after you have watered and the air will not contain excessive levels of water vapour, so the damping-off fungi will not be able to develop.

To provide good air circulation, set up an oscillating fan near your seedlings and run it day and night. It's worth any extra watering you will have to do to keep your seedlings healthy.

solution 8 Store seeds correctly

Seeds live for varying amounts of time. Those in the onion family, Alliaceae, lose viability quickly and aren't much good after only a year, but lotus seeds can last over a hundred years and show no change in their germination rate. Most of the seeds you will be using in the garden maintain good germination rates for three to five years, but only if they are stored correctly.

To keep your seeds viable, store them away from moisture, light and high temperatures. Put any unused portions of old seed packets in sealable plastic bags or glass jars with screw lids and duct tape over the lid. If you don't have a cool, dry, dark place in the house to store them, pop them in a plastic bag or sealed jar in the refrigerator or freezer. Kept this way, the seeds will remain viable for many years.

Slip a label into the jar with the plant name, colour and storage date.

problem
The container plants look ragged by midseason

In spring, when you first put out your potted plants and hang some in baskets, everything looks beautiful. If you hav[e]
planted well, some of the pots will look just a bit empty, but at the rate that most plants grow that will soon chang[e]
because the plants will fill all the available space within a couple of weeks.

By midsummer the picture will have changed, however. Straggly petunia stems with tired foliage may be hanging fro[m]
the sides of a basket; once-glorious verbenas might have yellowing foliage; the sweet alyssum could be nothing more tha[n]
a bunch of tired-looking leaves; and a mixed group of annuals could have developed a tangle of bare stems near the so[il]
line. The solutions below address the most common reasons for these midseason troubles.

solution 1 Trim the roots

Sometimes, a pot complements a plant so well that you can't bear to transplant it to another container. Fortunately, there is an effective way around the problem of the plant outgrowing the pot. Rather than transplanting, you can prune the roots.

Remove the root ball from the pot and gently shake the soil from the roots. If the plant is so potbound that you can't dislodge the soil, pull a layer away with your fingers.

Once you can see the root ends, give them a light prunin[g.] Cut back any that are circling the pot and trim those tha[t] were touching the sides. Put a few inches (centimeters) o[f] new soil mix in the pot and replace the pruned root bal[l.] Add new soil mix around the edges and give it a goo[d] watering to let it settle.

solution 2 Cut back annuals

Annuals vary in the length of time they will bloom before dying, so the techniques that are effective in keeping them blooming for a long period also vary from species to species. Some species, such as impatiens and wax begonia (*Begonia semperflorens*), are 'self-cleaning' – that is, the flowers drop by themselves. Although they set seeds, they continue to bloom for months without any help from the gardener.

A far greater number of annuals do require the gardener's hand – you have to deadhead, or remove faded flowers, before they set seeds, to keep the plants blooming. Zinnias, marigolds, petunias and China asters are only a few of the many plants that respond to deadheading.

Plants with tiny flowers are difficult, if not impossible, to deadhead. Some, such as lobelia and sweet alyssum, also tend to stop blooming in midseason. But you don't have to add them to the compost pile at this point. Instead, you can cut them back to a few centimetres above the soil line. If the potting mix gives them adequate nutrition, they will respond by growing new stems and blooming again within a few weeks. This technique is also good for revitalizing

plants that you deadhead but that tend to grow long, unat[-] tractive stems by mid- to late summer. Petunias[,] calendula and bachelor's buttons are excellent candidate[s] for this treatment, but you can try it on just about an[y] annual plant.

Zinnias bloom for months if you keep them deadheaded.

solution 3 Plant in succession and pot in succession

Plants outgrow containers fairly rapidly. If you initially plant so that the pot doesn't look half empty, your plants will be growing too close together before you know it. The solution for this isn't widely spaced planting, however. If you gave every plant all the room it could use during the whole season, your containers would be nothing more than a group of big pots with a tiny stem and a flower or two here and there. It is far better to space plants so they can grow comfortably for a few months and then, if necessary, do it again.

You have a choice between planting in succession or potting in succession. Successional planting involves removing the ragged-looking plants, getting rid of the soil, and washing the container thoroughly with a 10 percent solution of laundry bleach to kill any disease organisms or insect eggs before you refill and replant the pot. This solution is always the one you should adopt if the plants become diseased or infested with pests, but it may not be appropriate if the plants are just struggling for more space. In that case, it may be better to pot in succession.

Often the best remedy for potbound plants is to transplant them into larger quarters. If the roots of the plants are starting to grow out of the drainage holes at the bottom of the pot, and the top growth looks out of proportion with the size of the container, the plants are probably becoming rootbound. Move them to a pot that is at least 2.5cm (1 inch) larger in diameter than the previous pot, but not more than 5cm (2 inches) bigger. It's better to move them two or three times in a season than to put them into a pot that's too large.

1 Whoops – when you see roots coming out of the drainage holes, it's time to repot.

2 Gently tease out circling roots before you replant to let them grow into the new soil.

3 Center the plant's root ball in the new pot and add soil all around it, tapping to settle it.

4 Finish by watering the plant and letting it drain and then adding soil to an inch under the rim.

solution 4 Choose appropriate plants

You can grow just about any plant in a container, but some plants look better than others in certain situations. Trailing plants, for example, look more appropriate in window boxes and hanging baskets than in pots set on the ground. Cultivar selection matters, too. If you are growing plants in pots, you will be better off with those that have been bred to be compact rather than those with long stems.

Read cultivar descriptions in catalogues carefully. The huge popularity of container growing has meant that many plants have been bred especially for growing in pots. Sometimes the description will say this, but sometimes it will just note that the cultivar is particularly compact. Whenever possible, choose these plants over others. Particularly good container plants are listed opposite.

Different plant suit different pots. These miniature conifers have been specially cultivated to be grown in pots in the home.

The pelargonium suits a window box or raised planting area like this.

solution 5 Double-pot your plants

In the high temperatures and bright light of midsummer, many plants simply don't get enough water to keep them thriving. There are several remedies: You can find the time to water a couple of times a day, you can set up a drip irrigation system (see page 55), or you can double-pot them.

If you are double-potting, there are two options. If you want to raise humidity and slow down the rate at which the soil dries, use a pot at least 10cm (4 inches) larger than the plant's pot. Put a layer of peat moss in the bottom, centre the plant's pot and stuff peat moss around its sides. When you water, water the peat moss, too. When water evaporates from the peat moss, it will increase humidity levels around the plant. The wet peat moss around the pot will also serve as insulation, so the pot will take much longer to dry.

The second option is ideal for gardeners who simply can't water as frequently as their plants require. Double-pot as described above but don't leave it at that. Buy some lantern or candle wick from a hardware or crafts store. For a small plant, place one end of a wick several centimetres below the top of the peat moss between the pots and the other end a few centimetres below the soil surface in the plant's pot. For pots 20cm (8 inches) wide, use two wicks, spaced evenly around the rim, and for larger plants, use even more wicks. Water the peat moss thoroughly when you water. The wick will carry water from the wet peat moss to the soil in the pot. If the outside pot doesn't have drainage holes, you will be able to ignore watering for several days.

GOOD CONTAINER PLANTS

If you're looking for an unusual plant for your container or one that retains its good looks and compact growth habit far into the summer, try one of the following plants.

Compact cultivars for pots

Ageratum houstonianum 'Blue Blazer' (floss flower)

Antirrhinum majus 'Royal Carpet', 'Coronette' (snapdragon)

Artemisia 'Silver Mound', 'Silver Brocade'

Brachyscome cvs. (Swan river daisy)

Calendula officinalis Fiesta series (pot marigold)

Dianthus chinensis 'Magic Charms' (pinks)

Gaillardia grandiflora 'Goblin' (blanket flower)

Heliotropium arborescens 'Mini Marine' (heliotrope)

Isotoma axillaris (rock isotome), 'Shooting Stars' (laurentia)

Lobelia erinus 'Compact Royal Jewels', 'Crystal Palace', 'Rosamund'

Melampodium paludosum 'Million Gold'

Rudbeckia hirta 'Toto' (black-eyed Susan, coneflower)

Salvia farinacea 'Alba'

Scaevola aemula (fan flower)

Tagetes cvs. 'Disco Mixed Colours', Signet series (marigold)

Torenia cvs. 'Summer Blue Wave' (wishbone flower)

Tropaeolum majus 'Empress of India' (nasturtium)

Trailers for hanging baskets and window boxes

Acalypha reptans (cat's tail)

Anagallis monellii (pimpernel)

Helichrysum petiolare (liqorice plant)

Lantana montevidensis

Lotus berthelotii (parrot's beak)

Petunia Surfinia Series

LEFT *Artemisia* (Silver Mound)
BELOW *Gaillardia grandiflora* (blanket flower)

ABOVE *Tropaeolum majus* (nasturtium)

problem

The container plants look nutrient deficient

Nutrient deficiencies are the most frequent problems that containerized plants face. Roots can forage far and wide in the soil for the nutrients they need – even a small plant's roots can easily extend 30cm (1 foot) or so deep in the soil and 3r (10 feet) or more wide – but in a pot all the roots have to wrap around each other in a confined space. Roots often try to travel out of the drainage holes in search of new soil. But they will not get far and will soon become "air pruned" when they are not moist enough to survive.

Nutrient deficiencies show first as yellowing, purpling or mottled leaves. Next comes die back of growing tips and general stunting. Insects and disease problems soon follow because weak plants are more vulnerable than healthy ones. The following solutions will help to keep your plants from suffering deficiencies.

solution 1 Apply liquid fertilizers

Containerized plants need a great deal of water. Most require at least one watering a day, but in the hottest part of the season some require two waterings. It's important to water deeply (see 'Check for soluble salts,' opposite page 153), but when you do, you will also be washing nutrients out of the soil. More often than not, plants become nutrient deficient by midseason.

Liquid fertilizers are the remedy. If you want to work completely organically, choose a mixture of liquid seaweed and fish emulsion as your fertilizer. But rather than diluting it according to the directions on the bottle, use it at half-strength. This lighter concentration will allow you to apply it more frequently.

Synthetic liquid fertilizers are also available at any garden supply store. The plant label will generally recommend a dilution rate for plants in pots, but if it doesn't, begin by mixing it as directed on the package. Depending on how the plants respond, you can always adjust the mix.

Most plants do well with a weekly feed, but some especially vigorous growers may require feeding more often. Look at the leaves to determine nutrient needs. If the leaves are a strong green, the plants are getting enough nutrients. If they are a bit yellow or purple, they need feeding. If they are getting too much nitrogen and you need to cut back on fertilizing, the leaves will be too dark a colour and grow too large. In some cases, they will be a little bit floppy and look as if they don't contain enough cellulose.

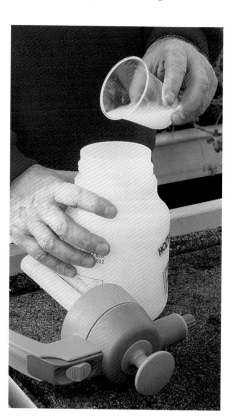

Mix fertilizers as directed on the package, using warm water. When possible, use filtered water with fertilizers.

Spray early in the morning so that leaves can dry before the sun is hot. This prevents fertilizer burn.

Solution 2 Check for soluble salts

Nutrient elements are made up of salts. In the garden, rain often washes excess nutrient salts out of the top layers of the soil, but in dry soils and containers salts can accumulate. If they do, plant roots have a very hard time picking up adequate moisture, even if the soil is wet, because the salts in the soil solution hold onto it. Without adequate levels of water, plants become drought-stressed and can also suffer nutrient deficiencies.

You can usually see salts building up. White crystals form on the surface of the soil and along the soil line on the inside of the pot. If the situation is not severe, you can leach the soil mix by top watering the plant until water freely pours from the drainage holes. Let a great deal of water wash through the soil. Subsequent to that, don't water unless the soil is really dry; when you do water, don't stop until water runs from the drainage holes, even if you are using drip irrigation.

If leaching the soil doesn't solve the problem, remove the plant from the pot and gently wash the roots with running water. Then pot it up again in new potting soil. Water thoroughly each time to avoid future problems.

Solution 3 Select the right soil mix

Soils with high levels of organic matter have several advantages. First, because nutrients are released slowly as microorganisms in the mix break them down and transform them into forms plants can use, fewer are available at any one time. This means that excess soluble salts are less likely to build up in the potting soil. Second, these mixes require less fertilization, therefore less maintenance time. Finally, the pH in these potting mixes stays more stable than it does in a mix composed only of peat moss, vermiculite, perlite and synthetic nutrients.

When you buy a potting soil, check the ingredients. Your guarantee that the mix has organic matter is the mention of compost or aged manure at the top of the list. Depending on where you live, you might have to check with several garden supply stores before you find a mix like this, but it will be well worth the trouble.

Solution 4 Add worms

Worms are the gardener's best friend, even in a potting mix. They tunnel up and down, creating pore spaces for air and water. They help to make nutrients available if the mix contains enough organic matter. And they help to maintain the slightly acid soils that plants require.

Worms will not fare well in a small pot, so there is no use adding them. But they do well in pots that are at least 20cm (8-inches) wide. You can add them anytime – when you first fill the pot or later, when plants are actively growing. If you add them later, loosen the soil first so they can burrow away from the light immediately. Don't put too many worms in a pot. For pots between 20–25cm (8–14-inches), use two worms. Add 4 in pots 40–60cm (16–24-inches), and eight or more in half-barrel and large tubs.

You can usually find worms at the bottom of your outside compost pile or in your garden. Or check the web or look in the back of gardening magazines for suppliers.

The worms in your garden are a different species than the ones you can buy, but either will work well in a pot.

chapter six

INSECT AND ANIMAL PESTS

All gardeners, even the most experienced, occasionally have problems with insects, animals, weeds or diseases. Insects can appear to be your worst problems, particularly when a garden is new, but weeds, animal pests and diseases can also take a toll on both your plants and your patience.

Insect pests and plant diseases usually decline as a garden becomes more established. For one thing, the soil becomes more fertile thanks to the organic matter you add every year, and, as it does so, the number of beneficial organisms that live in it increases. They prey on disease organisms as well as on the eggs, larvae and pupae of pest insects, so problem populations decline. Above ground, things improve, too. If you follow the suggestions in this chapter, you won't be using pesticides, and, in consequence, many beneficial insects will thrive to prey on pest insects. In most gardens, it only takes a few years to see a radical decrease in both disease and insect problems.

Weeds and animal pests do not decline in severity as a result of better soil health. As a matter of fact, some weeds become more troublesome as the soil becomes more fertile, and some animals will skip over the neighbours' plants in favor of your larger, healthier ones. Fortunately, if you keep up with the weeding and prevent new weed seeds from forming, weed problems will eventually become a memory. As for animal pests, repelling them by one means or another can solve your problems.

problem
Aphids

Aphids live everywhere in the temperate zone and prey on almost all plants. Members of the Aphidoideae family, they e[a]
by piercing plant tissues with their stylets and sucking out the fluids. They often transmit viruses and other diseases whil[e]
they feed. Fortunately, as you develop a diverse ecosystem in the garden, aphids become less and less of a problem becaus[e]
so many natural predators control them.

solution 1 Attract biological controls

Many other insects in the garden prey on aphids, either as predators or parasites. While the immature stages of these insects attack aphids, many of the adults require nectar and pollen from flowers. Ladybugs and hover flies can feed from fairly large blooms, but lacewings and the plethora of beneficial parasitic wasps must feed from small flowers. To attract and keep beneficial insects in the garden, set aside places where you can grow succession crops of three or four small-flowered species listed below, such as dill an[d] sweet alyssum, as well as a couple of those with larg[e] blooms, such as asters and feverfew, at all times. Thi[s] simple act will keep beneficial insects in your garden al[l] through the season.

Ψ ⋈🐖 ◑ 🥛 🍃

Aphids can carry virus diseases.   Aphid colonies contain all ages.

PLANTS TO ATTRACT BENEFICIAL INSECTS

Achillea spp. (yarrow)
Anethum graveolens (dill)
Aster spp.
Carum carvi (caraway)
Centaurea cyanus (bachelor's buttons)
Chamaemelum nobile (chamomile)
Coreopsis spp. (tickseed)
Coriandrum sativum (coriander)
Layia platyglossa (tidytips)
Lobularia maritima (sweet alyssum)
Mentha spp. (mint)
Nemophila menziesii (baby blue eyes)
Nepeta cataria (catnip)
Oenothera laciniata; O. biennis (evening primrose)
Tanacetum parthenium (feverfew); *T. vulgare* (tansy)

---

solution 2 Use aluminum foil

Aphids use the sky to tell them how to fly in an upright position. Because of this, you can use aluminum foil to confuse them so that they don't land on your plants. If aphids have been a serious problem on particular plants in the past, mulch the plants with aluminum foil in the early spring. When the aphids fly from their woody winter hosts to your garden plants, they'll avoid this confusing spot in the garden.

Ψ ⋈🐖 ◐ 🥛 🍃

APHID PREDATORS AND PARASITES

Aphid midges
Braconid wasps
Chalcid wasps
Lacewings
Ladybugs
Hover flies
Tachinid flies

solution 3 Soap to the rescue

Insects breath through small openings along the sides of their thorax. Soap is an effective control because it can clog these openings and suffocate the insect. Special insect-controlling soaps are available at garden supply stores. Mix soaps as directed and spray them on affected plants only in low light conditions such as early morning or twilight. Because soap clogs the stomata (pores) on plant leaves, too, you must wash it off the plants about 24 hours after spraying.

LAST RESORT

When soap and biological controls fail to keep aphid populations low, try a botanical control. Horticultural oils suffocate insects; use dormant oils on woody plants in late winter, but during the season use fine horticultural oil or garlic oil as directed on the bottle. If aphids survive an oil spraying, use neem, which kills more pests than beneficials. Next most generally lethal is sabadilla, and finally, pyrethrin. Avoid rotenone because even the 1 percent formulation kills most insects that touch it.

---

problem
Mexican bean beetles

Mexican bean beetles are the only members of the ladybug family that harm plants. The insects resemble fat, yellowish-brown ladybugs; the larvae look more like fuzzy mealybugs than ladybug larvae. Both bean beetle adults and larvae feed on the undersides of bean leaves, eventually skeletonizing them. If populations are high, bean beetles can kill a crop in a matter of days.

solution 1 Squash the eggs

The best way to prevent damage from bean beetles is to kill them before they hatch. The eggs look a great deal like ladybug eggs—a cluster of yellow cylinders standing on end. As they age, the eggs darken and turn increasingly orange. Check leaf undersides for the eggs every day. When you find a cluster, pick off the leaf so you can destroy the eggs or leave the leaf on the plant and squash the cluster by hand.

solution 2 Use a spray

If you don't kill all the eggs, you may be faced by a swarm of tiny bean beetle larvae. Because they eat from leaf undersides, it's easy to overlook them until the damage is severe. Should this happen, you can try to hand-squash as many larvae and adults as possible, but if populations seem too high spray plants with neem (see "Last Resort" box above).

solution 3 Cover the beans

To prevent adults from flying in and laying eggs on your plants, cover them with fleece. It's best to cover the area where they are planted before the seeds germinate, so even if a bean beetle notices that a new crop is up it will be unable to get to the plants to lay eggs on them.

problem
Flea beetles

Flea beetles can destroy seedlings in only a few hours. The adults overwinter in the soil and emerge to feed in midspring, so they can be a particularly serious problem after warmer than usual winters. They make numerous round holes in leaves and if populations are high enough, the holes converge until the leaf is gone. Adults lay eggs on plant roots. The larva feed on the roots for two to three weeks, pupate for two to three weeks, and then emerge as adults to start the cycle again. Depending on climate, there are between two and four generations a year.

The best biological controls are beneficial nematodes. You can import these with good compost or buy them from mail-order supplier.

solution 1 Spray with clay

Kaolin, a fine clay now available from most mail-order garden suppliers, repels many insects, including flea beetles. If caterpillars, Japanese beetles, grasshoppers, tarnished plant bugs, thrips, aphids, cucumber beetles, or even the disease powdery mildew are bothering your plants, try spraying with kaolin.

Fine as it is, the clay can clog spray nozzles. So rather than use your good backpack sprayer or a manually compressed sprayer, put it in a small bottle with a plastic trigger. Use a fairly large sewing needle to make the hole in the sprayer larger than normal; this will save you from having to clean out a clogged nozzle.

Though tiny, flea beetles can kill plants.

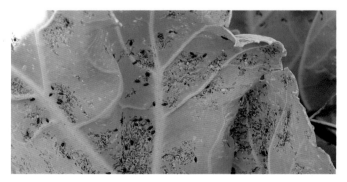
Flea beetles love cabbage family crops.

solution 2 Cover the crop

One of the best ways to deal with flea beetles is to avoid them altogether. As soon as you sow seed or transplant, cover the area with floating row cover material. Because adult flea beetles emerge from the soil, this works only if previous crops in the area did not host flea beetles. Remember to rotate the crops they love best – arugula and other members of the cabbage family, tomato family plants, and all the squashes – so they don't just pick up where they left off the year before.

solution 3 Trap them with tanglefoot

Tanglefoot is a sticky material available from most good garden stores. Use it against flea beetles by spreading it on the bottom third of two 1-m (3-foot) -long pieces of cardboard. Hold the uncoated part of the cardboard upright and close to the plants. The sticky parts should be on either side of the affected plants. Jostle the plants with your foot as you walk along. The flea beetles will jump away from the plants and get stuck on the cardboard.

problem
Caterpillars

Many caterpillars are benign, as all butterfly or moth lovers know. However, a few are dreadful garden pests. From army-worms to tomato hornworms, caterpillars can cause a great deal of damage. Some, such as parsley worms, turn into lovely butterflies, so a little damage is worth it, but when a caterpillar that doesn't turn into a lovely butterfly or moth poses a serious threat to your plants you may want to control it.

Birds are the best natural control. Attract them to the garden with birdbaths and birdseed and you will be rewarded by some good caterpillar control. Yellow jackets also prey on caterpillars; rather than killing them indiscriminately, allow those with nests far away from areas where people congregate to live in peace.

solution 1 Cover the crop

Caterpillars simply can't prey on plants under fleece (floating row covers) because the adult butterflies or moths can't lay eggs on the plant leaves. If you have a crop that is routinely bothered by caterpillars, invest in the lighter weight pest covers; you can leave them on in warm weather without baking the plants.

solution 2 Use a disease

Bacillus thuringiensis var. *kurstaki* (Btk) is a bacterial disease that kills young caterpillars if they eat it. Use this spray only as a last resort because it will kill benign butterflies and moths as readily as it kills pests. Only a few hours after a caterpillar ingests the bacteria, it stops feeding. It won't die for a day or two, but because it doesn't eat, it doesn't cause any more damage. Btk is available at most garden supply stores and mail-order suppliers.

solution 3 Look for the eggs

You will sometimes notice damage from caterpillars before you can see the pests. Huge holes suddenly appear in plant leaves where the tissue was smooth and unbroken only a day before. If you stoop down to investigate, you may see groups of darkish coloured globules. This is 'frass' or waste products from the caterpillars. Eventually, you may see the pests themselves. If you do, pick them off the plants and either crush them or put them in a jar of water with a skim of gasoline on the top of it. But don't stop there – look for eggs. Search on both sides of the leaves as well as in the axils between the main stem and leaf petioles. You will know they are eggs because they will be round and laid in rows or a definite pattern. Crush them or scrape them off the plant and put them into the jar with the gasoline skim.

Wise gardeners tolerate some caterpillars.

problem
Cutworms

Cutworms are the larvae, or caterpillars, of several different kinds of moth. The adult moths lay eggs on the ground or o
grass stems in early to midspring. The eggs hatch in about a week, and the cutworms burrow into the soil. At night, the
come out to feed. Most species cut through the stems of young plants and then eat the leaves, but a few climb the sten
to reach the leaves. After a month or so, some species pupate in the soil and emerge as a second generation of adult
These species lay eggs that overwinter but species with only one full generation a year may overwinter in the pupa stag

solution 1 Apply nematodes

The best biological controls for cutworms are beneficial nematodes. *Bacillus thuringiensis* var. *kurstaki* (Btk) works but is much less certain because the caterpillar has to ingest it. In contrast, beneficial nematodes will search out their prey and attack it.

Many companies sell nematodes, and you should buy a brand that is labelled for the pest you are trying to eliminate. Other than that, choose a brand that is sold locally because various nematode species are adapted to different regions.

Apply nematodes as directed on the package, which is generally by watering them into the soil near the plants you want to protect.

solution 2 Use toothpicks

One of the easiest ways to foil a cutworm's intentions is t
surround each transplant with toothpicks. As you put i
your seedlings, place three to four toothpicks with shar
ends around each stem. No cutworm can cut through th
toothpicks to topple the plant and the sharp end
will pierce the bellies of the climbing ones. This trick is s
effective that it's worth crawling down a row for direc
seeded plants to insert toothpicks around their stems.

solution 3 Put up a barrier

Old toilet paper rolls and tin cans make good cutworm barriers as long as the caterpillar isn't living right under the plant. Cut both ends out of cans and set either it or the toilet paper roll over the plant, burying the bottom inch (2.5cm) or so in the soil.

Cutworms aren't known for their beauty!

solution 4 Make a newspaper slurry

Make a newspaper slurry by tearing black and white newsprint into small pieces, putting them in a bucket, and covering them with water. Let this mixture sit for a few days to a week until the newspaper has broken down into mush. Use a wooden stick to pick up globs of the stuff and place it around your plant stems, patting it in place. Do this only on a bright, sunny day. Once the slurry has dried, it i
impenetrable to cutworms. A slurry mulch also works t
keep cabbage root fly maggots from burrowing down to ea
the roots of brassica crops.

problem
Earwigs

Earwigs, like cockroaches, can eat almost anything. They survive on a diet of rotting wood and old leaves as well as on ripe muskmelons, unopened rose blossoms, or tender new lettuce. They prey on aphids and other small insects, too.

If you see a few earwigs in the garden, let them be. It's likely that tachinid flies, their natural enemy, are keeping the population under control for you. But if every stone you turn over is crawling with earwigs or none of the roses opens undamaged, you should consider taking action.

solution 1 Trap them in pots

Earwigs like to sleep in a dark, protected spot during the day, so they are easy to catch. You can trap them on the soil surface by sinking a small pot so that the rim is level with the soil. Fill the pot with bread-crumbs soaked in vegetable oil, and set a "roof" of cardboard, creased to make a tent shape, over the pot.

To trap earwigs above the soil surface, stick a strong stake into the soil. Fill a small clay pot with cotton soaked in vegetable oil and hang this, upside down, over the stake.

Remove trapped earwigs every day.

solution 2 Clean up the garden

Earwigs love garden debris. It makes dark, cozy niches for resting in daytime and doubles as a handy food source right inside the bedroom. Discourage earwigs by cleaning up. Put away old pots, compost plant wastes, and pick up tools and boards. Between a clean, debris-free area and a few earwig traps, you should be able to control them.

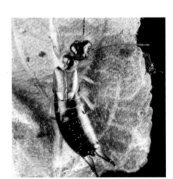

Earwigs are distinctive.

problem
Nematodes

Nematodes are microscopic worm-like creatures. Many nematodes are beneficial, including the sort we buy for controlling various soil-dwelling pests. But other nematodes are pests. Some attack roots while others feed on leaves. Hosts range from tomatoes to fruit trees to ornamentals. Both fungi and beneficial nematodes prey on them.

Nematode damage can be hard to diagnose. On roots, you may see lumps; plants tend to be stunted, and leaves yellow and wilt. Foliar nematodes make the areas between the veins on lower leaves yellow before the leaf turns brown and dies.

solution 1 Use marigold covers

'Nemagold' marigolds suppress root nematodes. But they won't work unless you cover the garden area with them for a complete season. Seeds are available from many seed companies, most particularly in areas where this problem is most prevalent.

solution 2 Apply chitin

Chitin, found in crustacean shells and insect exoskeletons, is an excellent nematode control. If you can get waste crab shells, cover the garden with a 13-mm (½-inch) layer of them in the autumn and work them into the top soil layers.

If you cannot get crab shells, use beneficial nematodes or drench the soil with neem, but do not use the two together.

problem
Cucumber beetles

Two types of cucumber beetles, striped and spotted, prey on garden plants. The larvae of both species hatch from eggs lai on the soil surface and tunnel down into the soil, where they feast on crop roots.

Spotted cucumber beetle larvae are also known in the U.S. as southern corn rootworms because they cause as muc damage to corn as they do to cucurbits, or squash family plants. After pupating in the soil, they emerge as adults and begi feeding. Striped cucumber beetles are fairly indiscriminate in their tastes. They munch on plants in your flower beds as hap pily as they do on squashes, but spotted cucumber beetles generally stick to corn and cucurbits.

solution 1 Mulch with straw

Straw is scratchy. Unlike hay, which mats down and becomes soft as it weathers, straw remains stiff and holds its sharp edges. As a consequence, insects don't like crawling on it. It makes a good mulch early in the season for plants that emerging adult beetles prey on. Because they tend to walk at first and also because these beetles lay eggs on the soil surface, it prevents many of them from attacking your plants.

The spotted cucumber beetle.

solution 2 Use a last-resort spray

If cucumber beetles are routinely devastating your flowe and vegetable crops, you may need to control them with spray. Eventually, the soil in your garden will be goo enough so that natural controls, such as beneficial nema todes, will take over for you, but until then, these beetle can give you a major headache. Pyrethrum sprays kill thes beetles. Mix and apply as recommended on the bottle, an remember to spray only early in the morning or at twiligh to avoid burning leaves under bright sunlight.

See also: 'Nematodes', page 160; 'Cover the crop', page 158

problem
Japanese beetles

Japanese beetles, mostly a problem in the eastern states of America, can skeletonize an entire garden. Adult beetles emerge from the soil in late spring or early summer and begin feeding on anything from basil to roses. They burrow under vege-tation in late summer to lay eggs. After hatching, the larvae burrow into the soil and feed on plant roots for a year or two. Irregularly shaped patches of dead grass in the spring and moles are both symptoms of larval infestation.

solution 1 Use milky spore disease

Milky spore disease (*Bacillus popilliae*) attacks and kills Japanese beetle grubs in the soil. This solution is extremely effective in warmer climates. However, in cooler northern areas, it will not survive the winter so is largely a waste of money. Use beneficial nematodes in these areas to avoid problems.

Apply the milky spore disease as directed on the package. It may take a year to be completely effective, but you will see a real reduction in beetle populations the following summer.

solution 2 Pick by hand

The most effective way to save plants from adult Japanese beetles is to remove the beetles by hand. It takes some patience but brings immediate rewards.

Wear gloves because their feet have tiny claws that are unpleasant to the touch. Arm yourself with a jar of water with a skim of gasoline on the surface. Pick off the beetles, one by one, and drop them into the jar.

Alternatively, you can vacuum them up with a small, handheld, battery-powered vacuum cleaner. Be prepared for them to try to disappear into crevices in the plant or to drop to the surface of the soil when they notice that they are under attack. You usually need to repeat this operation every day for a few days to catch them all.

Japanese beetles are best removed from plants by hand.

See also: **'Apply nematodes', page 160; 'Cover the crop', page 159**

DON'T USE TRAPS

Japanese beetle traps, baited with sexual attractants, are sold at almost every garden supply store. But unless you have a huge property, don't buy one. Beetles from miles around will fly to the lure, and many of them will decide to stop off for a bit of lunch and dinner rather than proceeding to their death. So you will end up with more beetles, not fewer.

problem
Leafhoppers

Leafhoppers are small, wedge-shaped insects that prey on numerous plant species. They are particularly troublesome to fruit trees and potatoes but eat lots of other vegetables as well as a wide range of ornamentals and grasses.

Both adults and nymphs suck plant juices from plant stems and the undersides of leaves. They release a somewhat toxic substance into the plants as they feed and also spread many viral diseases. Rather than noticing the leafhoppers themselves, you might first notice that plant leaves are puckered or mottled.

solution 1 Spray dormant oil

Adults of many leafhopper species overwinter on perennial plants, and this is particularly true of the species that attack fruit trees. Fortunately, there is an easy way to control these insects. In

One of many leafhopper species.

late winter, long before the buds finish swelling, spray dormant oil on the tree, covering it well. Not only will it kill leafhoppers, it will control many other insects and diseases on the tree. You can find dormant oil at any garden supply store or mail-order garden company.

solution 2 Coddle beneficial insects

Many beneficial organisms attack leafhoppers. In addition to ladybugs, lacewings and parasitic wasps, which prey on many small insects, parasitic flies, damsel bugs, minute pirate bugs, and spiders all prey on leafhoppers. Plant mixed groups of flowering plants to attract these species. But more than that, avoid using any pesticide sprays, even those that are supposedly fairly benign. A garden without poisons builds larger populations of beneficial organisms than one where they have to fight for survival.

solution 3 Use last-resort remedies

If worst comes to worst and you decide to spray for leafhoppers, use insecticidal soap as your first control. If that doesn't work, use neem. This substance, available from many mail-order garden suppliers, comes from the bark of a tree that grows in India. It attacks many more pests than beneficial insects, but can still disrupt the balance in your garden. If you can't find neem, use a pyrethrum formulation.

See also: 'Use biological controls', page 166; 'Cover the plants', page 167

problem
Mealybugs and scale insects

Mealybugs and scale insects are more serious pests in warm weather areas and on houseplants than they are where winters bring prolonged periods of freezing weather. However, there are exceptions; the comstock mealybug attacks apples and pears, and San Jose scale can be a problem for fruit trees in Canada.

Mealybugs are elliptical, pale-colored, and covered with short filaments and a white, waxy material. They suck cell sap from twigs, leaves or fruits and tend not to move much once they find a good feeding spot.

Scale insects can be oval or round and do not have a white covering. Instead, adult females look like small, raised bumps on the plant tissue. Males of all scale species have wings, and immature scales crawl for a few hours before settling down to feed and mature. Like mealybugs, they can kill a houseplant or even a large tree if populations get out of hand.

solution 1 Use alcohol swabs

Alcohol kills both scale insects and mealybugs. On a houseplant, even a large one, this remedy is so effective that it is worth taking the time to saturate cotton swabs with some ordinary methylated spirits and dab them on each mealybug or scale insect you see. Remember to look for these insects at leaf axils and buds as well as on leaf undersides and along the bark of small twigs. Check again in a few days; dead insects will drop off or shrivel up, so it will be a relatively quick task to kill any that remain alive.

Mealybugs on passion flowers.

See also: 'Use biological controls', page 167

solution 2 Release biological controls

Natural biological controls live where mealybugs and scale insects do. Consequently you may never have to worry about high populations. But the ecosystem is disturbed by weather extremes or if there aren't enough small flowers in bloom to feed the beneficials, import controls.

Mealybug destroyers are excellent controls on citrus, grapes, and indoor or greenhouse plants. For citrus mealybugs, buy a parasitic wasp called *Leptomastix dactylopii*. For both armoured and soft scales, use a beetle the supplier recommends or the parasitic wasp.

solution 3 Spray outdoors

When mealybugs and scale insects attack outdoor plants, you may have to spray. Dormant oil does an excellent job of killing both types of insects, but remember to use it only in areas where plants become dormant during the winter months and spray before blossoms open in the spring.

Fine horticultural oils are also effective against these insects and have the advantage of being light enough not to injure actively growing plant tissues. In frost-free areas, these oils are a better choice for control as long as you spray before the summer heat sets in. You are usually safe if you stop spraying in early summer.

problem
Slugs and snails

Slugs and snails cause enormous damage in gardens all over the world. Because they feed at night, you may not be able to determine what's causing the damage unless you've seen it before. The tip-off is the size of the holes. They have mouthparts shaped like metal files, so they rasp large, ragged holes. You may see dry silvery trails, made by the slime they leave behind. Aside from tender foliage, strawberries, and flower petals, they eat dead organic matter. Trap them at the edges of slow compost piles.

Adult slugs and snails lay eggs near the surface of moist soil. The eggs hatch in 2 to 4 weeks and, depending on species, mature in 5 months to 2 years. They overwinter as eggs or adults under the soil or plant debris and resume feeding once the soil warms up. Because their skins dry easily, they feed on cloudy, damp days or at night. Biological controls for eggs include fireflies and ground beetles, while snakes, frogs, toads and birds prey on those that are fully grown.

solution 1 Use traps

Beer is the traditional slug trap. Gardeners fill old tuna cans with a malty-smelling beer and set them at close intervals through the garden. To keep beneficial ground beetles from falling into these traps, remember not to set them flush with the soil. A slug or snail will gladly climb the 2.5cm (1 inch) or so it takes to get into a partially buried can, but a ground beetle won't.

Instead of beer, you can also use a mixture of flour, water, sugar, and baker's yeast in the traps. Mix up a new batch every day or so and refill the cans.

Empty grapefruit rinds are attractive because slugs are always interested in a cool, sweet-smelling place to spend the day. Set the rinds, upside down, around the compost pile or in an area of the garden where slugs have been feasting. Early in the morning, before the sun has had a chance to heat up the air, lift the rinds and shake out the slugs into a container. You can kill the slugs by crushing them or placing them in a can of water with a skim of gasoline on top.

Iron phosphate traps are relatively new and are effective. You can buy them from garden suppliers under several trade names. Check the ingredient list to make sure that you buy an iron phosphate trap rather than one filled with a poison that can lure and hurt other organisms.

1 Specialized slug traps are available at many garden shops. They come with covers to keep stray animals from drinking the beer.

2 Pour beer into the trap. Some people say it has to be fresh, but others report good results with stale beer. Experiment for yourself.

solution 2 Change mulching materials

Organic mulches are some of the gardener's best allies, except when it comes to slugs. Slugs love nothing more than a soft bed of straw, hay or even aged woodchips. Not only does this mulch give a cool, damp environment, but it also serves as lunch when the weather is too hot to go out.

If slugs are a major problem in your garden, lay down landscape fabric or black plastic mulch. The landscape cloth won't repel the slugs, but neither will it attract them. Any slug travelling across plastic mulch to get to a tasty-smelling plant will stick to it on a hot day as the heat of the plastic will dry up the slime trail on which it travels.

solution 3 Use copper wire

Slugs and snails cannot travel across copper because chemicals in the slime path they travel on react with the copper to create an unpleasant sensation in their feet. Make use of this characteristic by surrounding garden beds with copper or wrapping trees with it. You can find copper at many garden supply stores or through mail-order catalogues. Buy strips 5cm (2 inches) wide or apply thinner strips in bands 5cm (2 inches) wide.

problem
Spider mites

Spider mites can devastate a plant before you even notice them. Several different species of spider mite are common on garden plants, greenhouse crops and even houseplants. Some species make webs, which are the first thing you often notice, but not all do. What they do have in common is their minute size and the fact that they have eight legs. They can be red, brownish, pale green and yellow; some are marked with two dark coloured spots.

The first signs of damage are yellow or pale specks on leaves. You may also see fine webbing, depending on the species attacking your plants. As damage worsens, leaves turn white and die.

solution 1 Use biological controls

The best biological control for pest mites are other mites. These predatory mites occur naturally in some warm-weather areas. However, they are not always present and even when they do live in your area they may not be numerous enough to control the pest species. Fortunately, you can purchase predatory mites from almost any supplier of biological controls. It's important to let the supplier choose the species and amount that you should buy because the predators have specific temperature, day length and host requirements, and not all predatory mites will prey on all pest mites or work in all environmental conditions.

Spider mites are devastating.

solution 2 Keep conditions moist

Mites simply don't thrive in moist conditions. If they are a problem, water the soil frequently enough to keep it consistently moist. Raise relative humidity levels around the plant in other ways, too. Mist the leaves whenever you pass the plant early in the day and set up pans of stones on the soil surface around the plant. Fill the pans with water and let it evaporate during the daylight hours.

solution 3 Use sprays as a last resort

Fine horticultural oils are effective against spider mites. Use them on any woody plants that can tolerate a coating of oil, but spray it off the next day. Insecticidal soap can also be effective in some circumstances. Spray and check for living mites the following day. If a great many survive, use a neem spray. Neem is reliable; mites simply can't survive contact with it. Pyrethrums are the spray of last resort.

problem

Tarnished plant bugs

Tarnished plant bugs, or TPBs, can cause an amazing amount of damage before you even know what's causing the problem. They feed on flowers, leaves, buds, and fruits by sucking out plant juices. As they feed, they insert a toxin into the plant that causes discolouration and distorted growth. On yellow cultivars of annual statice (*Limonium* spp.), for example, florets dry and turn a brownish-tan colour before they have even fully opened.

TPBs do not go through a complete metamorphosis. Instead, they have a nymph stage that looks similar to the adult but lacks wings. The nymph stage is the most vulnerable, and natural predators, such as big-eyed bugs, damsel bugs and minute pirate bugs, feed on them.

solution 1 Cover the plants

Fleece prevents tarnished plant bugs from laying eggs on the plants. Because adult TPBs overwinter in plant debris and fly as soon as temperatures warm in the spring, cover susceptible plants as soon as you plant or transplant them.

Fleece simply isn't attractive enough for flower beds and borders, no matter how much you might want to protect your plants. You can use the covers in cutting gardens, of course, because those are working rather than ornamental gardens, but you will have to spray where the looks of your planting matter as much as its productivity.

solution 2 Use last-resort remedies

Fine horticultural oil will kill tarnished plant bugs but is useful only on woody plants with tough leaves, such as roses. On annual plants, where problems are likely to be more severe anyway, the best control is pyrethrum. Use as directed on the bottle, remembering not to spray under high light conditions.

problem

Thrips

Thrips are so tiny that you may not notice them until the damage they are causing forces you to search for them. They suck plant juices from flowers, leaves and stems, causing a silvery streaking or speckling on the plant tissue where light shines through the almost-empty cell. Plants sometimes become stunted or distorted and flower buds may drop, unopened. Thrips can also pass viruses from one plant to another while they feed.

solution 1 Use coloured traps

Thrips are attracted to bright blue. Commercial growers use this to their advantage by setting up bright blue plastic cards in the field or greenhouse and coating them with tanglefoot (see page 158). The thrips fly to the cards to investigate and get hopelessly stuck.

Home gardeners can use blue sticky traps as easily as commercial ones. Check the internet or call companies that serve small farms and inquire about them.

solution 2 Release biological controls

Both minute pirate bugs and *Amblyseius cucumeris*, a predatory mite, control thrips, and both are available from biological control suppliers. Talk to the company before you order because you will want to know which control will do the most good in your particular circumstances, how many you should release, and any special release instructions.

problem
Birds

Birds can be dreadful pests. Some species eat every corn kernal seed you plant while others peck away at ripe berries. Birds are too valuable to entirely discourage altogether, however, so it's wise to plant some crops just for them. Highbush cranberries and mulberries are good choices. Birds usually prefer these fruits to anything you have in the garden and leave your plants alone when they are in fruit. The following solutions can also save your crops.

solution 1 Net the crops

Bird netting works. If you have gone to the trouble of raising a bountiful crop of raspberries or strawberries, it's well worth going to the trouble of putting nets over the plants. Do this a few days before the first fruit is ripe. The birds will know better than you when it is at peak flavour and they'll get to it before you do, unless it is covered.

Cover your berries.

solution 3 Set up Scare-Eyes

Scare-Eyes terrify most birds. Most garden supply catalogues include these large, yellow balloons with a huge 'eye' painted on opposite sides. They come with long strings so you can tie them to stakes or outbuildings, and they are light enough so they'll bop around in the wind. Their constantly changing position and scary eyes are enough to frighten most birds. You can make them even more effective by tying them to a stake that you move around daily.

solution 2 Make sticky perches

Birds have an instinctive fear of being trapped, and you can use this to your advantage when you are trying to protect plants that you can't cover. Make wooden perches that sit at various heights and set them close to the plants. Paint the top of each perch with a layer of sticky tanglefoot. When birds land on the perch to investigate the crop, which they always do before eating it, the sticky stuff will frighten them, and they'll fly off to find a safer place.

solution 4 Use reflective tape

Flashtape works as well as Scare-Eyes and is much less obtrusive. The foil tape, which is about 6mm (½ inch) wide, is silver on one side and shiny red on the other. It bounces in the wind, showing first the red and then the silver, and birds think it looks like flames.

Unroll the tape so that it twists like a crepe-paper party streamer, leave some slack in it so it will bounce, and staple it or tie it to stakes all around the area you want to protect. If the crop is low growing – strawberries, for example – set the tape only 30–45cm (12–18 inches) above the ground, but if it is high—as with raspberries – set it up so that it is at the midlevel height of the bushes.

Aluminium flashes like fire in the sun.

problem
Rodents

All rodents have the potential to be serious garden pests. Some, such as mice, do more damage in winter than summer, and others, such as rabbits and groundhogs, are pests during the growing season. Cats and dogs are the best rodent deterrents, but if you don't have a pet that regularly roams the garden area you will have to find another way to discourage these pests.

solution 1 Pull back mulches

Wonderful as mulches are for building soil and minimizing weed problems, they can also provide a home for some pests, including mice. This is particularly true during the winter months, when mice burrow under mulch to find their favorite winter food, such as the bark of your fruit trees and other ornamentals.

Prevent problems by pulling mulches back at least 30cm (1 foot) from tree trunks. When there is no snow cover, this distance seems daunting to the average mouse and it will not cross it to get to the bark

solution 2 Use tree guards in winter

Plastic tree guards give the best protection against mice in areas where snow gives them winter cover. Choose white guards with air holes to protect the trees from overheating. While you are most likely to have trouble with mice during the winter months, it's best to install the tree guards when you plant the tree. Because they are constructed to expand as the tree grows, they will not constrict its growth.

solution 3 Surround the garden with gravel

Rodents do not like to cross gravel. If they have a choice between traveling over grass or traveling over sharp stones, they will always choose the grass. You can use this to your advantage if rodents have been causing serious problems.

Prepare for the gravel 'moat' by excavating an area at least 30–45cm (12–18 inches) wide by about 15cm (6 inches) deep all around the garden. Build a frame that extends 2.5cm (1 inch) or so above the surrounding area. Add 8cm (3 inches) of builder's sand to the bottom of the trench and top it off with 8cm (3 inches) of sharp gravel.

solution 4 Fence the garden

Fences are the best rodent deterrents, but unlike those designed to prevent jumping animals from getting into the garden, rodent fences must extend almost as far underground as they do aboveground.

Dig a trench at least 1 foot (30cm) deep all around the garden and set a small-mesh fencing material in it. To make certain that it stays upright, pound fence posts into the soil at reasonable intervals and staple the fencing to them. If rodents are the only creatures you are trying to exclude, the fence doesn't have to extend aboveground any more than a few metres (feet).

solution 5 Use a live trap

Live traps are the most humane way to catch animals, as long as you have a safe place to release the creature after you have caught it. Most animals love peanut butter. Put some on a piece of bread or a slice of apple and set it into the trap just before dark. Check the trap early the next morning.

solution 6 Remove brush piles

Rabbits love brier patches. Brush piles come in a close second, because, like briers, they make an almost impenetrable fort.

When you remove a brush pile from the garden, you are also removing a choice hiding spot. Rabbits and mice will be forced to find new quarters.

problem
Deer

Deer can be a serious pest, particularly in areas where building is displacing their natural habitat. More than one gardener has lost his love for 'Bambi' in the face of real-life deer that gorge on garden crops and devastate foundation plantings. Use the following suggestions to prevent problems before they begin – it's easier to keep deer from discovering your plantings than to get rid of them after they've found them.

solution 1 Put up tall fences

Fences lower than 2.5m (8 feet) do not keep out deer. The average deer can jump a 2m (7–foot) fence without a second thought but will reconsider trying to sail over one that is higher than this.

Width also discourages most deer. A simple, 2.5m (7-foot) wire fence, with wires strung 30–45cm (12–18 inches) apart from each other, will work if it juts out 60–90cm (2–3 feet) from the top. Buy angled braces from a fencing company and screw them to the top of your fence posts. Run wires along them just as you do on the vertical portion of the fence. No deer will jump that high and that wide simultaneously.

If you live in a rural area, put up an electric fence. Bait it with peanut butter on foil strips. Hang the baited strips from the wire. When a deer licks one it will get enough of a shock to discourage it from trying to broach that fence.

On a large plot of land, a tall fence is the best option for keeping out deer.

solution 2 Hang dancing mirrors

A new product is a wonderful deer deterrent. Small pieces of mirror are strung on clear, nylon threads. Hang these threads around the garden, leaving slack in the lines so the mirrors will swing and dance in the breeze. The mirrors frighten deer and they will stay away. Remember to move the lines each week so that they don't get used to them. For a homemade version, discarded CDs can be used instead of mirrors.

solution 3 Grow deer-resistant plants

If deer are a perpetual problem in your garden, try growing as many plants that they don't like as you can. Often, if you surround your tastier plants with these species as well as using some of the other deterrents discussed above, you can completely discourage deer visits, even in early spring when they are particularly hungry. The list at right is not complete, but does include many of the most common plants that deer will not touch.

solution 4 Fence the ground

Deer do not like poor footing. They simply will not walk over something that threatens to tangle them up.

Mesh netting, the sort you use to trellis sweet peas, can be an effective deer barrier. Rather than using it as a fence, lay it on the ground, all around the garden. Use ground staples to secure it to the soil, but leave it slack enough so

that it will frighten a deer. To prevent deer from simply jumping over it, use at least two widths so that it extends 3–4.5m (10–15 feet) from the cultivated area.

Solution 5 Use soap, hair, eggs and other deterrents

Deer have a wonderful sense of smell. They don't see well, but with their noses, they don't need to. They are frightened by some smells. Use this to repel them.

Hang smelly deodorant soap, still in its box, from trees or posts so it's about 1.2m (4 feet) off the ground. Secure it with a loop of wire poked through the centre of the box.

Human hair frightens deer. Hang it in old pantyhose or dirty socks, again at deer nose level. Or let some eggs sit out until they smell, add a little soap to make the mixture stick, and dip wooden stakes or markers into it. Place the stakes all around the plants you want to protect. Mix up a new batch every week and every time it rains.

Lions are deer predators. You can use this fear by getting some lion dung from a local zoo. Place is among the plants you want to protect. Refresh this regularly to get the maximum benefits.

DEER-RESISTANT PLANTS

Annuals

Agastache foeniculum (anise hyssop)
Ageratum houstonianum (floss flower)
Antirrhinum majus (snapdragon)
Begonia semperflorens (wax begonia);
  B. x tuberhybrida (tuberous begonia)
Bracteantha bracteatum (strawflower)
Brugmansia spp. (angel's trumpet)
Canna x generalis (canna lily)
Cleome hasslerana (spider flower)
Digitalis purpurea (foxglove)
Heliotropium arborescens (heliotrope)
Lobularia maritima (sweet alyssum)
Matthiola incana (stock)
Nicotiana spp (tobacco plant)
Papaver spp. (poppy)
Ricinus communis (castor oil plant)
Salvia spp. (ornamental sage)
Senecio cineraria (ragwort)
Solenostemon scutellaroides (coleus)
Tagetes cvs. (marigold)
Zinnia spp.

Bulbs

Allium spp. (ornamental onion)
Chionodoxa spp. (glory-of-the-snow)
Colchicum spp. (autumn crocus)
Eranthis hyemalis (winter aconite)
Fritillaria spp. (crown imperial, fritillary)
Galanthus spp. (snowdrop)
Hyacinthus spp.
Lycoris squamigera
Muscari spp. (grape hyacinth)
Narcissus spp. (daffodil)
Puschkinia libanotica (striped squill)
Scilla spp. (squill)

Perennials

Aconitum spp. (monkshood)
Ajuga reptans (bugle)
Alchemilla mollis (lady's mantle)
Aquilegia spp. (columbine)
Armeria maritima (thrift)
Asclepias tuberosa (butterfly weed)
Astilbe spp.
Baptisia spp. (false indigo)
Cerastium tomontosum (snow-in-summer
Cimicifuga spp. (bugbane)
Convallaria majalis (lily of the valley)
Dicentra spectabilis (bleeding heart)
Dictamnus albus (dittany, fraxinella)
Echinops spp. (globe thistle)
Eryngium spp. (sea holly)
Euphorbia spp. (spurge)
Filipendula vulgaris (meadowsweet)
Galium odoratum (sweet woodruff)
Geranium spp. (cranesbill)
Gypsophila spp. (baby's breath)
Hypericum spp. (St John's wort)
Kniphofia spp. (red hot poker)
Lamium maculatum (deadnettle)
Lavandula spp. (lavender)
Liatris spicata (gayfeather)
Ligularia spp.
Limonium latifolium (sea lavender)
Linum perenne (flax)
Lobelia cardinalis (cardinal flower)
Lychnis coronaria (rose campion)
Mertensia virginica (Virginia bluebells)
Mysotis spp. (forget-me-not)
Oenothera spp. (evening primrose)
Paeonia spp. *and* cvs. (peony)
Penstemon spp.

Perovskia atriplicfolia (Russian sage)
Polygonatum spp. (Solomon's seal)
Solidago spp. (goldenrod)
Verbascum spp. (mullein)
Veronica spp. (speedwell)
Yucca filamentosa (Adam's needle)

Shrubs

Abelia grandiflora (glossy abelia)
Berberis spp. (barberry)
Buddleia davidii (butterfly bush)
Buxus spp. (boxwood)
Calluna vulgaris (heather)
Calycanthus floridus (carolina allspice)
Chaenomeles japonica (flowering quince)
Cotinus coggygria (smokebush)
Cotoneaster spp.
Daphne spp.
Elaeagnus umbellata (autumn olive)
Forsythia spp.
Ilex spp. (holly)
Juniperus spp. (juniper)
Kerria japonica (Japanese kerria)
Ligustrum spp. (privet)
Mahonia spp.
Picea spp. (spruce)
Pieris japonica (lily-of-the-valley bush)
Pinus mugo (mountain pine); *P. parviflora*
  (dwarf white pine); *P. thunbergii*
  (Japanese black pine)
Potentilla fruticosa
Rosa rugosa (Japanese apple rose)
Skimmia japonica
Spiraea spp.
Syringa spp. (lilac)
Viburnum spp.

WEEDS AND DISEASES

Serious weed problems can plague even the best gardeners. All it takes is a small period of neglect – perhaps time when you are too busy with other matters to keep up with the weeding – to create a huge weed population. Or it could be that you have moved into a house with a garden that is already infested with weeds, both annual and perennial. In either case, you will have to tackle the weed problems with energy and dedication. With these two qualities, you will be able to defeat even the worst weed problems within a year or two.

Most plants can host a disease. But fortunately plants growing in good soils and appropriate environments are resistent to them. Nonetheless, you may see a disease on your plants. Look in these pages for solutions to common diseases.

problem
Annual and biennial weeds carpet the vegetable garden

Most annual weeds thrive in the high-fertility, fast-draining soils of a vegetable garden. Many of them are relatively benign plants, and in low concentrations they can even be desirable. For example, young fat-hen, redroot amaranth, and purslane are all highly nutritious salad crops with an excellent flavour, and plants such as jimsonweed and common mallow are pretty enough to be ornamentals. But these plants show no restraint. A single amaranth can spread several thousand seeds over the garden, and before you know it everything you plant will be struggling for light, water and nutrients in the face of this competition. It's at this point that you realize that weeds can be real garden problems.

---

solution 1 Weed early

Annual weeds are relatively easy to control when they are young. Remember to check the garden every day or two after you have tilled or seeded or transplanted. As soon as you see the tiny little seed leaves, use a hoe or a small hand-weeder to pull them out of the soil. It only takes a few minutes when weeds are this small; they become a major nuisance only if you let them get established.

KNOW YOUR ENEMIES

In temperate regions the following annual plants commonly cause weed problems. If you see just one or two of any of them, take them seriously. Dig them out, cut them off just under the surface of the soil, or snap off their flowers – anything to prevent them from going to seed.

Abutilon theophrasti (velvetleaf)
Agrostemma githago (corn cockle)
Amaranthus blitoides (prostrate pigweed); *A. retroflexus* (redroot pigweed)
Ambrosia artemisiifolia (ragweed); *A. trifida* (giant ragweed)
Anthemis cotula (stinking chamomile)
Bidens bipinnata (Spanish needles); *B. frondosa* (devil's beggarticks)
Brassica kaber (wild mustard); *B. nigra* (black mustard)
Capsella bursa-pastoris (shepherd's purse)
Chenopodium album (fat-hen)
Cuscuta pentagona (field dodder)
Datura stramonium (jimsonweed, thorn apple)
Dioda teres (poorjoe)
Erigeron annuus (fleabane)
Euphorbia maculata (spotted spurge)

Galinsoga parviflora (galant soldier)
Galium aparine (goosegrass, sticky willy)
Geranium carolinianum (Carolina geranium)
Ipomoea purpurea (morning glory)
Lactuca serriola (prickly lettuce)
Malva neglecta (common mallow)
Matricaria matricarioides (pineapple weed)
Mollugo verticillata (carpetweed)
Polygonum aviculare (knotgrass); *P. hydropiper* (marshpepper smartweed); *P. pensylvanicum* (Pennsylvania smartweed); *P. persicaria* (lady's thumb)
Portulaca oleracea (purslane)
Salsola iberica (Russian thistle)
Sida spinosa (prickly sida)
Solanum nigrum (black or deadly nightshade)
Sonchus oleraceus (smooth sow thistle)
Spergula arvensis (toadflax)
Stellaria media (chickweed)
Thlaspi arvense (field pennycress)
Tribulus terrestris (puncture vine)
Xanthium pensylvanicum (cocklebur)

See also: **'Mulches', page 54**

solution 2 Plant cover crops

Cover crops are plants that you grow to add nutrients and organic matter to the soil, but they can also go a long way toward eliminating your weed problems. Planted thickly enough, all cover crops suppress weeds by outcompeting them for light, water, and nutrients. Additionally, some release compounds that kill other plants, including weeds, while they are growing or while they are decomposing.

A good rule is to keep one-quarter of your garden under cover at all times. Plan for this from the beginning so that you will have the space. You can plant cold-hardy crops, such as clover, in early spring and let them grow for a full year as long as you remember to mow them whenever they come into bloom. Otherwise they will turn into

as big a weed problem as you are trying to correct. Plant tender cover crops, such as buckwheat, after all danger of frost has passed. If you want a second buckwheat crop, let your first planting set seed before you mow it. The seeds it spreads will produce plants that will be ready to mow by early fall when you want to plant a winter cover such as oats or winter rye to blanket the soil over the cold months. The table on page 176 lists common cover crops along with appropriate planting times and actions.

solution 3 Mulch in the paths

Bare soils – such as those in open pathways – are ideal habitats for weeds. If weed seeds aren't already in the soil, wind, water and passing birds and animals will deposit them and they will soon germinate.

Mulch is the best way around this problem. Depending on the garden, you can use a living mulch, such as a low-white Dutch clover, which you can keep mowed through the season, or cover the path with a more traditional mulch, such as straw or cocoa shells.

COMMON BIENNIAL WEEDS

Biennials take two years to complete their life cycles. They generally grow a basal rosette of leaves during the first season and send up a seed stock during the second. Like annuals, they produce huge numbers of seeds, so it is equally important to get them out of your garden as soon as you see their first leaves.

Arctium minus (burdock)
Conium maculatum (hemlock)
Daucus carota (Queen Anne's lace, wild carrot)
Dipsacus fullonum (teasel)
Lamium amplexicaule (henbit, deadnettle)
Senecio jacobaea (common ragwort)
Silene alba (white campion)
Verbascum blattaria (moth mullein); *V. thapsus* (great mullein)

Sonchus oleraceus (smooth sow thistle)

Stellaria (chickweed)

COMMON COVER CROPS

Crop	Season to plant	Effects	Notes
Alfalfa	Early spring	Adds nitrogen and organic matter; suppresses weeds	Expensive; leave in place 18 months to get value for your money
Buckwheat	Early to late summer	Suppresses weeds; adds phosphorus	Use anytime you have a 40-day window of bare soil and no frost.
Hairy vetch	Spring to autumn	Adds nitrogen and organic matter; suppresses weeds	Plant in 1:2 ratio with winter rye to get maximum benefits
Low-white Dutch clover	Early spring	Adds nitrogen and organic matter; suppresses weeds	Use on pathways for living mulch
Oats	Early spring to autumn	Suppresses weeds; adds organic matter	Not hardy; use in fall and let die over winter
Red clover	Late spring to summer	Adds nitrogen and organic matter; suppresses weeds	Grows tall; leave in place one year
Winter rye	Late summer to autumn	Kills many weed seedlings	Turn under when 20–30cm (8–12 inches); do not allow to go to seed

solution 4 Try a herbicide

Conventional herbicides kill more than weeds – they also kill micro-organisms in the soil where they are applied. As a consequence, gardeners who are trying to build soil health have had to find other ways to control their weeds. However, within the last few years, several products have come out that kill weeds more benignly.

Herbicides made of fatty acids (basically soaps) are effective against young annual weeds. They kill only the leaves they touch, so you can apply them to weeds growing up around established plants. But because they are so gentle, they don't kill perennials, so if you are concerned about your garden environment you will have pull or dig those out.

Corn gluten is another new product that helps to control weeds. Apply it to the soil just as early spring shrubs are blooming. The gluten kills seeds as they germinate. It can't discriminate between weeds and seeds you planted, so apply it with care. Because it is a by-product of corn syrup production, it adds nutrients to soils while it also kills germinating seeds.

An old-fashioned weed-killer, ordinary cider vinegar, is useful in some situations. Use it in the small cracks between paving and bricks or in a band close to the edging strip of a lawn or flower bed. It does kill some micro-organisms that come into contact with it, but damage is so slight that you don't need to worry about it if you apply it only to small spots.

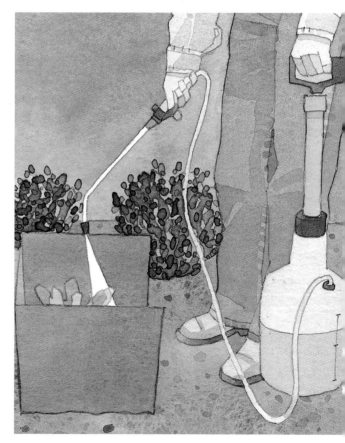

Direct herbicide sprays carefully.

problem

Perennial weeds sneak into the flower beds

Perennial weeds can be extremely difficult to eliminate. Because of the way most of them reproduce vegetatively, you don't want even to consider tilling them. After all, it only takes a little bit of a root for most of them to regrow. You will soon discover that you will have to get rid of them entirely if you don't want them to overrun your flowerbeds and other garden areas.

Early control is even more important with these plants than it is with annuals because the roots tend to grow more tenaciously into the soil. Check your perennial beds every few days during the early spring so you can pull out any weeds that appear as soon as they emerge from the soil. This early attention will pay you back in many weed-free hours later in the season.

Solution 1 Dig them up

Once a perennial weed becomes established, you will probably have to dig out its root system to get rid of it. But before you do, use a long thin spade or spading fork to really explore its root system. You will be frustrated if you go to the trouble of digging out a perennial weed only to see it reappear in a few weeks, so it's best to know what you are dealing with from the beginning.

Some weeds, such as the docks, have long, tough taproots. Others, such as bindweed, have roots that spread for many metres in all directions. Take the time to find and remove the whole root, no matter what type it is.

Sometimes weeds grow close to a treasured ornamental, wrapping their roots around its roots. You can't get rid of a weed like this by simply pulling and tugging. Instead, you will have to lift your plant and carefully remove the weed's roots before replanting the ornamental.

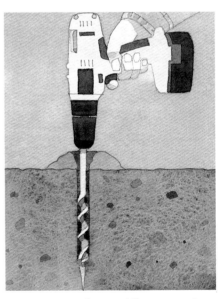

Above Many people use a drill to remove the long taproots of some perennial weeds.

Left *Stellaria* (chickweed) can blanket the ground.

See also: **'The garden is in an urban area', page 66; 'Low fertility soil', page 94, 'Plants won't bloom', page 150**

COMMON PERENNIAL WEEDS

Achillea millefolium (yarrow)	*Oxalis stricta* (wood sorrel)
Aegopodium podagraria (ground elder)	*Phytolacca americana* (pokeweed)
Allium spp. (wild garlic, wild onion)	*Plantago* spp. (plantain)
Artemisia vulgaris (mugwort)	*Prunella vulgaris* (self heal)
Asclepias syriaca (milkweed)	*Pueraria lobata* (kudzu)
Barbarea vulgaris (wintercress)	*Rhus radicans* (poison ivy); *R. toxicodendron* (poison oak)
Calystegia sepium (hedge bindweed)	*Rosa multiflora* (multiflora rose)
Cichorium intybus (chicory)	*Rumex acetosella* (sheep's sorrel); *R. crispus* (curled dock)
Cirsium arvense (creeping thistle); *C. vulgare* (spear thistle)	*Saponaria officinalis* (bouncing bet, soapwort)
Convolvulus arvensis (bindweed)	*Silene alba* (white campion)
Cyperus esculentus (yellow nutsedge)	*Solidago* spp. (goldenrod)
Equisetum arvense (field horsetail)	*Tanacetum vulgare* (tansy)
Glechoma hederacea (ground ivy)	*Taraxacum officinale* (dandelion)
Grasses, many species	*Tussilago farfara* (colt's-foot)
Hieracium spp. (hawkweed)	*Urtica dioica* (stinging nettle)
Hypericum perforatum (St John's wort)	*Verbena stricta* (hoary vervain)
Lythrum salicaria (purple loosestrife)	*Vernonia altissima* (tall ironweed)

solution 2 Spot-apply herbicides

Herbicides can be a last-resort remedy for difficult weed problems. Remember that you can correct whatever ecological disturbance the herbicide creates by applying 2.5cm (1 inch) or so of compost to the area and keeping it covered with an organic mulch. Before long, microbial populations will be as high as they ever were. This doesn't mean that you should just spray herbicides all over your yard, however. Instead, apply them only to the leaves of the weeds. If the weeds are growing close to other plants, use a paintbrush to apply the herbicide. Wear rubber gloves and a mask.

problem
Basal rot in bulbs

The first symptoms of basal rot (*Fusarium* spp.) can be subtle: Leaves and blossoms are small and sickly looking and then begin to yellow. If you do nothing about the disease, the plants will die. You won't notice this until the following year when bulbs fail to emerge from the soil. However, if you investigate when leaves look unhealthy, you will find that the bulb is rotting, generally from the base.

solution Prevent problems

Fusarium fungi move into susceptible plants through small wounds, bruises and cuts. Consequently, you can usually avoid problems by buying only healthy, uninjured bulbs and handling them carefully from purchase to planting.

Basal rot won't necessarily infect every bulb in a mass planting. If some of the plants in an area look unhealthy, take the time to dig them up. Inspect the bulbs carefully, discard any that look diseased, and replant those that are healthy.

Protect bulbs from basal rot.

problem
Aster yellows

Aster yellows affects many ornamentals as well as vegetables, ranging from carrots to strawberries. Symptoms vary according to the host plant but usually include growth distortions, excessive growth of secondary roots, and pale or discoloured growth. Leafhoppers transmit this disease, generally carrying it from its winter host plants – woody perennials – to both annuals and perennials in your garden.

Solution   Prevent problems

Fleece row covers offer the best protection for plants susceptible to aster yellows. This solution is suitable in the vegetable garden, where fleece isn't visually objectionable, but it doesn't work in ornamental areas. Because leafhoppers have to carry the disease from one plant to another, the first step in prevention is monitoring your garden and hedgerows for signs of the disease. Remove any plant that looks infected. Even if the plant has another disease, you will still be doing your garden a favour by getting rid of an infected plant. Second, try to control leafhoppers as directed on page 163.

A calendula affected by aster yellows.

See also: **'Leafhoppers', page 163; 'Cover the plants', page 167**

problem
Bacterial wilt

Bacterial wilt (*Erwinia* spp., *Pseudomonas* spp.) can seem mysterious. The first symptom is wilting in one area of the plant in the afternoon. The next morning, the plant looks fine and the wilting is gone. But by that afternoon, the plant has wilted again. This cycle repeats itself for a few days. The area of wilting gradually increases, and the first tissue that was infected browns and dies. Eventually, the whole plant may die.

Bacterial wilt diseases live in the vascular system of the plant. Leaves wilt because the bacteria become so numerous that they plug up the vascular system and the leaf can't get water or nutrients.

solution   Prevent problems

Avoidance is the best policy when it comes to wilt diseases. Begin by choosing disease-free seed and wilt-resistant cultivars. Then, cover all susceptible plants with fleece when you first transplant or plant them. You will have to remove the fleece from squash when the plants bloom so that insects can pollinate them. Once you do this, cucumber beetles can transmit the disease, so most people make two or three plantings a season of susceptible crops, including courgettes and cucumbers.

To avoid problems with the bacteria that cause wilt on tomato family crops, make sure you rotate their location in the garden so that four years will go by before they are in the same spot again.

See also: **'Cucumber beetles', page 162; 'Flea beetles', page 158**

problem
Botrytis blight, grey mould

One or another of these fungi, *Botrytis allii* or *B. cinerea*, can infect almost every plant you grow. On plants with soft flowers, such as geraniums and begonias, botrytis usually begins as a rot on the wilted blooms. If they are lying on a leaf below, the disease rapidly spreads to the leaf and then to the rest of the plant. Tiny, water-soaked spots are the first symptoms on leaves, stems, and fruit, but it doesn't take long for a fuzzy gray mold to begin growing from the enlarging spots.

solution 1 Prevent problems

You're likely to see more botrytis on annuals than perennials.

Botrytis fungi overwinter on plant material that they infected and killed during the summer. As soon as spring comes, they form spores. Wind, water, dirty tools, and even your hands carry the spores to new plants. But gray mold fungi don't infect healthy tissue; they need a wound, bruise, or dying tissue to enter a plant.

Prevention is largely a matter of keeping plants healthy and the environment unfriendly to these fungi. Work to improve soil drainage in any boggy areas; if you cannot do this, choose plants that prefer moist ground to grow in these spots. In the rest of the garden, space plants to allow maximum air circulation because spores germinate best in humid conditions. Remove old leaves and flowers from plants before they rot, even those lying on the soil surface. If you see any grey mould, pick off the infected tissue immediately. Spray compost tea on susceptible plants every two or three weeks during the growing season; compounds in the tea kill botrytis spores as they germinate.

problem
Crown gall

The bacterial disease crown gall (*Agrobacterium tumefasciens*) affects many perennial plants, but it is most troublesome on roses, fruit trees, brambles grapes, beets, turnips, and tomatoes. The first symptom is a general look of ill health. Leaves yellow and wilt, and some branches may begin to die back. If you see these symptoms, remember to check the stem or trunk near the soil line. Crown gall bacteria live in the roots and crown of a plant, exuding chemicals that stimulate abnormal growth—the lumpy, irregularly shaped galls that form just above and below the soil line.

solution 1 Prevent problems

Crown gall is so ugly that it's unforgettable.

Crown gall bacteria live in infected roots but can also survive in the soil without a host for several years. Soil water carries the bacteria along. When they come into contact with a root of a susceptible plant, they can enter it through wounds, bruises, and even natural openings.

Prevent problems by excluding infected plants from your yard. Examine roots closely before introducing a plant to your soil. If you see any irregular formations, no matter how small and insignificant they seem, don't plant it.

When you plant highly susceptible species, such as brambles and roses, take advantage of a biological control, the bacterium *Agrobacterium radiobacter*, which preys on the crown gall species. Make up a solution of the bacteria and soak the roots in it before planting.

solution 2 Control problems

Agrobacterium radiobacter and other organisms that live in a well-made compost kill crown gall bacteria, but the best control is prevention. However, there is one control measure you can take if you catch the disease when infection is slight.

Dig up the infected plant, taking as much of the root system as you can. Wash it off and inspect it closely for signs of infection. Prune out all diseased tissue, cutting back to healthy growth and dipping your tools in a solution of *Agrobacterium radiobacter* between cuts. To make doubly sure that you have removed all the disease organisms, dig out even more of the soil in the area where the plant grew and fill the hole with a mix containing a high proportion of well-made compost. Replant, backfilling with a compost mixture, and watch the plant carefully for signs of the disease. If it recurs, remove the plant and grow a nonsusceptible species in its place.

problem
Damping-off and root rot

Damping-off diseases, which are caused by many fungal species, attack plants as they are germinating and while they are tiny seedlings. The organisms that cause these diseases are in all environments. Even if you sterilize a soil mix, spores for one of these diseases can travel through the air to reinfect the medium.

Many of the same disease organisms that cause damping-off diseases cause root rot. The difference is one of location. Damping-off diseases are most likely to attack plants in seed trays, but root rot attacks them in the garden.

solution Prevent problems

Damping-off and root rot diseases are most likely to strike in humid conditions, when soil drainage or air circulation is poor. Plant only in fast-draining media and soils, and space plants so air can circulate freely around them. If you are starting seeds inside and damping-off has been a problem, set up an oscillating fan to blow air over the trays as seedlings germinate. If root rot has been a problem, wait to plant susceptible plants until the soil has had a chance to dry in spring.

The soil may have been too wet for these crowded lettuce seedlings.

solution 2 Control problems

Chamomile tea kills some of the damping-off organisms, so many people water seed trays with it. While this treatment might be effective, be cautious about relying on it. When plants are infected by damping-off fungi, some of their stem tissue is injured. You can often see this damage, wire stem, as a slight indentation just at the soil line. Therefore, although you might be able to halt the spread of the disease with chamomile tea, the plant will never regain the lost tissue and will never be as vigorous as an uninfected plant. It is usually wiser to throw out infected plants than try to save them.

Compost contains organisms that kill many of the pathogenic species that cause root rot and damping-off. In early spring, apply about 2.5cm (1 inch) of fully finished compost to garden areas that have hosted these diseases.

It may take a year or two to see results, but disease populations will decline as the beneficial organisms increase.

problem
Rust

There are many rust fungi, including *Puccinia* spp. and *Uromyces* spp., and they typically have complicated life cycles. Many of them, such as cedar-apple rust, must prey on more than one host to develop from a spore to a spore-bearing organism. Some of these organisms produce as many as five different types of spore forms, too.

Rusts are easy to diagnose once they have developed because they produce brightly colored spots on the leaf undersides of at least one of their hosts. The spots can be rust coloured, but they are also sometimes yellow, red, or orange.

solution 1   Prevent problems

Good cultural care helps to prevent rust problems. Water early in the day, space plants so air circulates freely, and plant only in well-drained soils. Balanced nutrition is particularly important because some rusts attack plants with the sappy growth that excess nitrogen produces.

An example of rust affecting a plant.

solution 2   Control problems

When rust strikes an annual plant, pull it and dispose of it in a hot compost pile or a trash bag destined for the landfill. For perennials, the best control is sulfur. Pick off infected leaves and then spray; the sulfur won't kill the rust organisms once they have developed, but it does kill spores.

problem
Scab

Scab (*Cladosporium cucumerinum, Streptomyces scabies*) is a disease of vegetable crops. Cucumbers, beets, cabbages, carrots, aubergines, spinach, onions, parsnips, potatoes and turnips are all susceptible.

Scab infections are well named because the spots on most plants look like scabs, whether they are on the roots or the above-ground parts of the plant. On leaves of members of the squash family, the spots are angular and don't look scabby, but the disease spreads quickly to make scabby-looking spots on cucumbers or rotting areas at the stem ends of melons.

solution   Prevent problems

Resistant cultivars of many vegetables are commonly available, and it is worth choosing them when possible. For potatoes, check planting stock carefully and discard any potatoes with scabby spots.

The scab that infects crops other than cucurbits is encouraged by alkaline soil. If possible, keep soils at a pH of 5.5 or so, particularly in areas where you are growing potatoes. Apply 13–25mm (1 inch) of compost before planting, too, because it contains organisms that prey on those that cause scab. Finally, practise rotations of at least four years to avoid problems.

Potato crops are susceptible to scab.

problem
Downy mildew

Downy mildew is caused by a number of fungi, most of them species-specific. They are grouped together because they cause symptoms that look similar and because they behave in much the same way, even if they are different organisms. These diseases attack leaves first, creating pale or yellow spots on the upper sides. Spores form on the lower sides of the leaves and may be purplish, white, grey, or a light blue-grey colour. Infected tissue eventually withers and drops. On fruit, you will see a purplish or white mould on the skin, which gradually spreads.

solution 1 Prevent problems

Some of the fungi that cause downy mildew overwinter on plant tissue that they infected the previous season. Others form resting spores in infected tissue and can live in the soil without a host for some years. Regularly removing all diseased and dying plant debris from the garden goes a long way toward eliminating the problem.

All of the organisms responsible for these diseases can germinate in only a film of water. Keep air circulation high, make sure soil mixes are well drained, and water early in the day so that plants dry by nightfall.

Some vegetable cultivars are resistant to downy mildew; choose them whenever possible.

solution 2 Control problems

Bordeaux mixture kills most of the organisms that cause downy mildew. While it is never worth spraying vegetable crops with Bordeaux mixture, it's wise to use it on perennials, such as grapes, if the disease strikes. Bordeaux mixture can injure delicate plant tissue; test it on a few leaves before spraying the whole plant and wait five days to check for damage. If the leaves are uninjured, spray the plant at weekly intervals and just before rain to kill downy mildew spores.

problem
Fusarium wilt

This wilt is caused by species of *Fusarium*, that live in regions without prolonged periods of below-freezing temperatures in the winter. As you can guess from the common name, wilting is the first symptom of this disease.

Fusarium fungi colonize the vascular tissues of a plant. They secrete a toxin that kills the cells, releasing nutrients for the fungus to feed on. Because this disease enters plants through roots and wounds, the wilting may be localized on one side or area of the plant at first, but as the disease spreads the whole plant may be affected.

A wide range of plants, including spring bulbs, vegetables, annual and perennial ornamentals, and even trees, can host *Fusarium* wilt.

solution 1 Prevent problems

Good soil drainage and air circulation discourage this disease. Add compost to the soil, space plants well, and water early in the day. In addition, both potassium deficiencies and nitrogen excesses seem to encourage the problem. Test soils frequently and adjust nutrient levels accordingly.

Some vegetable cultivars have been bred to be resistant to this disease, and you should choose them whenever possible. When you are buying bulbs, check to make certain that there are no soft spots. Inspect the roots of other perennials thoroughly to make sure that you do not plant anything with roots that look as if they might be infected.

solution 2 Control problems

The only control for *Fusarium* wilt is removal. If plants become infected, you will need to dig them up and discard them. Take as much of the surrounding soil as possible because it's likely to be infected with the disease spores. Replace it with a mix that contains high quantities of compost. If possible, don't replant the area for a season so that you do not give the remaining spores a new host right away.

Ψ ⁀ᑕᙣ ◑ ▯ 𝌆

Plants suffering from *Fusarium* wilt droop in any soil.

problem
Leaf spot

Like damping-off and downy mildew, leaf spot diseases are actually caused by a number of different fungal and bacteria organisms. They are grouped together only because they all cause spots on leaves and most of them respond to the same sorts of preventive and control measures.

Leaf spot diseases attack trees, fruit plants, perennials, annuals, grasses, herbs, and vegetables. In short, if a plant has leaves, it's likely that one or another organism creates spots on them when it attacks.

solution 1 Prevent problems

Good cultural care gives plants more resistance to all diseases, but this is particularly so when it comes to leaf spots. Space plants well, keep air circulation high, test soil and adjust nutrient levels accordingly, water early in the day, and take care not to touch plants when you are working around them. It's also important to stay out of the garden when plants are wet from dew or rain, because just brushing against them can spread these diseases.

Compost tea, sprayed on plants at intervals of a week to ten days, will kill or disable the spores for many of the leaf spot diseases. Begin your spraying program well before you see problems; it may prevent them so well that you will never know if it is effective or not.

Ψ ⁀ᑕᙣ ◔ ▯ 𝌆

solution 2 Control problems

Depending on the plant species, sulfur, copper, and Bordeaux mixture will control leaf spot diseases. Check the label on each of these preparations to see if the plant you are trying to protect is listed. Spray as directed on the bottle, but remember not to spray in bright light conditions.

Ψ ⁀ᑕᙣ ◔ ▯ 𝌆

Leaf spot diseases range in severity from mild to devastating.

problem
Mosaic diseases

Various viruses cause mottled leaves, usually with fairly sharply demarked areas of yellow or pale green. Leaves may also be puckered or otherwise deformed, and the plants may be stunted. Some plants develop unnaturally brittle stems that break easily.

Plants ranging from ornamentals to vegetables are susceptible to mosaic diseases, but you are most likely to see them on tomatoes, cucumbers, brambles, and roses.

solution 1 Prevent problems

Cucumber mosaic virus.

Small sucking insects, such as aphids and leafhoppers, frequently transmit viruses from one plant to another. Wherever possible, use row covers to protect plants early in the season. Encourage beneficial insects, too, by growing the plants that feed them during the adult stage of their lifecycles.

Resistant cultivars of many vegetables are widely available, and it is worth looking for them while you are shopping for plants or seeds. When you are buying plants, inspect the leaves carefully and pass over any that look diseased.

solution 2 Control problems

The only good control for a virus disease is eradication. If any plants display symptoms, harden your heart and pull them out. No matter how painful this is, leaving them in place where they will be a source of viral material to transmit to other plants will be even more painful.

Many viruses, including those that cause mosaics, can survive the temperatures in a hot compost pile. When you remove infected plants, either bury them far away from your cultivated plants or put them in a trash bag and send them to the local landfill. Remember to wash your hands after touching infected plants, too, and sterilize any tools that may have come into contact with them.

Sometimes the only way to deal with mosaic diseases is to pull out the plant.

See also: **"Attract biological controls," page 156**

GLOSSARY

Acid soil A soil that is below 7 on the pH scale. Acid soils generally occur in high rainfall areas.

Alkaline soil A soil that is above 7 on the pH scale. Alkaline soils generally occur in low rainfall areas or where the bedrock is limestone.

Beneficial insects (Sometimes called Beneficial Controls.) Insects that prey on pest insects.

Bordeaux Mixture A fungicide made by mixing lime, copper sulfate, and water together.

Botanical controls Pesticides and herbicides manufactured or derived from a botanical substance.

Cation A positively charged ion.

Chilling hours The number of hours below 7°C (45°F) that a plant requires to break dormancy in the spring.

Collar The slight bulge where a branch grows from the trunk or branch on a tree or shrub.

Compost tea A spray that protects against many diseases and which can also act as a fertilizer or stimulate the growth of soil organisms. Soak a quart of compost in 5 gallons of water for 5 to 10 days to make a disease-preventive tea. Use teas in which the compost has soaked for a longer time as fertilizers and soil stimulants.

Cultivar A plant variety that breeders have modified from the parent stock, often by crossing two or more varieties of the same species. Technically, a cultivar must be a cultivated variety.

Cucurbits Members of the squash family, including all types of winter and summer squash, including pumpkins, as well as cucumbers and all melons.

Deadhead To remove faded flowers from plants before they set seed.

Divide To separate a plant – roots, crown, stems – into two or more pieces.

Fish emulsion A fertilizer made from waste products from fish. Some fish emulsions are fermented.

Fertilizer A material used primarily to provide nutrients to plants. Fertilizers can be 'organic' or 'synthetic'.

Flowers of sulfur Finely ground, 100 percent sulfur, used to acidify soil and sometimes as a fungicide.

Foliar feed A nutrient source that is sprayed on the foliage of a plant rather than the soil in which it is growing.

Friable A term used to describe a soil with an easily penetrated structure. Friable soils contain spaces for both air and water.

Genus The plant classification that includes species that are related by common characteristics such as flower shape or seed formation.

Graft To attach a part from one plant to another plant. For example, breeders commonly graft selected rose cultivars onto hardy rootstocks.

Green manure A crop grown for the purpose of adding nutrients to the soil.

Greensand A naturally occurring sedimentary deposit that contains large quantities of glauconite, a mineral that contains iron potassium silicate. Used to add potassium to a soil.

Hardy A descriptive term meaning that a plant is able to survive temperatures of 3°C (32°F) or lower.

Hardiness Zone The U.S. and Canada are both divided into geographic regions, or hardiness zones, according to their average minimum winter temperatures. Plants are rated as being hardy to particular zones.

Hardscaping A term used to describe constructed garden features ranging from stone paths and walls to wooden trellises and arbors.

Hybrid A plant with two parents that belong to different varieties, species, or in some cases, genera.

Insecticidal soap A fatty acid sold as a pesticide that kills insects by clogging their breathing holes and suffocating them or eroding their cell walls.

Ion An atom or group of atoms that has lost or gained one or more electrons and as a consequence, carries a positive or negative electric charge.

Leaf mould Decomposed leaves from hardwood trees.

Microclimate The climate in a local area. One yard may have several different microclimates as a consequence of such things as slopes, buildings, or windbreaks.

Mycelium A group of the hyphae, or strands, that make up the body of a fungus. The mycelium of powdery mildew may be visible on a leaf surface, but most fungal pathogens grow inside plant tissues.

Neem A tree in India from which a pesticide is manufactured. Neem is a botanical pesticide that legislation allows organic growers to use.

Organic Technically, a living or dead material that contains carbon. The word is used by gardeners to mean that a substance is derived from once-living organisms and by farmers and the government to mean that a substance or technique is allowable under legislation that sets the standards for 'certified organic' growers.

Pathogen A microorganism that causes a disease in another organism when it preys on it.

Pea Stone A type of washed gravel that ranges between ½-inch to slightly over an inch in diameter. In gardens, it is often used for walkways and as a mulch under ornamental plantings.

pH A measure of the acid/alkaline content of a material. On this scale, 7 is neutral, that is, neither acid nor alkaline, while numbers below 7 indicate acid conditions and those over 7 indicate alkaline conditions.

Pheromones Chemical compounds that insects and animals release to attract other insects, usually as mates.

Scarify To scratch or nick a seedcoat to make it easier for water to penetrate and germination to begin. In nature, the acids in the guts or birds or other animals often scarify seeds.

Soil Amendments Materials that are applied to soils to stimulate soil life or to improve the texture, drainage, organic matter content, or fertility of the soil. They differ from fertilizers in that they generally perform more than one function.

Species The plant classification that distinguishes plants within a particular genus. One species may contain plants that are classified as subspecies, varieties, or cultivars of that species.

Stratify To expose seeds to fluctuating temperatures for varying periods of time to stimulate germination. Some seeds must be frozen for specific periods of time and some must be chilled to 5°C (40°F) or lower.

Tender The term used to describe a plant that cannot withstand freezing temperatures.

Synthetic A descriptive term frequently used for pesticides, herbicides, or fertilizers that have been manufactured from gasses or fossil fuels or, in the case of fertilizers, minerals that have been treated with strong acids to make their nutrients immediately available.

Variegated A multi-coloured leaf. Most variegations are white and yellow with green, but variegations can also be rose, magenta, purple, or silver.

Vegetative reproduction Plant reproduction from a tissue such as a root, stem, or leaf rather than that from a seed. Most perennial plants reproduce vegetatively in addition to sexually, or through seed production.

INDEX

A
Abelia x grandiflora 41, 51, 171
Abelmoschus moschatus 144, 146
Abies 77
   A. balsamea 67
Abraham's balm see Vitex agnus-castae
Abutilon theophrasti 174
Acalypha reptans 151
Acanthus
   A. mollis 49, 51
   A. spinosissimus 49
   A. spinosus 49
Acer
   A. griseum 46
   A. negundo 80
   A. platanoides 46
Achillea 14, 21, 89, 97, 143, 156
   A. clavennae 69
   A. filipendulina 51, 59
   A. millefolium 61, 178
acid soil 74, 75, 77
aconite winter see Eranthis hyemalis
Aconitum 19, 91, 171
   A. carmichaelii 145
   A. napellus 14
Acorus calamus 93
Adam's needle see Yucca filamentosum
additives for poor soils 94
Adiantum pedatum 12
Aegopodium podagraria 103
   A. p. 'Variegatum', 12, 49, 178
aeration 83, 110
Aesculus parviflora 51

Aethionema grandiflorum 69
African daisy see Arctotis acaulis
Agastache foeniculum 171
Ageratum houstonianum 171
   A. h. 'Blue Blazer', 151
Agrobacterium
   A. radiobacter 181
   A. tumefasciens 181
Agrostemma githago 174
Agrostis 75
air circulation for seedlings 147
Ajuga 12, 12, 77, 91
   A. reptans 21, 39, 65, 65, 103, 171
Akebia quinata 19
Alcea rosea 80, 146
Alchemilla mollis 37, 49, 80, 87, 171
alcohol swabs for insect control 164
alfalfa 84, 84, 176
Alisma plantago-aquatica 93
alkaline soil 78–81
   plants for 80, 81
   plants indicating 78, 79
Allium 51, 61, 61, 171, 178
   A. cristophii 35
allspice Carolina see Calycanthus
alpine barrenwort see Epimedium alpinum
alpine rockcress see Alyssum montanum
Alstroemeria aurea 66
alum root see Heuchera/cvs.
aluminum foil to deter insects 156
Alyssum montanum 69
alyssum
   sweet see Lobularia maritima
   yellow see Aurinia saxatilis
amaranth globe see Gomphrena globosa
Amaranthus
   A. biltoides 174
   A. retroflexus 174
Amblyseius cucumeris 167
Ambrosia
   A. artemisifolia 174
   A. trifida 174
Amelanchier 77, 87
American columbine see Aquilegia canadensis
American euonymus see Euonymus americana
Ammi majus 142, 143
Amorpha 66
Anagallis monellii 151
Anchusa azurea cvs., 14
Anemone 51
   A. blanda 47, 49
   A. hupehensis 12, 59
   A.x hybrida 12, 59
   A. nemorosa 19, 75, 117
Anethum graveolens 156
Angelica archangelica 75
angel's trumpet see Brugmansia
animal problems 154, 169–71
anise hyssope see Agastache foeniculum
annuals
   for alkaline soils 80, 97
   cutting back 148
   deer-resistant 171
   easy-care 21
   for high heat and dry soil 66
   high-nutrition planting holes 97
   for illusion 19
   for poor soils 91, 97
   for salty soils 99
   for sandy soils 89
   for shade 49
   weeds 174–6
Anthemis
   A. cotula 174
   A. tinctoria 51
Anthriscus
   A. cerefolium 39
   A. sylvestris 79
Antirrhinum majus 66, 143, 145, 151, 171
aphids 156–7
apples 139
apricots 138–9
Aquilegia 47, 49, 67, 80, 80, 142, 143,

145, 171
rabis 39, 69
ralia five-leaved *see Akebia quinata*
rctium minus, 175
rctostaphylos uva-ursi 61, 65, 77
rctotis acaulis 66
risaema 91
 A. triphyllum 12, 49, 117, 143
ristolochia macrophylla 19
rmeria 21, 57, 99, 143, 144
 A. juniperifolia 69
 A. maritima 69, 99, 171
 A. plumbaginaceae 65
 A. pseudarmeria 14, 42, 63
rmyworms 119, *119*
rrowhead see Sagittaria sagittifolia
rtemesia 89, 97, 143
 A. absinthium 42, 51
 A. 'Silver Brocade', 151, *151*
 A. 'Silver Mound', *151*, 151
 A. stellariana 65
 A. vulgaris 178
rum see Arisaema; Arum
 bog *see Calla palustris*
Arum italicum 'Pictum', 57
runcus sylvester 19
Asarum caudatum 116, 117
sclepias
 A. syriaca 178
 A. tuberosa 14, 51, 61, 77, 89, 97, 143, 171
sh mountain *see Sorbus acuparia*
Asplenium scolopendrium 12
aster see Aster
 china *see Callistephus chinensis*
Aster 89, 99, 156
 A. x frikartii 61
 A. novae-angliae 61
 A. novi-belgii 61
ster yellows 179
Astilbe 50, 91, 171
 A. arendsii 12, 47
Astrantia
 A. major 51
 A. maxima 51
Athyrium filix-femina 12
Aubrieta deltoidea 57
Aurinia saxatilis 57
autumn color 35
avens see Geum
azalea 11
 see also *Rhododendron*

B
baby blue eyes *see Nemophila menziesii*
baby's breath *see Gypsophila paniculata*
Baccharis halimifolia 63
bachelor's buttons *see Centaura cyanus*
Bacillus
 B. popilliae 118, 162
 B. thuringensis 92, 159, 160
bacterial wilt 179
bagasse mulch 80
balloon flower *see Platycodon grandiflorus*
balsam *see Abies balsamea*
bamboo 32, 59
Baptisia 146, 171
 B. australis 19, 51, 61, 66, 87
Barbarea vulgaris 178
bare strips 38
bark
 chips 21, 54, 80
 shredded 80
barrenwort *see Epimedium x versicolor*
 alpine *see Epimedium alpinum*
barriers
 against cutworms 160
 against salt and wind 62
basal rot 178
Bassia scoparia 19
bats 92
bayberry *see Myrica pensylvanica*
beach heather *see Hudsonia tomentosa*
beach plum *see Prunus maritima*
beakrush white *see Rhynchospora alba*

bean beetles Mexican 157
bearberry red *see Arctostaphylos uva-ursi*
beard tongue *see Penstemon hirsutus*
bear's breeches *see Acanthus mollis*
beauty berry *see Callicarpa bodinieri*
beauty bush *see Kolkwitzia amabalis*
beds 13, 26, 27, 42, *43*, 52
beebalm *see Monarda didyma*
beech European *see Fagus sylvatica*
beer traps 165
beetles 158, 162-3
beggar's ticks *see Bidens ferulifolia*
Begonia 67, 143
 B. semperflorens 171
 B. semperflorens-cultorum hybrids 49
 B. x tuberhybrida 49, 171
bellflower *see Campanula*
Bellis perennis 37
bells of Ireland *see Molucella laevis*
bentgrass common *see Agrostis*
Berberis 33, 71, 87, 89, 171
 B. thunbergii 35, 57, 80, *81*, 97
bergamot *see Monarda didyma*
Bergenia 12, 12, 39, 80, 87
 B. cordifolia 57
 B. 'Sunningdale', 36
berms 90
Bermuda grass *see Cynodon dactylon*
Betula pendula 46, 67
Bidens
 B. bipinnata 174
 B. ferulifolia 66
 B. frondosa 174
biennials 49, 174–6
billbugs 119
bindweed *see Convolvulus arvensis*
 hedge *see Calystegia sepium*
biological controls for insects 156
birch silver *see Betula pendula*
bird problems 168
bishop's mitre *see Epimedium x versicolor*
bishop's weed *see Ammi majus*
bittercress *see Cardamine*
black cohosh *see Cimicifuga racemosa*
blackberries 139
black currants 139
black-eyed Susan *see Rudbeckia hirta*
blanket flower *see Gaillardia grandiflora*
bleeding heart *see Dicentra*
blight 180
bloodroot *see Sanguinaria canadensis*
blooming problems 130–7
bluebell *see Hyacinthoides*
 Spanish *see Hyacinthoides hispanica*
 Virginia *see Mertensia virginica*
blueberry 139, see also *Vaccinium*
bog arum *see Calla palustris*
bog gardens 93
bog sage *see Salvia ulginosa*
bog sedge *see Carex oligosperma*
Boltonia asteroides 61
Bordeaux mixture 183
borders narrow 38
Boston ivy *see Parthenocissus tricuspidata*
botrytis blight 180
bottle gourd *see Lagenaria siceraria*
bottlebrush buckeye *see Aesculus parvi-flora*
bouncing Bet *see Saponaria officinalis*
box mountain *see Arctostaphylos uva-ursi; Berberis*
box elder *see Acer negundo*
boxwood *see Buxus*
boysenberries 139
Brachyscome cvs. 151
braconid wasps 156
Bracteantha bracteata 66, 142, 143, 171
bramble *see Rubus*
Brassica
 B. hirta 39
 B. juncea 84
 B. kaber 174
 B. napus 84
 B. nigra 174
 B. rapa var. *nipponsinica* 39
bridal wreath *see Spiraea*

broom *see Cytisus*
 Spanish *see Spartium junceum*
Browallia 143
brown patch *121*, 121
Brugmansia 19, 66, 146, 171
Brunnera macrophylla 49
brush piles as hiding places 169
buckeye bottlebrush *see Aesculus parvi-flora*
buckthorn sea *see Hippophae rhamnoides*
buckwheat hulls 54, 176
Buddleja davidii 42, 66, 80, *80*, 89, 171
bugle *see Ajuga*
bugloss *see Anchusa azurea*
bulbs 37, 42, 47, 49, 171, 178
bulrush *see Typha*
Bupleurum 63, 145
burdock *see Arctium minus*
burning bush *see Dictamnus*
burr oak *see Quercus macrocarpa*
bush groundsel *see Baccharis halimifolia*
bush violet *see Browallia*
busy Lizzie *see Impatiens*
Butomus umbellatus 93
butterfly verbena *see Verbena bonariensis*
butterfly weed *see Asclepias tuberosa*
Buxus 33, 171

C
cactus prickly pear *see Opuntia compressa*
Caladium x hortulanum 49
Calamintha 66
calcitic lime additions 76
Calendula officinalis 21, 67, 143, 151
California lilac *see Ceanothus*
California poppy *see Eschscholzia californica*
Calla palustris 91, 93
Callicarpa bodinieri 35
Callistephus chinensis 67
Calluna vulgaris 35, 59, 63, 69, 77, 89, 93, 171
Caltha palustris 93
Calycanthus 19
 C. floridus 171
Calystegia sepium 178
Camellia japonica 49
Campanula 61
 C. carpatica 14, 57, 99
 C. persicifolia 19, 61
 C. rotundifolia 75
campion
 red *see Silene dioica*
 rose *see Lychnis coronaria*
Campsis grandiflora 16
candleberry *see Myrica pensylvanica*
candytuft *see Iberis sempervirens*
Canna x generalis 144, 146, 171
Capsella bursa-pastoris 174
Caragana arborescens 66
caraway *see Carum carvi*
Cardamine 91
cardboard mulch 54
cardinal flower *see Lobelia cardinalis*
 blue *see Lobelia siphilitica*
Carex
 C. aquitilis 93
 C. grayi 93
 C. oligosperma 93
carnivorous plants 92
Caroline geranium *see Geranium carolinianum*
carpetweed *see Mollugo verticillata*
carrot wild *see Dauca carota*
Carum carvi 156
Carya illinoiensis 77
Caryopteris clandonensis 51
castor oil plant *see Ricinus communis*
Catalpa 80
Catananche caerulea 66
caterpillars 159
Catharantus rosea 143
catmint *see Nepeta hederacea*
catnip *see Nepeta cataria*
cat's tail *see Acalypha reptans*
Ceanothus 63

cedar mulch 21, 54, 70
Cedrus 77
celandine lesser *see Ranunculus ficaria*
Celosia 89, 143
Celtis 80
Centaurea 97
 C. cyanus 16, 21, 89, 156
 C. macrocephala 21
Centranthus ruber 21, 51, 63
Cerastium tomentosum 97, 171
Ceratostigma plumbaginoides 14, 116
Cercis canadensis 51
Chaenomeles 89
 C. japonica 171
 C. speciosa 41
chalcid wasps 156
Chamaecyparis 63, *63*
 C. obtusa 69
 C. o. 'Nana', 59
Chamaedaphne calyculata 93
Chamaemelum nobile 156
chamomile *see Chamaemelum nobile;
 Anthemis tinctoria*
 false *see Boltonia asteroides*
 stinking *see Anthemis cotula*
chamomile tea for damping-off 181
Chasmanthium latifolium 63
chaste tree *see Vitex agnus-castus*
checkerberry *see Gaultheria procumbens*
Chelone 14, 19
Chelone glabra 93
Chenopodium
 C. album 174
 C. bonus-henricus 79, *79*
cherries 138–9
cherry Cornelian *see Cornus mas*
chervil 39
chickweed *see Stellaria media*
chicory *see Cichorium intybus*
Chinese fringe tree *see Chionanthus
 retusus*
Chinese lanterns *see Phyalis alkekengi*
Chionanthus retusus 51
Chionodoxa 49, 171
chitin for nematode control 161
Christmas rose *see Helleborus niger*
Chrysanthemum 67, 77, 80
Chrysogonum virginianum 116
Cichorium intybus 78, 79, 178
cider vinegar herbicide 176
Cimicifuga 171
 C. racemosa 50
cinch bugs 120
cinnamon clethra *see Clethra acuminata*
cinquefoil *see Potentilla*
circular beds 42, 43
Cirsium
 C. arvense 178
Cistus 89
 C. vulgare 178
citrus fruit 139
Cladosporium cucumerinum 187
Clarkia 135
clay for insect control 158
clay soil 76, 86–7
Claytonia perfoliata 39
cleavers *see Galium aparine*
Clematis 80, 145
 C. maximowicziana 42
 C. 'Rosy O'Grady', 35
 pruning 133
Cleome hassleriana 19, 21, 171
Clethra 99
 C. acuminata 91
 C. alnifolia 41, 61, 91, *91*, 97
 C. spinosa 99
climbing plants 19, 35, 36
 styles *31*
Clintonia umbellatus 117
clover 84, 176
Cobaea scandens 19
cocoa shells 21
cocklebur *see Xanthium pensylvanicum*
cockspur hawthorn *see Crataegus
 crus-galli*
cocoa bean hulls 54, 83

coffee grounds mulch 80
cold gardens 60–1
coleus *see Coleus; Solenostemon*
Coleus x *hybridus* 49
colour 10, *16*, 16, *17*, 28, 29, 35, 48
coloured traps 167
colts'-foot *see Tussilago farfara*
columbine *see Aquilegia*
companion planting for bulbs 37
compost 54, 83, 95, 107, 111, 129
coneflower *see Echinacea; Rudbeckia*
Conium maculatum 174
Consolida 142, 143, 145
containers 57, 92, 148–53
    see also hanging baskets
Convallaria majalis 12, 21, 49, 77, 116,
    171
Convolvulus 97
    C. arvensis 178
cool gardens increasing temperature 135
copper wire to control slugs and snails
    166
coral gem *see Lotus berthelotii*
Coreopsis 66, 99, 156
    C. basalis 21, 89
    C. lanceolata 97
    C. verticillata 21, 51, 59, 61
Coriandrum sativum 156
corn cockle *see Agrostemma githago*
corn gluten herbicide 176
Cornelian cherry *see Cornus mas*
Cornus 77, 87
    C. alba 21
    C. canadensis 116, 117
    C. florida 67
    C. mas 36, 51
    C. sanguinea 'Winter Berry', 35
Coronilla varia 84
Corydalis 47
Cosmos 21, 80
Cotinus coggygria 19, 51, 89, 171
Cotoneaster 71, 171
    C. 'Cornubia', 49
    C. horizontalis 35, *71*
    C. lacteus 35
    C. lucidus 33
    C. salicifolia 65, *65*
cottage gardens 29
cottongrass *see Eriophorum virginicum*
courtyard *67*
cover crops 84, 175, 176
cow parsley *see Anthriscus sylvestris*
crab flowering *see Malus*
Crambe maritima 63, 66
cranberry highbush *see Viburnum
    trilobum*
cranesbill *see Geranium*
Crataegus 59, 75, 80
crazy paving 18
creeping dogwood *see Cornus canadensis*
creeping Jenny *see
    Lysimachia nummularia*
creeping snowberry *see
    Gaultheria hispidula*
creeping thistle *see Cirsium arvense*
creeping wintergreen *see Gaultheria
    procumbens*
Crepis incana 66
Crinum pedunculatum 91
Crocus 49
    C. speciosus 57
crown gall 181
crown imperial *see Fritillaria*
crownvetch *see Coronilla varia*
cuckoo flower *see Cardamine*
cucumber beetles 162
cup-and-saucer vine *see Cobaea scandens*
cupid's dart *see Catananche caerulea*
currants 139
Cuscuta pentagona 174
cutworms 119, 160
Cyclamen hederifolium 35, 117
Cynodon dactylon 79
Cyperus esculentus 178
cypress summer *see Bassia scoparia*
cypress vine *see Ipomoea*

Cyrilla racemiflora 91
Cytisus 89, 89

D
Dactylorhiza elata 93
daffodil *see Narcissus*
daikon radish *see Raphanus sativus*
daisy
    African *see Arctotis acaulis*
    English *see Bellis perennis*
    Michaelmas *see Aster* x *frikartii*
    ox-eye *see Leucanthemum vulgare*
    painted *see Tanacetum coccineum*
    swan river *see Brachyscome* cvs
dame's violet *see Hesperis matronalis*
damp gardens 49, 52–3
damping-off 147, 182
dandelion *see Taraxacum officinale*
Daphne 171
Datura stramonium 174
Daucus carota 79, 175
daylily *see Hemerocallis* cvs.
dead nettle *see Lamium maculatum*
deadheading 136, 148
deadly nightshade *see Solanum nigrum*
deer problems 170–1
Delphinium 16, 19, 61, 142, 143, 145
Dendranthemum 67, 77, 80
designing gardens 8–43
devil's beggarticks *see Bidens frondosa*
dewberries 139
Dianthus 14, 49, 67, 97, 99, 145, 151
Dicentra 14, 49
    D. spectabilis 21, 145, 171
Dictamnus albus 35, 66, 171
Diervilla lonicera 19
digging double-, 85
Digitalis 49, 143
    D. grandiflora 48, 51, 66
    D. purpurea 49, 171
dill *see Anethum graveolens*
Dioda teres 174
diseases 172, 178–87
ditches 91
dittany *see Dictamnus albus* var.
    purpureus
dock curled *see Rumex crispus*
dodder field *see Cuscuta pentagona*
dogwood *see Cornus*
    creeping *see C. canadensis*
    common *see C. sanguinea*
    Tatarian *see C. alba*
dollar spot 121
dolomitic lime additions 76
dormant oil *see* oils for insect control
Doronicum 146
double-digging 85
Douglas fir *see Pseudotsuga menziesii*
downy mildew 183
Dracocephalum 145
dragon's head *see Dracocephalum*
drainage 82, 90–1
drip irrigation 55, 57, 67, 88
Drosera 92, 93
drought-tolerant grasses 106
dry gardens 49, 54–7, 71
dusty miller *see Artemisia stellariana;
    Lychnis coronaria*
Dutchman's breeches *see Dicentra*
Dutchman's pipe vine *see
    Aristolochia macrophylla*

E
earwigs 161
Eastern trout lily *see
    Erythronium americanum*
easy-care *see* low-maintenance
eaves gardens under 70–1
Echinacea 14, 19, 21, 51, 143, 145
Echinops 14, 51, 171
edelweiss *see Leontopodium alpinum*
Egyptian star *see Pentas lanceolata*
Elaeagnus 80, 87, 89, 171
elder box *see Acer negundo*
elderberries 139, *see also* Sambucus nigra

elephant's ear *see Bergenia*
Elymus arenarius 63, 63
endophytes in grasses 120
English daisy *see Bellis perennis*
English ivy *see Hedera helix*
English primrose *see Primula vulgaris*
Epimedium 87
    E. alpinum 65
    E. x *versicolor* 'Sulphureum', 35
Epsom salts 134
Equisetum arvense 178
Equisetum scirpoides 93
Eranthis hyemalis 49, 171
Erica 39, 77, 93
    E. carnea 36, 59, 69, 69
Erigeron annuus 174
Eriophorum virginicum 93
Erwinia 179
Eryngium cvs., 14, 35, 51, 61, 145, 171
Erysimum cheiri 57
Erythronium americanum 117
Eschscholzia californica 21, 57, 67, 97, 99
Euonymus 49, 77
    E. alatus 35, 61
    E. americana 91
    E. europaeus 87
    E. fortunei 39, 65, 71
    E. japonica 33
    E. obovatus 19
    E. radicans 19
Euphorbia 91, 171
    E. characias 57
    C. c. subsp. *wulfenii* 57
    E. griffithii 142, 144, 145
    E. maculata 79, 174
    E. myrsinites 57
European beech *see Fagus sylvatica*
European white birch *see Betula pendula*
evening primrose *see Oenothera speciosa*
everlasting *see Bracteantha bracteata*
eyesores 30–3

F
Fagus sylvatica 46, 59, 80
fairy lanterns *see Disporum flavum*
fairy rings *122*, 122
false dragonhead *see
    Physostegia virginiana*
false goat's beard *see Astilbe arendsi*
false indigo *see Baptisia australis*
false spikenard *see Smilacina*
fan flower *see Scaevola aemula*
fat hen *see Chenopodium album*
Fatsia japonica 49
felt mulch 54
fences 32, 56, 61, 113, 169, 170
fern 49
    lady *see Athyrium filix-femina*
    royal *see Osmunda regale*
    sensitive *see Onoclea*
fertilizers
    for annuals 97
    for high salt levels 98
    for lawns 109
    liquid 152
    for perennials 137
    for poor soils 96
    for sandy soils 88
    types 96
    water-in 68
fescue sheep's *see Festuca ovina*
Festuca glauca 63
Festuca ovina 75
feverfew *see Tanacetum parthenium*
field dodder *see Cuscuta pentagona*
field horsetail *see Equisetum arvense*
field pennycress *see Thlaspi arvense*
figs 139
Filipendula 51, 75, 79, 91, 171
fir *see Abies*
    Douglas *see Pseudotsuga menziesii*
flag
    sweet *see Acorus calamus*
    yellow *see Iris pseudacorus*
Flashtape 168

flax *see Linum narbonense*
flea beetles 158
fleabane annual *see Erigeron annuus*
flies beneficial 156
floating row cover *see* row covers
floss flower *see Ageratum houstonianum*
flower beds *see* beds
flowering problems 130–7
foamflower *see Tiarella*
foliar feed 95
forget-me-not water *see
    Myositis scorpioides*
formal gardens 17, 28
forms tiered 13
Forsythia 21, 171
    F. intermedia 41
Fothergilla 91
    F. gardenii 21
    F. major 35
foundation plants for dry soils 71
foxglove *see Digitalis grandiflora*
Fragaria vesca 75
fraxinella *see Dictamnus albus*
fringe tree Chinese *see Chionanthus
    retusus*
Fritillaria 171
frost pockets 60
fruit 11, 38, 138–9
furniture for garden 34
fusarium blight 123
Fusarium 123, 178, 183–4

G
Gaillardia 14, 19, 21, 67, 99, 143, 151
galant soldier *see Galinsoga parviflora*
Galanthus 49, 49, 91, 171
Galinsoga parviflora 174
Galium
    G. aparine 174
    G. odoratum 39, *116*, 116, 171
garden design 8–43
garden furniture 34
garden rooms 17
Gaultheria
    G. hispidula 117
    G. procumbens 77, 116, 117, *117*
Gaura 21, 66, 97
gayfeather *see Liatris*
gazebos *34*, 51
Gentiana 69, 145
geranium rock *see Heuchera americana*
German statice *see Goniolimon tataricum*
germander *see Teucrium chamaedrys*
germination poor 142–7
Geum 14, 80, 142
ginger wild *see Asarum caudatum*
Gingko biloba 67
Glechoma hederacea 178
Gleditsia triacanthos 80, 89
globe amaranth *see Gomphrena globosa*
globe thistle *see Echinops ritro*
globeflower *see Trollius* x *cultorum*
glory of the snow *see Chionodoxa*
goat willow *see Salix caprea*
goatsbeard *see Aruncus sylvester*
gold dust *see Aurinia saxatilis*
golden glow *see Rudbeckia lacineata*
goldenrod seaside *see
    Solidago sempervirens*
Gomphrena globosa 143, 144
Goniolimon tataricum 143
good King Henry *see
    Chenopodium bonus-henricus*
gooseberries 139
goosegrass *see Galium aparine*
gourd bottle *see Lagenaria siceraria*
goutweed *see Aegopodium podagraria*
    'Variegatum'
grape hyacinth *see Muscari*
grapefruit traps 165
grapes 139
grasses as weeds 178
grasses for lawns

drought-tolerant 106
endophytes in 120
low thatch-producing 111
pest-resistant 119
slow-growing 102
suited to climates 107
tough 113
grasses ornamental 59
indicating acid soil 75
fountain grass *see Pennisetum alopecuroides*
lyme grass *see Elymus arenarius*
short dunegrass *see Panicum amarum*
ground elder *see Aegopodium podagraria*
ground ivy *see Glechoma hederacea*
ground staples 64
groundhog problems 169
groundsel bush *see Baccharis halimifolia*
grow-bags/sacs 13, 41
guelder rose *see Viburnum opulus*
gutters 13, 71
Gypsophila 97, 171
  G. elegans 143
  G. paniculata 66, 80
gypsum for clay soil 87

H
hackberry *see Celtis*
Hamamelis 36, 89
hanging baskets 13, 41, 151
hare's ear shrubby *see Bupleurum fruticosum*
hawk's-beard *see Crepis incana*
hawkweed *see Hieracium*
hawthorn see *Crataegus*
hay mulch spoiled 54
heath winter *see Erica carnea*
heather *see Calluna vulgaris*
Hedera 12, *31*, 36, 39, 49, 103
hedge bindweed *see Calystegia sepium*
hedgehog juniper *see Juniperus chinensis* 'Echiniformis'
hedges 33
  for garden rooms 17
  plants for 33, 41
  for privacy 67
  for protection 58, 61
  pruning 33
heeling-in 128
Helenium autumnale 19, 143
Helianthemum 57,
Helianthus 19,
Helichrysum petiolare 151
Heliopsis helantheoides 145
Heliotropium arborescens 151,
Helleborus 49, 57, 87
  H. foetidus 36
  H. niger 37, 145
  H. orientalis 12
Hemerocallis cvs., 14, 19, 21, *26*, 51, 65, 77, 87, 99, 144, 145
hemlock *see Conium maculatum*
  Canadian *see Tsuga canadensis*
henbit *see Lamium amplexicaule*
Hepatica americana 117
herbicides 176, 178
herbs for partial shade 39
Hesperis matronalis 49, 66
Heuchera/cvs., 14, 51, 67, 99, 143
Hibiscus/cvs., 19, 67, 146
  H. moscheutos 14, 143, 144
  H. syriacus 19, 41, 89, 91
hickory *see Carya illinoiensis*
Hieracium 178
highbush cranberry *see Viburnum trilobum*
Hinoki cypress *see Chamaecyparis obtusa*
Hippophae rhamnoides 63
hoary vervain *see Verbena stricta*
holly *see Ilex*
  sea *see Eryngium*
hollyhock *see Alcea rosea*
honesty *see Lunaria annua*
honey locust *see Gleditsia triacanthos*
honeysuckle *see Lonicera tatarica*
  dwarf *see Diervilla lonicera*

horsemint *see Monarda didyma*
horsetail field *see Equisetum arvense*
Hosta/cvs., 12, 19, 49, 99
hot dry sites 67
house extending into garden 10
hover flies 156
Huntsman's cup *see Sarracenia purpurea*
hyacinth *see Hyacinthus*
  grape *see Muscari*
hyacinth bean *see Lablab purpureus*
Hyacinthoides
  H. hispanica 12
  H. non-scripta 49
Hyacinthus 171
Hydrangea 19
  H. macrophylla 'Compacta', 63
  H. quercifolia 35
Hypericum 171
  H. calycinum 65
  H. hirsutum 145
  H. perforatum 178

I
Iberis sempervirens 14, 57
Ilex 33, 58, 59, 67, 75, 171
  I. aquifolium 59
  I. glabra 'Nordic', 21
  I. verticillata 71
illusion creating 10, 16, 18, 19
Impatiens 21, 67, 49, 143
Indian bean *see Catalpa*
indigo false *see Baptisia australis*
informal gardens 29
inkberry *see Ilex glabra*
insects beneficial 118–20, 154–67
Ipomoea 11, 146
  I. alba 19
  I. purpurea 174
Iris/cvs., 77, 80
  I. cvs., 51
  I. foetidissima 49
  I. pseudacorus 91, 93, *93*
iron phosphate traps 165
ironweed tall *see Vermona altissima*
irrigation drip 55, 67, 88
Isotoma axillaries 151
Itea viriginica 21
ivy
  English *see Hedera helix*
  ground *see Glechoma hederacea*
  Mexican *see Cobaea scandens*
  poison *see Rhus radicans*

J
Jack-in-the-pulpit *see Arisaema triphyllum*
Jacob's ladder *see Polemonium boreale*
Japanese anemone *see Anemone hybrida*
Japanese apple rose *see Rosa rugosa*
Japanese beetles 118, *118*, 162–3
Japanese bitter orange *see Poncirus trifoliata*
Japanese black pine *see Pinus thunburgii*
Japanese greens *see Brassica rapa var. nipposinica*
Japanese kerria *see Kerria japonica*
Japanese rush *see Acorus calamus*
jasmine *see Jasminum*
Jasminum nudiflorum 57
J. effusus f. *spiralis* 93
Jerusalem sage *see Phlomis russeliana*
jimsonweed *see Datura stramonium*
jostaberries 139
juniper *see Juniperus*
  creeping *see Juniperus horizontalis*
Juniperus 89, 171
  J. chinensis 'Echiniformis', 59, 69
  J. horizontalis 12, 39, 65, *71*, 71, 97, 99

K
kaffir lily *see Schizostylis coccinea*
Kalmia latifolia 77
Kansas gayfeather *see Liatris pycnostachya*
kaolin for insect control 158
Kerria japonica 51, 61, 171
Kirengeshoma palmata 48, 49

kiwifruit 139
knapweed *see Centaurea macrocephala*
Kniphofia/cvs., 63, 89, 97, 142, 171
knotgrass *see Polygonatum aviculare*
knotted rush *see Juncus nodosus*
Kolkwitzia amabalis 19, 51, 66
kudzu *see Pueraria lobata*

L
Lablab purpureus 19
Labrador tea *see Ledum groenlandicum*
lacewings 156
Lactuca
  L. sativa 39
  L. serriola 174
lady fern *see Athyrium filix-femina*
ladybugs 156
lady's mantle *see Alchemilla mollis*
lady's thumb *see Polygonatum persicaria*
Lagenaria siceraria 19
lamb's ear *see Stachys*
Lamium 91, 116
  L. amplexicaule 175
  L. maculatum 49, 103, 171
lance-leaved coriopsis *see Coreopsis lanceolata*
landscape fabric 21, 36, 54
Lantana camera 66
Lantana montevidensis 151
large gardens 16–21, 29
larkspur see *Consolida*
Lathyrus 14, *31*, 80, 143, 144, 145
laurel mountain *see Kalmia latifolia*
laurentia see *Isotoma axillaris*
Lavandula 42, 51, 65, *65*, 80, 145, 171
Lavatera 89
lavender *see Lavandula*
  sea *see Limonium latifolium*
lavender cotton see *Santolina chamaecyparissus*
lawns 24, 100–25
layered gardens 12
Layia platyglossa 156
lead plant *see Amorpha*
leaf mould 54
leaf size 11, 18
leaf spot 123, 184
leafhoppers 163–4
leatherleaf *see Chamaedaphne calycylata*
leaves shredded 54, 80
Ledum groenlandicum 93
Lenten rose *see Helleborus orientialis*
Leontopodium alpinum 69
leopard's bane *see Doronicum*
Leptomastix dactylopii 164
lettuce 39
Leucanthemum vulgare 75
Leucothoe 39
Levisticum officinale 39
Liatris 14, 77, 145
  L. pycnostachya 87
  L. scariosa 19, 61
  L. spicata 171
licorice plant *see Helichrysum petiolare*
light requirements filtered 12
lighting for germination 143
Ligularia 171
Ligustrum 33, 89, 99, 171
  L. obtusifolium 17
  L. ovalifolium 59, 63
lilac *see Syringa*
  California *see Ceanothus*
Lilium 19, 67, 77
lily
  Asiatic and Oriental 19
  canna *see Canna x generalis*
  crimson *see Schizostylis coccinea*
  Eastern trout *see Erythronium americanum*
  kaffir *see Schizostylis coccinea*
  Peruvian see Alstroemeria aurea
  river *see Schizostylis coccinea*
  speckled wood *see Clintonia umbellatus*
  veratrum *see Veratrum*
lily of the valley *see Convallaria majalis*
lily-of-the-valley bush *see Pieris japonica*

lilyturf *see Liriope muscari*
  creeping *see Liriope platyphylla*
liming soil 69, 76, *124*
Limonium 66, 99, 99
  L. latifolium 14, 89, 97, 171
  L. sinuatum 143
Linnaea borealis 117
Linum 57, 171
Liriope
  L. muscari 14, 49, 65
  L. platyphylla 49
  L. spicata 49, 103
liverwort round-lobed *see Hepatica americana*
loam adding lime to 76
Lobelia 14, *14*, 67, 80, 143, 145
  L. cardinalis 14, 19, 77, *87*, 91, 171
  L. erinus 151
  L. siphilitica 14
Lobularia maritima 21, 99, 156, 171
loganberries 139
Lonicera 80
  L. tatarica 19
loosestrife purple *see Lythrum salicaria*
lords and ladies *see Arum italicum*
Lotus berthelotii 151
lovage 39
love-in-a-mist *see Nigella damascena*
low-maintenance gardens 20, 21
Lunaria annua 49, 142
Lupinus 66, 77, 84, 143, 144
Lychnis 145
  L. coronaria 66, 143, 171
Lycoris squamigera 171
lyme grass *see Elymus arenarius*
Lysimachia nummularia 21, 103
Lythrum salicaria 178

M
Mache 39
madwort *see Aurinia saxatilis*
magnesium deficiency 134
Mahonia 71, 80, 171
  M. aquifolium 21, 39, 49, 57
  M. japonica 36
maidenhair fern *see Adiantum pedatum*
mail-order plants 128–9
mallow
  common *see Malva neglecta*
  musk *see Abelmoschus moschatus*
  tree *see Lavatera*
Malus 46, 77, *139*
Malva neglecta 174
maple
  hedge *see Acer campestre*
  Norway *see Acer platanoides*
  paper bark *see Acer griseum*
mapping the garden 22–3
Marasmius oreades 122
marigold *see Tagetes*
  marsh *see Caltha palustris*
  pot *see Calendula officinalis*
marjoram sweet 39
marsh fern *see Thelypteris*
marsh marigold *see Caltha palustris*
marsh rosemary *see Ledum groenlandicum*
marshpepper smartweed *see Polygonatum hydropiper*
martins 92
Matricaria matricarioides 174
Matthiola incana 142, 143, 171
mayapple *see Podophyllum peltatum*
Mazus pumilo 93
meadowsweet *see Filipendula palmata*
mealybugs 164–5
mealycup sage *see Salvia farinacea*
Meconopsis cambrica 19
Medicago sativa 84, *84*
Melampodium paludosum 151
Mentha 39, 156
Mertensia virginica 47, 117, 171
Mexican bean beetles 157
Mexican ivy *see Cobaea scandens*
Mexican sunflower *see Tithonia rotundifolia*

mice problems 169
Michaelmas daisy see *Aster* x *frikartii*
Microbiota decussata 39
mignonette see *Reseda odorata*
mildews 183, 186
milkweed see *Asclepias syriaca*
million bells see *Calibrochoa*
Mimulus 145
    M. luteus 91
miner's lettuce 39
mint 39
Minuarta verna 69
mirrors to protect against deer 170
Missouri primrose see *Oenethera*
mizuna 39
mock orange see *Philadelphus*
mould gray 180
moles 125
Mollugo verticillata 174
Molucella laevis 143, 144, 145
Monarda 19, 39, 87, 97, 142
monastery bells see *Cobaea scandens*
moneywort see *Lysimachia nummularia*
monkshood see *Achillea napellus;*
    Aconitus
morning glory see *Convolvulus; Ipomoea*
mosaic diseases 185
mosquitoes 92
moss 86
    purple swamp see *Mazus pumilo*
moss phlox see *Phlox subulata*
moss pink see *Phlox subulata*
moss sandwort see *Minuarta verna*
moth mullein see *Verbasum blattaria*
mountain ash see *Sorbus acuparia*
mountain box see
    Arctostaphylos uva-ursi; Berberis
mountain laurel see *Kalmia latifolia*
mountain phlox see *Phlox subulata*
mountain pine see *Pinus mugo*
mountain rockcress see *Arabis caucasica*
mountain spurge see
    Pachysandra terminalis
mowing strips 104
mugwort see *Artemisia vulgaris*
mulches 21
    for alkaline soils 80
    to clear weeds 64
    to control slugs and snails 166
    for dry gardens 54, 67
    paths 175
    perennials 137
    rodents and 169
    for sites under eaves 70
mullein see *Verbascum*
Muscari 171
musk mallow see *Abelmoschus*
    moschatus
mustard 39, *see also Brassica juncea*
Myosotis
    M. alpestris 37
    M. scorpioides 61, 93
    M. sylvatica 37
Myrica 63, 77, 89, 91, 97
periwinkle lesser see *Vinca minor*

N
Narcissus 67, 171
narrow borders 38
nasturtium see *Tropaeolum majus*
nectarines 139
neem 157
neglected garden 22–7
Nemagold marigolds 161
nematodes 160, 161
Nemophila menziesii 156
Nepeta
    N. cataria 156
    N. hederacea 103
Nerium oleander 41
netting crops 168
nettle see *Urtica dioica*
nettle tree see *Celtis*
newspaper mulch 54, 160
Nicotiana 77, 143, 171
Nigella damascena 21

nightshade see *Solanum nigrum*
nitrogen inhibiting blooming 130
Norway maple see *Acer platanoides*
nutrients 94, 152–3
nutsedge yellow see *Cyperus esculentus*

O
oak see Quercus
    poison see *Rhus toxicodendron*
oats 176
obedient plant see *Physostegia*
Oenothera 97, 143, 171
    O. biennis 156
    O. laciniata 156
    O. speciosa 37, 65
oils for insect control 157, 163, 165, 166,
    167
oleander see *Nerium oleander*
oleaster see *Elaeagnus*
onion ornamental see *Allium cristophii*
Onoclea 91
Opuntia compressa 63, *63*
orange Japanese bitter see
    Poncirus trifoliata
Oregon grape see *Mahonia aquifolium*
organic matter 83, 107, 140
Oriental poppy see *P. orientalis*
Origanum majorana 39
Osmunda regale 91
Oxalis 75
    O. oregana , 117
    O. stricta 178
ox eye see *Anthemis tinctoria*
oxeye see *Heliopsis helantheoides*
ox-eye daisy see *Leucanthemum vulgare*
Oxydendrum arboreum 77
Ozarks sundrops see *Oenethera*
ozone levels high 66

P
Pachysandra 103, 103
    P. procumbens 12, 21, 49, 66
    P. terminalis 12, 21, *39*, 49, 66
Paeonia/cvs., 14, 131, *131*, 145, 171
painted daisy see *Tanacetum coccineum*
pansy see *Viola*
Papaver 97, 171
    P. orientalis 99
paper bark maple see *Acer griseum*
parrot's beak see *Lotus berthelotii*
parsley 39
Parthenocissus
    P. henryana 35
    P. quinquefolia 31
    P. tricuspidata 31
paths 42, 175
paving 18, *67*, 112
pawpaws 139
pea stone 36, 54, 57
peach bells see *Campanula persicifolia*
peaches 139
peanut hull mulch 54
pearly everlasting see *Anaphalis*
pears 139
peat moss for clay soil 86
pecan see *Carya illinoiensis*
pelican's beak see *Lotus berthelotii*
Pennisetum alopecuroides 63
Pennsylvania smartweed see *Polygonatum*
    pensylvanicum
pennycress field see *Thlaspi arvense*
Penstemon 59, 80, 143, 145, 171
    P. hirstutus 51
Pentas lanceolata 143
peony see *Paeonia*/cvs.
perennials
    for alkaline soils 77, 80
    for autumn interest 35
    for clay soils 87
    cold-hardy 61
    deer-resistant 171
    for dry soils 51, 57, 66
    easy-care 21
    fertilizing 137
    for illusion 19
    long-blooming 14

for moist sunny spots 51
    pollution-tolerant 67
    for poor soils 91, 97
    rock garden 69
    for salty soils 99
    for sandy soils 89
    seaside 63
    for shade 49
    weeds 177–8
    wind-tolerant 59
    for winter interest 36
periwinkle see *Catharantus; Vinca*
Perovskia atriplicifolia 21, 51, 89, 171
peroxyacetyl nitrate (PAN) levels 66
Persian stonecress see
    Aethionema grandiflorum
persimmons 139
Peruvian lily see *Alstroemeria aurea*
Petroselinum crispum 39
Petunia/cvs., 21, 80, 99, 143
Petunia Surfinia Series 151
Philadelphus 19, 21, 80
Phlomis russeliana 51
Phlox 80, 99, 143
    P. drummondii 21
    P. paniculata 19, 51, 61
    P. subulata 21, 59, 66
Phragmites australis 63
Physalis alkekengi 143
Physostegia 142
    P. virginiana 14, 21
Phytolacca americana 178
Picea 89
pickerel weed see *Pontederia cordata*
Pieris japonica 51, 171
pigweed see *Amaranthus*
pimpernel see *Anagallis monellii*
pine see *Pinus*
    dwarf see *Pinus mugo*
    dwarf white see *Pinus parviflora*
    Japanese black see *Pinus thunburgii*
    mountain see *Pinus mugo*
pine needle mulch 54, 80
pineapple weed see *Matricaria matricari-*
    oides
pinks see *Dianthus*
Pinus 77, 89
    P. mugo 59, 171
    P. parviflora 171
    P. thunbergii 171
pipsissewa common see *Chimaphila*
pirate bugs 167
pitcher plant see *Sarracenia purpurea*
Plantago 75, 178
plantain see *Plantago*
    water see *Alisma plantago-aquatica*
planting 140–1
plants (*general only*)
    see also specific plants e.g. shrubs
    for autumn interest 35
    for bottom layers 12
    to distract the eye 32
    dividing 26
    establishing 140
    heeling-in 128
    layers 12
    long-flowering 14
    moving 25
    for screens 41
    size small gardens and 11
    spacing out 53
plastic film 54, 61
plastic netting planting through 64
plastic tree guards 169
Platanus 80
Platycodon 16, 42, 50, 51, 77, 143
plum beach see *Prunus maritima*
plumbago blue see *Ceratostigma*
    plumbaginoides
plums 139
Podophyllum peltatum 117, 117
poison hemlock see *Conium maculatum*
poison ivy see *Rhus radicans*
poison oak see *Rhus toxicodendron*
pokeweed see *Phytolacca americana*
Polemonium boreale 145

pollinators 138–9
pollution-tolerant plants 66–7
Polygonatum 14, 49, 91, 117, 171
    P. aviculare 174
    P. hydropiper 174
    P. persicaria 174
Poncirus trifoliata 57, 66
pond edging 14
Pontederia cordata 93
poorjoe see *Dioda teres*
poppy see *Papaver*
    California see *Eschscholzia californica*
    Oriental see *P. orientalis*
    Welsh see *Meconopsis cambrica*
Portulaca 143
    P. grandoflora 21, 66, 89, 97, 99
    P. oleracea 174
pot marigold see *Calendula officinalis*
potato scab 187
Potentilla 14, 89
    P. fruticosa 57, 59, 87, *87*, 171
    P. tabernaemontani 65
powdery mildew 186
prickly pear cactus see *Opuntia compress*
primrose see *Primula*
    Missouri see *Oenethera*
Primula 12, 21, 47, 49, 77, 143, 145
    P. elatior 61
    P. marginata 37
    P. vulgaris 61
privacy design for 67
privet see *Ligustrum*
Prunella vulgaris 178
pruning 130
    clematis 133
    fruit 139
    lilacs 130
    roses 132
    trees 48
    wisteria 132
Prunus maritima 63
Pseudomonas 179
Pseudotsuga menziesii 33
Puccinia 187
puccoon red see *Sanguinaria canadensis*
Pueraria lobata 178
puncture vine see *Tribulus terrestris*
purslane see *Portulaca*
Puschkinia 49, 171
Pyracantha 63
    P. coccinea 33
    P. 'Orange Glow', 35
pyrethrin 157
pyrethrum 162
pythium blight 123

Q
Queen Anne's lace see *Dauca carota*
Quercus 77
    Q. macrocarpa 80
quince flowering see *Chaenomeles*
    speciosa
quinces 139

R
rabbit problems 169
radish daikon see *Raphanus sativus*
ragweed see *Ambrosia*
ragwort
    common see *Senecio jacobaea*
    sea see *Senecio cineraria*
rain barrel 70
raised beds 52
Ranunculus ficaria 75
rape see *Brassica napus*
Raphanus sativus 84
raspberries 139
red-barked dogwood see *Cornus alba*
redbud see *Cercis canadensis*
red currants 139
red-hot poker see *Kniphofia*
red thread 124
redwood sorrel see *Oxalis oregana*
reedmace see *Typha*
reflective surfaces 46
reflective tape 168

refridgerating plants 128
Reseda odorata 80
Rhododendron 19, 49, *71*, 71, 75, 77
    R. impeditum 59, 69
    R. vaseyi 91
    R. viscosum 91, 93
Rhus
    R. radicans 178
    R. toxicodendron 178
Ribes 75
Ricinus communis 19, 171
river lily *see Schizostylis coccinea*
rockcress *see Aurinia saxatilis*
    mountain *see Arabis caucasica*
rock gardens 69
rock geranium *see Heuchera americana*
rock rose *see Helianthemum*
    nummularium
rocket 39
rocks water conservation with 57
rocky gardens 68–9
rodent problems 169
root ball splitting 140
root rots 182
root trimming in containers 148
Rosa 145
    miniature climbing 11
    pruning 132
    R. multiflora 178
    R. rugosa 32, 33, 77, 89, 99, *99*, 171
    R. virginiana 91
rose *see Rosa*
    Christmas *see Helleborus* niger
    guelder *see Viburnum opulus*
    Japanese apple *see Rosa rugosa*
rose campion *see Lychnis coronaria*
rose mallow *see Hibiscus*
rose moss *see Portulaca grandiflora*
rose periwinkle *see Catharanthus rosea*
rosemary *see Rosmarinus*
    marsh *see Ledum groenlandicum*
Rosmarinus 63
row covers 61, 157, 158, 159, 167
rowan *see Sorbus aucuparia*
royal fern *see Osmunda regale*
Rubus tricolor 49
Rudbeckia
    R. hirta 14, 19, 21, 61, 77, 87, 151
    R. laciniata 19, 21
Rumex
    R. acetosella 178
    R. crispus 75, 178
    R. scutatus 39
rush
    corkscrew *see J. effusus* f. *spiralis*
    flowering *see Butomus umbellatus*
    Japanese *see Acorus calamus*
Russian sage *see Perovskia atriplicifolia*
Russian thistle *see Salsola iberica*
rust 124, 187
rye winter 176

S
sage
    bog *see Salvia ulginosa*
    Jerusalem sage *see Phlomis russeliana*
    mealycup *see Salvia farinacea*
    Russian *see Perovskia atriplicifolia*
Sagittaria sagittifolia 93
Salix
    S. babylonica 93
    S. caprea 19
Salpiglossis sinuata 143
Salsola iberica 174
salt levels in soil 98–9, 153
Salvia 80, 97, 142, 171
    S. farinacea 21, 151
    S. uliginosa 91
Sambucus 59, 75
sand 36, 86
sandwort moss *see Minuarta verna*
sandy soil 76, 88–9
Sanguinaria canadensis 117
Santolina 14, 57, 89, 97
Santolina chamaecyparissus 63
Saponaria officinalis 178

Sarracenia purpurea 93
satinroot *see Heuchera americana*
sawdust mulch 54, 80
scab 187
Scabiosa 143
    S. caucasica 14, 21, 51, 80
scabious *see Scabiosa caucasica*
Scaevola aemula 151
scale insects 164–5
scale of gardens 29
Scare-Eyes 168
scarification of seeds 146
Schizostylis coccinea 91
Scilla 171
screens 31, 41, 46, 63
sea buckthorn *see Hippophae rhamnoides*
sea holly *see Eryngium* cvs.
sea kale *see Crambe maritima*
sea lavender *see Limonium latifolium*
sea ragwort *see Senecio cineraria*
seaside gardens 62–3
seaweed mulch 54
sedge
    bog *see Carex oligosperma*
    mace *see Carex grayi*
    water *see Carex aquitilis*
Sedum 14, 21, 57, 69, 77, 89, 99
seedlings damping-off 147, 182
seeds poor germination 142–7
self-heal *see Prunella vulgaris*
Senecio
    S. cineraria 171
    S. jacobaea 175
sensitive fern *see Onoclea*
shade-loving plants
    damp shade 49
    dry shade 49
    herbs and vegetables 39
    layered gardens 12
    providing shade for 137
    spring 47
    under trees 116
    white and pastel 48
shady gardens 46–9, 50–1, 134, 137
shape for illusion 18
sheep's fescue *see Festuca ovina*
sheep's sorrel *see Rumex acetosella*
shellflower *see Molucella laevis*
shepherd's purse *see*
    Capsella bursa-pastoris
shrubby hare's ear *see*
    Bupleurum fruticosum
shrubs
    for alkaline soils 77, 80
    for autumn interest 35
    for clay soils 87
    cold-hardy 61
    deer-resistant 171
    to distract the eye 32
    for dry soils 51, 57, 71
    easy-care 21
    for high heat and dry soil 66
    for illusion 19
    indicating acid soil 75
    for shade 49
    moving 25
    pollution-tolerant 67
    for poor soils 91, 97
    rocky garden 69
    for salty soils 99
    for sandy soils 89
    seaside 63
    for sloping gardens 65
    wind-tolerant 59
    for winter interest 36
Siberian pea shrub *see Caragena*
    arborescens
sicky perches 168
Sida spinosa 174
Silene
    S. alba 175, 178
    S. dioica 75
silver birch *see Betula pendula*
site maps 22–3
site problems 44–71
size of plants small gardens 11

Skimmia japonica 57, 171
sloping gardens 64–5
slugs 165–6
small gardens 10–15, 29
smartweed
    marshpepper *see*
        Polygonatum hydropiper
    Pennsylvania *see*
        Polygonatum pensylvanicum
Smilacina 117
smoke bush *see Cotinus coggygria*
snails 165–6
snapdragon *see Antirrhinum majus*
sneezeweed *see Helenium autumnale*
snow-in-summer *see*
    Cerastium tomentosum
snow mould 124
snowberry *see Symphoricarpus*
    creeping *see Gaultheria hispidula*
snowdrop *see Galanthus nivalis*
snowflake *see Leucojum*
snowy mespilus *see Amelanchier*
soaking seeds 144
soap for insect control 157
soapwort *see Saponaria officinalis*
sod webworms 120
soil
    acid 74
    alkaline 78–81
    boggy 92–3
    compacted 82–5
    double-digging 85
    high salt content 98–9, 153
    low-fertility 94–7
    mixes for containers 153
    pH 26, 69, 74, 78, 86–7
    poorly drained 90–1
    problems 72–99
    sampling 74
    testing for nutrients 94
    warming 60
Solanum nigrum 174
Solenostemon 67, 171
Solidago 87, 171, 178
    S. sempervirens 63, 99
Solomon's seal *see Polygonatum*
Sonchus oleraceus 174, *175*
Sorbus acuparia 59
sorrel 39
    see also Oxalis
    redwood *see Oxalis oregana*
    sheep's *see Rumex acetosella*
sourwood *see Oxydendrum arboreum*
sow thistle smooth *see Sonchus oleraceus*
Spanish bluebell *see*
    Hyacinthoides hispanica
Spanish broom *see Spartium junceum*
Spanish needles *see Bidens bipinnata*
Spartium junceum 59
spear thistle *see Cirsium vulgare*
speedwell spiked *see Veronica spicata*
Spergula arvensis 174
spider flower *see Cleome hassleriana*
spider mites 166
spiderwort *see Tradescantia*
spike grass *see Distichlis spicata*
spiked speedwell *see Veronica spicata*
spikenard false *see Smilacina*
spinach 39
Spinacia oleracea 39
spindle winged *see Euonymus* alatus
spindle European *see Euonymus*
    europaeus
spiraea *see Spiraea*
    blue mist *see Caryopteris clandonensis*
Spiraea 33, 61, 80, 87, 171
spleenwort ebony *see*
    Asplenium platyneuron
spring garden 37
    bulbs 42, 47
spruce *see Picea*
spurge *see Euphorbia*
    mountain *see Pachysandra terminalis*
squill *see Scilla*
    striped *see Puschkinia*
St John's wort creeping *see Hypericum*

    calycinum
Stachys 57, 142
star cluster *see Pentas lanceolata*
statice *see Goniolimon tataricum;*
    Limonium sinuatum
Stellaria media 75, 79, 174, *175*
stepping stone path 112
sticky traps 167
sticky willy *see Galium aparine*
stinging nettle *see Urtica dioica*
stinking chamomile *see Anthemis cotula*
stinking hellebore *see Helleborus foetidus*
Stoke's aster *see Stokesia aster*
Stokesia laevis 14
stone wall *62*
stonecress Persian *see*
    Aethionema grandiflorum
stonecrop *see Sedum*
storage of seeds 147
storing plants 129
stratifying seeds 145
straw mulches 21, 54, 83, 162
strawberry wild *see Fragaria vesca*
strawberry shrub *see Calycanthus floridus*
strawflower *see Bracteantha bracteata*
Streptomyces scabies 187
sugarcane mulch 80
sulfur flowers of 78
sulfur dioxide levels 66
summersweet *see Clethra alnifolia*
sun rose *see Cistus*
sundew *see Drosera*
sunflower *see Helianthus annuus*
    Mexican *see Tithonia rotundifolia*
sunny gardens 50–1
sunplant *see Portulaca*
swamp azalea *see Rhododendron*
    viscosum
swamp cyrilla *see Cyrilla racemiflora*
swamp moss purple *see Mazus pumilo*
sweet flag *see Acorus calamus*
sweet pea *see Lathyrus latifolius*
sweet pepper bush *see Clethra alnifolia*
sweet rocket *see Hesperis matronalis*
Carolina allspice *see Calycanthus*
sweet woodruff *see Galium odoratum*
Symphoricarpus 49
Syringa 87, *87*, 130, 171

T
tachinid flies 156
Tagetes cvs., 21, 77, 151, 161, 171
Tamarix 19, 63
Tanacetum
    T. coccineum 21
    T. parthenium 156
    T. vulgare 39, 156, 178
tanglefoot 158, 167
tansy 39
Taraxacum officinale 75, 178
tarnished plant bugs 167
Taxus baccata 39, 49, 58
temperatures for germination 142
terraced garden 14, 15
Teucrium chamaedrys 69
thatch in lawns 110–11
Thelypteris 91
thistle
    creeping *see Cirsium arvense*
    globe *see Echinops ritro*
    Russian *see Salsola iberica*
    smooth sow *see Sonchus oleraceus*
    spear , *see Cirsium vulgare*
Thlaspi arvense 174
thorn apple *see Datura stramonium*
thrift *see Armeria pseudarmeria*
thrips 167
Thunberg's barberry *see Berberis*
    thunbergii
thyme creeping *see Thymus serpyllum*
Thymus 39
    T. serpyllum 21, 65, 103
Tiarella 77, 116
tickseed *see Bidens ferulifolia; Coreopsis*
tidytips *see Layia platyglossa*
tiered beds 13, 14

tires chipped 114
Tithonia 19, 32, 143
toadflax *see Spergula arvensis*
tobacco plant *see Nicotiana*
toothpicks to deter cutworms 160
torch lily *see Kniphofia uvaria*
Torenia cvs. 49, 151
Tradescantia 117
trailing plants for containers 151
transplants 98
traps 165, 167, 169
tree mallow *see Lavatera*
trees
  for alkaline soils 80
  assessing existing 25
  for clay soils 87
  lime-tolerant 77
  plastic guards 169
  pollution-tolerant 67
  pruning 48
  refuge area under 116
  for sandy soils 89
  shade under 46
  tree islands 20, 29, 104
  unwanted 25
  wind-tolerant 59
trellis 12, 30, *34*, 40, 51, 67
Tribulus terrestris 174
Trifolium pratense 84
Trillium 117
trinity flower *see Tradescantia*
Trollius 51, 61, 91, 145
Tropaeolum majus 21, 67, 80, 89, 97, 99, 143, 151, *151*
trout lily Eastern
  see Erythronium americanum
trumpet vine *see Campsis grandiflora*
Tsuga canadensis 41
tulips *37*
turtlehead *see Chelone lyonii*
Tussilago farfara 178
twinflower *see Linnaea borealis*
Typha 93

U
urban gardens 66–7

Uromyces 187
Urtica dioica 178

V
Vaccinium 75
valerian red *see Centranthus ruber*
Valerianella locusta , 39
vegetables 13, 38, 39, 50, 51, 56
velvetleaf *see Abutilon theophrasti*
Veratrum 91
Verbascum 171
  V. blattaria 175
  V. bombyciferum 19
  V. thapsus 175
Verbena 89, 97, 99
  V. bonariensis 142
  V. hybrida 143
  V. strica 178
vermiculite for seed germination 146
Vermona altissima 178
Veronica 171
  V. longifolia 145
  V. prostrata 69
  V. spicata 59, 69
Verticillium wilt 186
vervain hoary *see Verbena strica*
vetch hairy 176
Viburnum 51, 57, 87, 171
  V. davidii 49
  V. opulus 19, 35
  V. trilobum 63, 75
Vinca
  V. major 49
  V. minor 12, 21, 39, 49, 65, 103
vine
  cup-and-saucer *see Cobaea scandens*
  Dutchman's pipe *see* *Aristolochia macrophylla*
  puncture *see Tribulus terrestris*
vinegar 79, 176
Viola 103, 145
  V. odorata 103, *103*
  V. tricolor 37
  V. x wittrockiana 21, 50, 67, 77
violet bush *see Browallia*
Virginia bluebells *see Mertensia virginica*

Virginia ivy *31*
Virginia rose *see Rosa virginiana*
Virginia sweetspire *see Itea virginica*
Viriginia creeper *see* *Parthenocissus henryana; P. quinquefolia*
viruses 185
Vitex agnus-castus 51, 57

W
wake robin *see Trillium*
wallcress *see Arabis caucasica*
wallflower *see Erysimum cheiri*
walls 40–1, 46, 59, 61, *62*
wasps beneficial 156
water conservation 57, 70, 71
water features 14, 36, 55
water forget-me-not *see* *Myosotis scorpioides*
water plantain *see* *Alisma plantago-aquatica*
water sedge *see Carex aquitilis*
water treatment of seeds 144
watering gardens 55, 79, 92, 109, *141*
wax begonia *see Begonia semperflorens*
webworms 120
weeding 174
weeping willow *see Salix babylonica*
weeds 64, 75, 78, 172–8
Weigela 41, 99
Welsh poppy *see Meconopsis cambrica*
white currants 139
wildflowers 75, 79, 117
willow *see Salix*
willow bellflower *see* *Campanula persicifolia*
willowleaf cotoneaster *see* *Cotoneaster salicifolia*
wilt 179, 183–4, 186
windbreaks 58, 59, 62
windflower *see Anemone blanda*
window boxes trailers 151
windy gardens 53, 58–9
winter aconite *see Eranthis hyemalis*
winter plants for interest 36
winterberry *see Ilex verticillata*
wintercress *see Barbarea vulgaris*

wintergreen creeping *see Gaultheria procumbens*
wishbone flower *see Torenia*
Wisteria 19, *31*, 36, 132
witch hazel *see Hamamelis x intermedia* mountain *see Fothergilla major*
wood anemone *see Anemone nemorosa*
wood chips 54
wood lily speckled *see Clintonia umbellatus*
wood shavings 54
woodland garden plants 117
woodruff sweet *see Galium odoratum*
worms 111, 135
wormwood *see Artemisia absinthum*

X
Xanthium pensylvanicum 174

Y
yarrow *see Achillea*
yellow flag *see Iris pseudacorus*
yew *see Taxus baccata*
Yucca 89, 97
  Y. filamentosum 19, *89*, 89, 171

Z
Zen garden 36
Zinnia 67, *148*, 171

ACKNOWLEDGEMENTS

The publisher wishes to thank all those who kindly supplied the photography and illustrations for this book, as follows:

Inside
Mark Winwood (© Collins & Brown): 2, 26 (both), 27 (top left, middle and right), 60 (top left and right), 64 (left and right), 76 (all), 82 (all), 83 (both), 88, 95, 107 (all), 108 (all), 110, 111 (both), 125, 128, 134 (top), 135 (left), 140, 141, 142, 143, 144, 146 (all), 147 (bottom), 149 (all), 152 (both), 153 and 181 (bottom); © Garden Picture Library/Steven Wooster: 4 and 41; © Collins & Brown: 5, 12 (all), 18 (bottom, all), 40 (all), 46, 48 (top, centre and right), 49 (both), 52 (bottom, all), 54, 55 (all), 61 (all), 65 (bottom, centre and right), 72-73, 74 (all), 77, 80 (left), 81, 87 (all), 89 (both), 97 (top and bottom right), 99 (top right), 106, 109 (both), 112 (all), 113 (top, all), 114 (all), 115 (bottom, all), 116 (both), 126-127, 131, 135 (right) and 139; © Garden Picture Library/Howard Rice: 8-9, 20, 29 (bottom), 36 (top), 37, 103 (bottom), 105, 133, 145 (bottom), 147 (top) and 166; © Garden Picture Library/Michael Paul: 10; © Garden Picture Library/Clive Nichols: 11 and 38 (right); © Garden Picture Library/Sunniva Harte: 14; © Holt Studios/Bob Gibbons: 16 and 79 (left); © Garden Picture Library/ John Ferro Sims: 17 and 63 (right); © Garden Picture Library/Juliette Wade: 18 (top) and 103 (top); © Steven Wooster: 19 and 48 (bottom); © Garden Picture Library/ Zara McCalmont: 24; © Garden Picture Library/ Brigitte Thomas: 27 (bottom) and 43; © Garden Picture Library/ Mark Bolton: 28 and 93 (bottom right); © Garden Picture Library/ Marie O'hara: 29 (top), 44-45, 67 and 156 (left); © Garden Picture Library/ John Glover: 30, 51 (middle), 58, 100-101, 115 (top) and 151 (bottom left); © Garden Picture Library/ JS Sira: 34 (top), 36 (bottom), 47, 51 (right), 53, 69 (bottom), 99 (left) and 164; © Garden Picture Library/ Mel Watson: 34 (bottom left); © Garden Picture Library/Mayer/Le Scanff: 34 (bottom right) and 50; © Garden Picture Library/ Neil Holmes: 35, 39, 51 (left) and 75; © Garden Picture Library/Graham Strong: 38 (left); Chrysalis Images: 56, 102 and 113 (bottom); © Holt Studios/Rosie Mayer: 57 and 86 (top); © Garden Picture Library/Ron Sutherland: 62; © Garden Picture Library/A.I. Lord: 63 (left); © Garden Picture Library/David Askham: 63 (middle) and 97 (bottom left); © Garden Picture Library/Didier Willery: 65 (bottom left); © Holt Studios/Primrose Peacock: 69 (top); © Holt Studios/Alan & Linda Detrick: 70 (top); © Garden Picture Library/Jerry

Pavia: 71 (top), 99 (bottom right) and 117 (right); © Garden Picture Library/David Cavagnaro: 71 (bottom left), 172-173 and 179; © Garden Picture Library/David Russell: 71 (bottom right) and 91; © Holt Studios/Nigel Cattlin: 79 (right), 84, 121, 138, 148, 158 (right), 159, 160 (both), 161 (both), 162, 168, 175, 178, 180 (top), 181 (top), 184 (both), 185 (both) and 187 (both); © Garden Picture Library/Chris Burrows: 80 (right); © Garden Picture Library/Henk Dijkman: 93 (top); © Garden Picture Library/Eric Crichton: 93 (bottom left) and 122; © Photos Horticultural/Robin Williams: 104; © Garden Picture Library/Lamontagne: 117 (left) and 150 (right); © Joseph Sohm; ChromoSohm Inc./CORBIS: 118 (left); © Karen Tweedy-Holmes/CORBIS: 118 (right); © Gary W. Carter/CORBIS: 119; © Pat Jerrold; Papilio/CORBIS: 124; © Garden Picture Library/NouN: 136; © Garden Picture Library/Ron Evans: 145 (top); © Garden Picture Library/Suzie Gibbons: 150 (left); © Garden Picture Library/Christi Carter: 151 (top); © Garden Picture Library/Pernilla Bergdahl: 151 (bottom right); © Garden Picture Library/David England: 154-155 and 177 (left); © Garden Picture Library/Rex Butcher: 156 (right); © Garden Picture Library/Philippe Bonduel: 158 (left); © Garden Picture Library/Michael Howes: 161 (left), 180 (bottom) and 182; © Hal Horwitz/CORBIS: 163 (top); © Anthony Bannister; Gallo Images/CORBIS: 163 (bottom); © Photos Horticultural: 165 (left), 165 (right) and 168; © Garden Picture Library/Vaughan Fleming: 175 (left);

All illustrations in this book were created by Ian Sidaway (© Collins & Brown).

Special thanks to Tornado Deer & Wildlife Fencing (www.tornadowire.co.uk) for providing the photograph on page 170.

Cover
Ian Sidaway (© Collins & Brown): front cover (top left, bottom centre right and bottom centre left), and back cover (left). Mark Winwood (© Collins & Brown): front cover (top centre left, top centre right), and back cover (centre right). © Collins & Brown: front cover (top right, centre above left, centre below left, centre right, bottom left and bottom right), and back cover (right, centre left).